THE LECTIONARY LAB COMMENTARY

WITH STORIES AND SERMONS FOR YEAR B

JOHN FAIRLESS AND DELMER CHILTON

Copyright © 2014 The Lectionary Lab
All rights reserved.
ISBN: 1502906945
ISBN-13: 978-1502906946

DEDICATION

William Shakespeare reminds us that, when one is seeking to follow his or her true calling, "…it must follow, as the night the day, thou canst not then be false to any man." (Polonius, in *Hamlet*, Act I, Scene 3.)

We were never quite sure when we offered **Volume 1** (for Year A) that there would be enough interest in our ramblings to justify a second volume, that night would follow day, as it were; to say that we have been humbled at the response would mark only the barest beginnings of our sentiment.

So, true to our calling, we have here more insights, thoughts, ideas, stories and sermons for those who do the work of preaching and teaching the scriptures. You have our highest regards and best wishes.

Thanks once again to all who bless us with your support and feedback, to our families that put up with our weekly distraction due to writing/reading/podcasting, etc., and to God and the churches of God that allow us to do what we want to do.

Mostly.

Contents

The First Sunday of Advent 3

The Second Sunday of Advent 8

The Third Sunday of Advent 12

The Fourth Sunday of Advent 18

Christmas Eve/Christmas Day 25

The First Sunday after Christmas 30

The Epiphany of the Lord 36

The Baptism of the Lord (First Sunday after the Epiphany) 40

The Second Sunday after the Epiphany 45

The Third Sunday after the Epiphany 52

The Fourth Sunday after the Epiphany 57

The Fifth Sunday after the Epiphany 64

The Sixth Sunday after the Epiphany 71

Transfiguration Sunday (Last Sunday before Lent) 79

The Seventh Sunday after the Epiphany 84

Eighth Sunday after the Epiphany (see Proper 3 – Season after Pentecost) 88

Ninth Sunday after the Epiphany (see Proper 4 – Season after Pentecost) . 88

Ash Wednesday 89

The First Sunday in Lent 93

The Second Sunday in Lent 98

The Third Sunday in Lent 106

The Fourth Sunday in Lent 114

The Fifth Sunday in Lent 120

The Sixth Sunday in Lent (Palm/Passion) 128

Maundy Thursday/Good Friday 135

Resurrection of the Lord (Easter) 141

The Second Sunday of Easter 145

The Third Sunday of Easter 153

The Fourth Sunday of Easter 160

The Fifth Sunday of Easter 168

The Sixth Sunday of Easter 173

The Ascension of Our Lord 178

The Seventh Sunday of Easter 181

Day of Pentecost 187

Trinity Sunday 191

Proper 3 – Season after Pentecost Sunday Closest to May 25 197

Proper 4 – Season after Pentecost Sunday Closest to June 1 202

Proper 5 – Season after Pentecost Sunday Closest to June 8 207

Proper 6 – Season after Pentecost Sunday Closest to June 15 215

Proper 7 – Season after Pentecost Sunday Closest to June 22 220

Proper 8 – Season after Pentecost Sunday Closest to June 29 227

Proper 9 – Season after Pentecost Sunday Closest to July 6 232

Proper 10 – Season after Pentecost Sunday Closest to July 13 239

Proper 11 – Season after Pentecost Sunday Closest to July 20 244

Proper 12 – Season after Pentecost Sunday Closest to July 27 251

Proper 13 – Season after Advent Sunday Closest to August 3 257

Proper 14 – Season after Pentecost Sunday Closest to August 10 265

Proper 15 – Season after Pentecost Sunday Closest to August 17 270

Proper 16 – Season after Pentecost Sunday Closest to August 24 277

Proper 17 – Season after Pentecost Sunday Closest to August 31 283

Proper 18 – Season after Pentecost Sunday Closest to September 7 290

Proper 19 – Season after Pentecost Sunday Closest to September 14 296

Proper 20 -- Season after Pentecost Sunday Closest to September 21 303

Proper 21 – Season after Pentecost Sunday Closest to September 28 309

Proper 22 – Season after Pentecost Sunday Closest to October 5 316

Proper 23 – Season after Pentecost Sunday Closest to October 12 323

Proper 24 – Season after Pentecost Sunday Closest to October 19 330

Proper 25 – Season after Pentecost Sunday Closest to October 26 337

Proper 26 – Season after Pentecost Sunday Closest to November 2 343

Proper 27 – Season after Pentecost Sunday Closest to November 9 350

Proper 28 – Season after Pentecost Sunday Closest to November 16 356

Proper 29 – The Reign of Christ   Sunday Closest to November 23 364

ACKNOWLEDGMENTS

With gratitude for the work of the **Consultation on Common Texts** in the United States and Canada, which is responsible for the readings cited herein as part of the Revised Common Lectionary.

The **Revised Common Lectionary** is housed online as a service of the Vanderbilt Divinity Library at Vanderbilt University, Nashville, TN

http://lectionary.library.vanderbilt.edu

Every attempt is made to give credit to owners and originators of all works quoted or referenced in any way within the pages of the commentary.

The First Sunday of Advent

Isaiah 64:1-9

Upon reading through Isaiah's text, one can't help but notice how terribly ACTIVE the language is! The heavens are torn, the mountains are quaking, there is fire all around, and adversaries are trembling. God is coming down, by God!

Or, at least, that is what we think we hope for at this opening of the season of Advent. We've heard that God has come down in the past, and that the results were generally positive.

But wait — if God is coming to judge sinners, and we're all sinners — doesn't that mean we might be in for a bit of judgment ourselves? Is that what we really want "for the holidays?"

Good thing that in our waiting, we remember that God is our Father, that we are God's people — and that God will not remember our iniquity forever.

HERE'S A THOUGHT: Ever thought about what it means to be "clay in the hands of the potter?" Here's a quick video clip that demonstrates what happens first in order for clay to be usable and moldable. Might not be an entirely comfortable process!

http://on.aol.com/video/preparing-the-clay-for-throwing-149485337

Psalm 80:1-7, 17-19

Three times in this psalm, the request is made of God, "let your face shine, that we may be saved."

What is salvific about the light of God's face? In a season of darkness, what does it feel like to see a light shining in the distance? How is light an image of hope?

1 Corinthians 1:3-9

In Advent, we become a "waiting people" — something that is not always that easy to do. What do we wait for?

For some reason I get a flashback image to my elementary school days, when Principal Nielsen would call us all to gather in the gymnasium for a special program. There was a huge purple curtain that covered the stage, and we knew that whatever we were about to see was behind that curtain. There wasn't a lot of excitement in my little hometown growing up, so it was mysterious and intriguing to wait for that curtain to be pulled back. It was almost as exciting to wait as it was to have the feature of the day revealed to us.

We are waiting on God to "reveal" something — or rather, someone — very important. It is the Lord Jesus Christ that God reveals to the world.

Mark 13:24-37

Again, we are reminded that Advent has a bit of an edge to it — I would almost call it "weird" or "funky." A darkening sun, the lack of moonlight, stars falling and the powers of heaven shaken — all of these things give an almost queasy feeling to the coming of the Son of Man.

Certainly, none of us wants to get caught short in our responsibility to serve God. If you snooze, you lose. Perhaps that is why we also remember that it takes all of us to be the church; none of us is alone, because it's just flat out impossible for one person to stay awake all the time.

Help a brother out, would you? Let's work and watch together through this, okay?

Sermon

"A Message from God"

Have you seen those billboards out on the interstates that purport to be messages from God?

I ride the roads a lot and I see a lot of those signs and they always make me laugh and sometimes
they make me think.

I saw one up in East Tennessee that went like this:

DON'T MAKE ME COME DOWN THERE!
— GOD.

The writer of our text from Isaiah would like that, I think. Though it is likely that he would be thinking, WHY DON'T YOU COME ON DOWN ALREADY, WHAT'S KEEPING YOU?

This text is part of a lament, an argumentative prayer, in which the prophet struggles with God over the fact that God has not been heard from in a while and things aren't going so well for God's people in the midst of God's absence.

The NRSV (and the RSV and the KJV) translates Isaiah 64:1 as something of a sighing request,

"Oh, that you would tear open the heavens and come down."

The Revised English Bible frames it as a question and makes the prophet's complaint much clearer:

"Why do you not tear asunder the heavens and come down?"

The first part of our text has a tone of wondering and smoldering anger that God has left and abandoned the people.

This accusatory theme barely lets up in verses 5 through 7 where, although the prophet admits that the people have sinned and turned from God and are in trouble because of it; he also lays the blame for this sinfulness squarely in God's lap for having gone away and left them to their own devices.

It's like the old Mark Twain joke about the man who killed his parents and then pleaded for mercy from the court because he was an orphan.

Then, at the beginning of verse 8, one word changes the tone and the meaning of the entire text.

"Yet, O Lord, you are our Father. We are the clay, you are the potter, we are all the work of your hand."

The Hebrew here is variously translated yet, but, however, nevertheless.

After making a serious and passionate case that things are really, really, bad and that God is, honestly, just as much to blame as the folk; the prophet speaks a word of hope and promise; yet, you are our Father.

This word of hope and promise is rooted in an awareness of the mighty acts of God that have come before and in trust that God will act again.

Advent is the season of YET, of BUT, of HOWEVER, of NEVERTHELESS.

Advent is a time when we stare into the face of the present data of the world's sorry state and dare to believe that God still cares and God still plans to do something about it.

Advent is a time when we wrestle with and confess the reality that we in the church all too often
live out of a practical atheism, in which we say with our lips that we believe in God, but we say with our lives that we really believe, really put our trust, in armies and governments and savings accounts.

Advent is a time when we wait for the Lord to come, and while we wait, we seek to become people who gladly do right, who remember God and God's ways.

Advent is a time when we do, indeed, wait for God to come down here; but it is not a fearful waiting, for it is promised that when God comes, our iniquity, our sin, our sorrow, will be remembered no more.

Amen, come Lord Jesus.

The Second Sunday of Advent

Isaiah 40:1-11

"The grass withers, the flower fades; but the word of our God will stand forever."

I live in the Appalachian Mountains. I recently ran across a coffee table book in a local book store. It was a collection of "Then and Now" photographs from various small towns in western North Carolina. The photographer had taken great pains in his 1990s shots to exactly recreate the camera angle and location of the 1880s photos in order to show how things had changed in 100+ years.

As fascinating as the commercial changes in buildings roads and utility poles were, I was even more fascinated by the changes one could detect in the environment; changes that were not man made but were natural and ongoing. "Nothing lasts forever," I thought.

And then I remembered this text. These early Sundays in Advent remind us that to put our hope and trust in anything but God's promises is a fool's bargain. Whether we trust in technology or psychology or political movements or, or, or . . . it is all like the grass and the flower; they fade and wither and only God's word, God's promise of hope and blessing, will endure.

Psalm 85:1-2; 8-13

A very important struggle for those of us who embrace any form of the Social Gospel, the Good News for the poor and the dispossessed, is to avoid works righteousness. It's a difficult tight rope to walk between the quietism of doing nothing and the activism of thinking the coming of the Kingdom of God depends totally on (our) human effort. This Psalm is a good reminder that God builds the Kingdom through us; we don't build the kingdom for God. Verse 12:"The Lord will give what is good."

2 Peter 3:8-15a

"While you are waiting…"

Waiting takes up a lot of our lives. Waiting in traffic, waiting at the doctor's office, waiting on hold, waiting in security lines at airports, waiting for the computer to update. I always carry a book or a newspaper with me wherever I go, so that I'll have something to bide the time while waiting. As much as I hate listening to other people talking on their cellphones in public, I do understand that it is something to do to fill up the emptiness of their waiting.

We, the Christian Church, have been waiting for Jesus for a very long time now, haven't we? Sometimes I think that a lot of what we do is the spiritual equivalent of doing the crossword, reading a novel or texting and talking nonsense on cell phones; just passing the time while waiting between getting saved and going to heaven. Peter calls us to another sort of waiting, an active waiting, a waiting full of striving for peace and justice in the world. As Peter says, the Lord is not slow, the Lord is patient, giving all every opportunity to get with the program.

Mark 1:1-8

My son David was an early riser when he was 3 or 4 years old. His room was across the hall from our bedroom and my side of the bed was closest to the door. Most mornings I opened my eyes to find him standing in the floor by the bed, his cabbage patch doll Webster in hand, staring me in the eye from about an inch away. When my eyes fluttered open he would shout, "It's day! Time to get up!" for several years, I began each day in a startled and confused state of mind.

Mark begins his Gospel in a similarly abrupt and urgent manner. No philosophical musing (John), no genealogical charting (Matthew), no historical scene-setting (Luke); just straight up proclamation. Like little David jumped right into the day, Mark jumps right into the Gospel and sin and salvation. "Baptism of repentance" and "forgiveness of sins," show up in verse 4. In the Greek text, "metanoias" (repentance) is the 50th word of Mark and "amartion" (of sins) is the 53. WAKE UP! IT'S DAY!

Sermon

"Well, Bless Your Heart!"

It's kind of a Southern thing – and it's meant to be a statement of comfort and support. It's also a subtle sort of way to evoke pity for a person that you really don't pity much at all – sort of a genteel put-down...a back-handed compliment... I am speaking, of course, of the phrase, "Well, bless your heart!"

We Southerners use it as a genuine form of solidarity in suffering; for example, when someone loses a loved one, "well, bless your heart." When there is an accident or a serious illness, the phrase comes in handy: "Well, bless your heart."

There is also the more insidious usage, say when someone is prattling on about this or that which doesn't really interest or concern us; it becomes more of a conversational foil or means of avoidance – "oh, well bless your heart."

Then, there is the third-person form of the phrase – most often used when sharing a "concern" [hear the word judgment, or our really favorite form of juicy gossip.] "Yes, poor Margaret – I don't know why she puts up with Ralph's shenanigans, bless her heart!"

Comfort really is a curious thing, isn't it? What does it require to comfort, or to be comforted, in a time of distress or need? At Advent, we wait for the kind of comfort that only God can bring. It is the kind of comfort spoken tenderly, offered graciously.

It's not easy to wait. We are accustomed to fast food, fast (and friendly!) service, fast responses to our problems and issues (think of emergency departments and urgent care.) My colleague, Dr. Chilton, told me recently about sitting bemusedly, listening to a fellow customer at Jiffy Lube complaining obviously and ostentatiously about the 30 minutes — for heaven's sake! –he would have to wait for his car to be ready.

But the gospel at Advent reminds us that we are only at the beginning of God's great work in our lives; there is much yet to be told, experienced, endured, and accomplished.

And God — the very God of creation and re-creation, according to Peter — is with us through every struggle and challenge and joy. God waits — with us. It's a whispered refrain that accompanies us on the journey of our lives.

Now, I don't know that God is a Southerner – or a Northerner, or an Easterner or a Westerner. I don't suppose God is American, or British, or African or Asian, really. Rather, God is found on all points of the compass, in every race and culture. God is everywhere and always God.

But I do know that God's intent is always loving, always with the best of our interest in mind - and that, with the coming of the Christ, God's desire is to comfort - to bless our hearts - truly and indeed.

The Third Sunday of Advent

Isaiah 61:1-4, 8-11

Fresh.

That's the word that comes to my mind as I read Isaiah's words. Maybe it's more like "refresh" — but either way, it's good news for those who are oppressed, brokenhearted, held captive and imprisoned.

None of these experiences are pleasant; they deplete us, destroy us, demean us. They dry us up — oppression is a desiccating wind that blows its ill effects into our lives. "Suck the life right out of you," is a phrase that comes to mind. Most of us identify with that experience at one time or another — actually, we identify a lot more than ONE time!

So, the Lord's word comes as a refreshing, renewing promise: no more ashes for you who have been tossed on the midden heap of life. Here's a beautiful green garland to adorn your brow, instead. Wash away the worn lines of your mourning; use this oil of gladness as a salve for the pain you've felt. The spirit within you — your humanity, your dignity — that light that flickers so faintly — here's a mantle of praise to wrap it up in. Chin up, head high — you belong to God! You matter!

God is making everything new — fresh!

Psalm 126

Psalm 126:1 has to be one of my all-time favorite Bible phrases: "When the Lord restored the fortunes of Zion, we were like those who dream."

Dreams are the stuff of our hopes, our best wishes, our life's aspirations. When we dream, we are transported beyond the world of the mundane; for a time, in our dream-like state, it seems that anything is possible. We can fly!

God's presence among us is the stuff of dreams — but, it is more than that. When God's hand moves, people know it: "The Lord has done great things for them!" (v. 2)

Interesting, isn't it, that the "great things" of the Lord are so often sown in the midst of tears? The God of Advent and of Christmas is the God Who Brings Forth Joy from Weeping. Weeping, we certainly have plenty of…may we find the patience and the wisdom to endure till the joy comes.

Luke 1:46b-55

This bit of Mary's "Magnificat" (the opening phrase in the traditional Latin setting) reflects God's propensity for turning things upside down — some would say, "right side up." We read Isaiah last week, who spoke of valleys being lifted and mountains being brought low.

Similarly, Mary highlights God's acting to bring down the powerful, lift up the lowly, fill up those who are hungry and empty the purses of those who (perhaps) trust vainly in their riches.

Oh, and one other thing — God has helped his servant. The newly-chosen mother of the Lord is already ahead of the game. Mary gets it. As her offspring will someday say, "Whoever wants to become great, must learn to be a servant." (Matthew 20:26)

1 Thessalonians 5:16-24

There is a great debate among preachers about the inherent usefulness (or devil-spawned evil) of sermons with titles like, "Ten Ways to Live the Successful Life God Wants You to Have!"

Well, apparently the apostle was wont to throw out the occasional list of actionable items for Christ-like living. There are at least 8 pretty cool things to do here that lead to a much-to-be-desired result: sanctification.

God's work in our lives, through Christ, is a process of becoming. It is ever God's work, to be sure, though we are co-workers/participants/beneficiaries; what we are becoming is more "holy" — more like Christ.

John 1:6-8, 19-28

John, who would become the Baptizer, sure had to get through an awful lot of negativity in order to do his job.

Notice all of the "nots" in this passage. He is not the light; he is not the Messiah. He is not Elijah, he is not "the prophet" — that voice of help and salvation that every generation seems to long for.

I imagine those gathered around John — the people famously described by former Vice-President Spiro Agnew as "nattering nabobs of negativity" — surmising that he must not be worth much. So many "nots."

When they finally asked him what he thought of himself, who he was, John's reply is laser-focused: "I am the voice of one crying in the wilderness — get it straight, people! Get ready for God's way!"

Sermon

"The Lord's Favor"

Trying to preach on this lesson from Isaiah reminds me of an old preacher story about the pastor and the Children's sermon.

Pastor says, "Well, boys and girls, what has a bushy tail and runs around in trees?" Nobody says anything. Pastor waits a bit, then says, "You know, it gathers nuts and puts them in holes in the tree and makes chirping noises, doesn't anybody know?" Again, a long silence.

Pastor sighs and says, "Help me out, boys and girls; surely somebody knows what animal I'm talking about."

After another awkward silence, one little boy slowly raises his hand. Pastor smiles and says, "Yes, Jackie"

Jackie swallows hard and says, "Well Pastor, we all know it sounds like a squirrel; but since this is church, we all know it'll turn out to be Jesus."

None of us can hear this text from Isaiah without also seeing in our imagination Jesus standing in his little home synagogue, reading this text and then saying to his friends, neighbors and relatives, "Today this scripture has been fulfilled in your hearing."

And because of this, even though we seminary trained folk are aware that that which was running around in the Prophet's brain might have been a political Messiah like Cyrus, or it might have been the tiny community of folk who had returned from Babylon to find Jerusalem in ruins, it might even have been the writer himself;

But, since this is church we immediately think of Jesus. And, like the children listening to the Pastor, we are both wrong and right in that assumption.

We are wrong if we think it is primarily, or only about Jesus, but we are right if we think it has something to do with Jesus, and us.

This text is set among those who have returned to Jerusalem after exile in Babylon. They have come home to find their city in ruins and their lives in disarray.

There are two important things that the texts calls upon that community to do:

1) Proclaim the year of the Lord's favor and
2) Thank God even before it happens.

Most scholars agree that "the year of the Lord's favor" refers to a Jubilee year, when all debts are cancelled and land is returned to its original owners. (Ummm? Sounds a little like Occupy Wall Street.)

The "servant" is sent by God to proclaim a year of God's favor to a group of down-hearted folk and to invite them to praise and thank God not for the good God has done, but for the good God will do.

John Goldingay, in his commentary on Isaiah, says they are to offer this response before the event actually happens. (Isaiah, p. 349)

That line, "before the event actually happens," made me rethink Advent a bit. Most of the time we talk about Advent as a time of waiting for the LORD to act.

Perhaps our call is to recognize that, like the folk in beat-up old Jerusalem, we are called to proclaim a year of the Lord's favor and thank God for the Good News before it happens.

Most folks could use a bit of Jubilee, I think. Things have been hard in the world and in this country for some time now.

Long years of war and social conflict have raged all over the globe, most countries are struggling economically; there is very little political stability anywhere in the world.

In the midst of all this we are called to both proclaim and live out a year of the LORD's favor. Jesus claimed this text for himself and his life on earth, we are called to do the same.

This is the cross that Christ called us to take up when he invited us to follow him, this cross of proclaiming God's preference for those whom the world despises, this is what we are called to do while we wait in the time between his coming years ago in Bethlehem and his coming again.

Amen.

The Fourth Sunday of Advent

2 Samuel 7:1-11, 16

This text turns on a play on the word: "house." This is one of the few times the pun works just as well in English as it does in Hebrew. David wants to do something for God by building God a house (physical structure). God turns that about by promising to build David a "house," that is "a family dynasty." There are two connections in this text to Advent.

1) The obvious connection to Joseph being "of the house and lineage of David," and all that that language implies in the Gospel stories.

2) More important is the promise of God's presence.

In one way or another, we all are prone to trying to keep God in God's place, aren't we? Whether it be between the pages of a black book or inside the restraints of a confessional system, we are not unlike King David in wanting to build a "house of cedar," where we can keep the divine under control. And God is not having any of it.

God reminds Nathan and David that God's place is where it has always been and always will be; in the midst of God's people. Advent is the promise that the uncontrollable, uncontainable and unlimited God will once again push through our restrictions and fear to stand in our midst.

Psalm 89:1-4, 19-26

Isn't "forever" a great word? The psalmist uses it three times in those first four verses. Makes me think of that great refrain from Handel's Messiah, choruses of "forever, forever" rolling and tumbling over each other like a sparkling waterfall. In secular music I think of Randy Travis' country song, "I'm gonna love you forever and ever, amen."

Yes forever is a lovely word. The Hebrew is ad olam, which "applied to David and his descendants, emphasizes the ever-continued, ever-acting presence of the blessing extended into the "indefinite future." (Vine's Dictionary of Biblical Words, p. 72)

What is the blessing that goes on forever? God's "steadfast love" and "faithfulness." God's gonna love us forever and ever, amen.

Romans 16:25-27

"The revelation of the mystery," that is best summation of Advent that I know. The mystery is the mystery of life, the mystery of meaning, the mystery of what it all means, the mystery of how we are to behave, the mystery of God and spirituality and life and death.

In the coming of the Christ, all is revealed, all is explained. Or so Paul says. Personally, I am still very often quite mystified by the whole thing, but I have to admit that clinging to the love of God in Christ gives me a good anchor to hold on to as I seek to understand the rest of it.

Luke 1:26-38

Two words leap out at me in this text: "favored" and "perplexed." For good reason is Mary perplexed. First of all, she knows she's a virgin; how can she be pregnant? Secondly, what sort of "favored" status is it to be pregnant without having had relations with your husband in a culture in which stoning is the proposed punishment for adultery?

If I had been Mary, perplexed would have been much too sedate a word to describe my feelings. "Angry and scared out of my wits" would have probably come closer. A bigger mystery to me than the virgin birth is Mary's reaction to the whole thing. Not just the perplexity and the polite questioning instead of the screaming heebie-jeebies; but the quiet acceptance and obedience in the words, "Here am I, the servant of the Lord; let it be with me according to your word."

Whether she actually said it or not, Mary lived those words. The question for me is whether or not I am ready to quietly and obediently live into the mystery of whatever God's steadfast love and faithfulness have in store? For me? Forever? Amen.

Sermon

"It's Good to Be the King!"

I've always heard that "it's good to be the king!"

You get to live in a palace, there are lots of people around to do what you say…they bring you food and wine and entertainment of all sorts. In fact, most everybody in your life is there to do pretty much whatever you want. After all, nobody outranks the king!

And so, we meet King David — the Shepherd Boy/Giant Killer/turned Warrior Prince and King. As Samuel records, David had no more worlds to conquer; God have "given him rest." All well and good, correct?

As it turns out, the whole "given him rest" thing wasn't all that it was cracked up to be — and David soon found himself restless. He needed something to do, some plan to conceive, some great deed to achieve. So, he cooked a little project up for himself. He was going to build God a house!

Oh, it would be glorious! David began to imagine the details in all their rich variety. One can almost feel his excitement as he shared his vision with his pastor — otherwise known as the prophet, Nathan. Brother Nathan liked the sound of the idea (remember, who's going to tell the king, "No, that sounds really stupid?") He gave David his spiritual imprimatur — "Go, do what you have in mind. The LORD is with you!"

There was only one problem with this awesome undertaking for God. Neither David nor Nathan had stopped long enough to ask God what it was that God wanted them to do.

So, Nathan gets a wake-up call around midnight one night; God has a message to be delivered to David.

"Do you think that I need you to build me a house? I've been doing pretty well for the last thousand years or so, in case you haven't noticed — I got Moses and your great-great-great granddaddy out of a pretty tight squeeze there in Egypt. I managed to keep your whole straggling lot of ancestors together for forty years in the wilderness. I got them all here to the Promised Land and have been with all of you every step of the way.

"And in all that time, I've lived in a tent and a tabernacle and I've never, ever asked anybody to build me a house. What makes you think that I need you to build me one, David?

"Remember, I picked you fresh from the sheep shift, young man — I stayed with you, helped you, and strengthened you— why, I made you, David! And I'm here to tell you, I didn't grant you victory over Goliath and Saul and the Philistines and Me-knows-whoever-else just to turn you into a glorified building contractor!

"I have something else in mind — something greater that I have planned for you to do. So, what I need from you is for you to just settle down, take care of the business I have set before you — and get back to being a king who cares for his people. Is that too much for me to ask?"

I would imagine you could have heard the veritable pin drop after God finished that comeuppance with both Nathan and with David.

The gentle correction of God is sometimes not so gentle in our lives. God needed David to understand — as I'm sure God sometimes is trying to get us to understand — that God was building David's life for a purpose. He was to be the progenitor of the family line that would lead to Joseph and Mary and to the baby in Bethlehem — the baby that was born to be the Savior of the world.

That's a pretty awesome assignment!

As we bring the season of Advent to a close and prepare to welcome the Christ anew into our lives, perhaps we can hear the word of the Lord for us in the midst of David's call:

Be careful when you think you have finally arrived; it is often most difficult to live successfully right after our greatest victories have been won.

Telling God what it is that you want to do can be a dangerous proposition. While God often works according to the desires of our hearts — and God certainly understands the ways that we are fearfully and wonderfully made — the basic commitment of our lives remains, "nevertheless, not my will but thine be done."

Even preachers get it wrong sometimes! Nathan got ahead of himself, or got a little carried away with the ambition of his most powerful and influential parishioner. Ministers are not perfect (in case you haven't figured that out) and shouldn't be expected to be. But, both members and ministers should be people of prayer — and certainly willing to admit it when they are wrong!

Whatever God has planned for you, you can trust that it will be better than anything that you may have imagined for yourself.

In his book, The Man God Uses, Dr. Henry Blackaby tells of reading the gospel story of the devoted friends who brought their paralyzed friend to Jesus one day. They wanted Jesus to heal their friend so that he could walk again. And yet, Jesus' response was, "Friend, your sins are forgiven." (see Mark 2:1-12)

Why did Jesus not respond according the wishes/prayers/faith of the friends? They asked for healing; Jesus offered forgiveness.

Dr. Blackaby says, "I began meditating on this passage…it was as if God said to me, 'Henry, these men were asking for one thing but I had so much more to give them.' If God had healed the man without forgiving his sins, he would have lost out on so much more God had to offer. Jesus not only provided for a physical problem, he provided for the spiritual one as well.

"When I realized this, I began to pray, 'Lord, if I ever make a request and you have something better in mind for me, please cancel my request.'" (Blackaby, Broadman and Holman Publishing Group, 1999, p. 90)

Lord, at the ending of Advent and at the coming of your Son at Christmas…if we have made requests and you have better things in mind, please cancel our requests.

Amen.

Christmas Eve/Christmas Day

Isaiah 9:2-7

I always wanted my family to hear from Ed McMahon when I was growing up. You know, the annual Publisher's Clearinghouse Sweepstakes? Ed and his crew would show up at your front door with a giant, over-sized check made out to "The Fairless Family" for One Million and no/100Dollars!

That's what I imagine when I read the line in Isaiah day about "as people exult when dividing plunder." How thrilled would I have been to divide the "plunder" of an unexpected bonus with my family members? Is that how I feel about the coming of the Wonderful Counselor, the Mighty God, the Everlasting Father, the Prince of Peace?

Psalm 96

I'm interested in the repeated admonition to "ascribe to the Lord" the glory due God's name. Ascribing something generally means to give credit where credit is due. I like that.

But, of course the original meaning goes even deeper; scribere is "to write," or even more literally, "to make a mark." When it comes to praising God for the wonder of creation, of Christ — we need to write it down — "book it," if you will.

Mark this day — this holy day — as the day we give God all the glory for Christmas!

Titus 2:11-14

Paul reminds us, in his words to Titus, that we have been waiting for a blessed hope, a manifestation (an outward demonstration, a materialization of something that has previously only been imagined) of the glory of God. And now, that for which we have been waiting has appeared.

Salvation is actually here, right in front of us — all around us, actually. Open your eyes, see it, feel it, hear it. Know it to be true to the depths of your soul. Jesus Christ is God, with us!

Luke 2:1-14, (15-20)

Cue Linus.

The Christmas speech from Charlie Brown's best bud is indelibly burned in the consciousness of the Peanuts generation; happily, through the magic of DVD's and Blu-Ray, the immortal moment lives on for new generations, as well.

Have you stopped to consider what a joy it is to continue to tell this story, year after year? We don't want to let it ever become blasé, just another story that we read.

Whether it's the "terror" of the shepherds at the first sighting of the angels, or the deep pondering of the Holy Mother at all that was happening around her…may we recover some of the mystery and awe of the events described in the gospel in our own hearing and telling.

Sermon

"Something for Christmas"

A few years ago I went down to a retirement center to hear the Choir sing. It was a good show.

They did a very hilarious version of "I ain't getting nuttin' for Christmas."

Do you know the song? A little boy sings about all the mischief he's been in, and then the chorus goes:

"I ain't getting nuttin' for Christmas, 'cuz I ain't been nuttin' but bad."

After I finished laughing, I started thinking and realized that while that line sums up a lot of our thinking about how God works, it's just not true.

Indeed, it is the exact opposite of the Gospel truth of this night; it is because we "ain't been nuttin' but bad" that we have received the one gift we needed, which is Jesus Christ Our Lord.

Not just or primarily us as individuals, but us as the human race, us as humanity.

As the Bible says, God so loved the World, the Cosmos, that he sent his only beloved Son.
No, it's not that we are individually evil; it's that the world is in a mess, and can find no way out.

The Christ was born at a time of political and social unrest.

Israel was once again a conquered country, living under the domination of the Romans, ruled by King Herod, a cruel, cruel man.
When Christ came, there was hunger and social injustice and war raged upon innocents, all in the name of such things as Truth and Justice and National Security.

Then as now, the old values had become skewed and obscured and unrecognizable, and no one knew whom they could trust.

And into such a world God sent the Son.

The message then and the message now is that we are not alone in the midst of the world's evil,

Though we, collectively," ain't been nuttin' but bad, we're still gettin' something for Christmas."
God has come to us in the midst of our distress. In the middle of our loneliness and despair,

God has sent us a sign of his love.

Into a world filled with hopelessness, God comes to us in the hopeful form of new life and new birth.
Christ came to be a beacon of light in a dark world.

Christ came to show us love in the midst of hatred and strife.

Christ came to bring life in the midst of death. The cross is a reminder to us that Christ did not come to be cute. Christ came to preach, teach, heal, suffer and die.

Just as the Cross looms over our altars, the cross hovers over the manger of the Christ Child.

Christ did not come so that we can have parties and give gifts.

Christ did not come, to reward us for being good, but to save us from being bad.

Christ came to show us the love and care of God in the midst of a deadly and dangerous world.

Christ came to show us how to live and how to die.

Christ came to die upon the cross for us, to save us from sin, death and the devil.

When we realize that, we are ready to celebrate with somber joy and reverent jubilation.

"I'm getting' sum-thin' for Christmas, even though I been nuttin' but bad."

"For unto us a child is born, who is Christ the LORD."

Amen and amen.

The First Sunday after Christmas
Isaiah 61:10-62:3

"My whole being shall exult in my God…."

Think about what it means for one's "whole being" to get involved in exultation — most of us are from very word-oriented traditions when it comes to worship. We listen a lot; we sometimes think about what we're hearing. And — occasionally — we actually do something with what we've heard (though we don't want to be too spontaneous or obvious with our actions.)

Our holiness brothers and sisters may have one up on us here — Shakers, Quakers, Rattlers, Rollers, Pentecostals of all varieties, even "Amen!" Baptists. That's probably a bit more of "whole body" experience when it comes to exultation.

Of course, there are some quiet ways to involve the whole being, as well. Prayer posturing (in the most positive sense of the word) such as kneeling, standing, or even falling prostrate would certainly qualify. Incense involves a different realm of the sensual; visual elements in worship can help.

I don't think Isaiah's point is necessarily about trying to come up with "the next new thing" in worship in order to attract the masses. But I do think a bit of consideration about stepping away from our potentially over-Reformed, hyper-sensitive aversion to anything "bodily" as part of living out our faith might be in order. Is God the God of the senses as well as of the mind?

Psalm 148

This psalm text has a whole lot of praising going on! The Bible is one of the first texts to promote inter-generational worship. Don't you just love the image of v.12? " Young men and women alike, old and young together!"

Galatians 4:4-7

Talk about a "pregnant moment!" God's timing was "full" — it was "ripe"- when Jesus entered the world as a human. The Christ was "born" to redeem us — actually, so that we could be "adopted" (a different form of birth) as children of God.

Gotta love the opportunity to call God "Daddy" — nothing sexist or exclusionist in this image. "Abba" is a term of endearment, a transliteration of the word spoken (or babbled) by children in cultures around the world. It comes through to us from the Aramaic term for a father...that moment of recognition that occurs with a grin and a stream of "abbabababa" gibberish from the mouth of a baby.

Warms the heart, you know...as God's heart must be warmed by our recognition and calling out for "Abba."

Luke 2:22-40

Simeon and Anna speak for the "senior generation" concerning this child that has been born. Their words are both wise and warning. This one brings light and glory — but risk, danger and soul-piercing emotion, as well.

Sermon

"The Main Event"

I don't attend big league sporting events very often. I take a yearly pilgrimage to Turner Field to see the Braves; otherwise I can count the number of NFL, NHL or NBA games I've seen live on both hands without using my thumbs.

But every time I go I find myself a bit overwhelmed by all the stuff that happens that has nothing to do with the game. Noise, lights, noise, food, noise, huge video screens, noise, fan contests. Did I say noise?

The last time I went to something like that I realized how easy it would be to lose track of the main event in the midst of all the loud and gaudy distractions.
And so it is with the Mass of Christ. There are so many loud and flashy and strident voices crying for our attention during this season that we can easily get distracted and lose track of the main event.

There is the commercial push that tries to convince us that the core to happiness is more stuff and that the best Christmas gift ever is the particular piece of stuff being advertised.

And while we all know that isn't true, we still find ourselves inundated with the commercials and almost against our own wishes and better judgment, we find ourselves buying a lot of stuff to give away to others.

Then there is the noise of standard American secular "Holiday Season." I kind of like some Christmas songs; "I'll have a bluuuuuuuuuue Christmas without you," for example, but few of us want those songs as our public soundtrack from the first day of November until Dec. 25th.

Then there's the Church related stuff which is intended to help us remember the coming of Christ but sometimes gets in the way too. We can get so carried away with and worried about the Choir cantata and the Children's Christmas program that we center more on the choral performance and the cuteness of the children than we do on the mystery of God made flesh.

Yes, the main event of the Incarnation can get lost in noise and lights and sentimentality of our celebration. It's like the crowd at a baseball game getting so involved in doing the wave that they miss an unassisted triple play on the field.

"The Word became flesh and tented among us."(Reynolds Price, Three Gospels)

The core of that main event, that unassisted triple play, that Incarnation we remember and celebrate today, is summarized in those few words; the Word became flesh and "made his home among us," "tented among us," "lived among us," (NRSV), "moved into the neighborhood" (Eugene Peterson, The Message)

But why? Why did "the Word," the Christ, the Son of God, do this? What is this Incarnation all about, and what does it mean for us?

Years ago, in the 1840's, Soren Kierkegaard, a Danish Christian writer, created a parable to help us understand this. It is called "The King and the Maiden." (Parables of Kierkegaard, T. Oden, ed.)

Kierkegaard tells the story of a king who was in love with poor peasant girl. She did not know him personally; he saw her from afar and wanted her for his bride.

At first the king thought he would do what kings normally did; he would send for her, announce his attention to marry her, she would accept and be eternally grateful that he had rescued her from her poor village, etc.

Then the King thought;" I do not want her to love me like that. I want a real love, a real marriage, a real relationship. I want her to love me for me!"

So, the king thought, in order to win his beloved's hand, he would cover his royalty with a beggar's cloak and go forth to woo her.

But then he realized that this was a ruse, a trick, and love can only be love if it is completely honest and true. He not only had to appear to be a beggar, he had to really be a beggar. American writer Phillip Yancey summarizes the conclusion of Kierkegaard's parable like this:

The king, convinced that he could not elevate the maiden without crushing her freedom, resolved to DESCEND. He clothed himself as a beggar and approached her cottage incognito, with a worn cloak fluttering loosely about him. It was no mere disguise, but a new identity he took on. He renounced the throne to win her hand. (Disappointment with God, 1988, p.110)

This is what Christ did. The Word renounced the throne to win the hand of the Bride of Christ; which is the church; which is us.

Philippians 2: 6-8 is a hymn, one of the first Christian hymns, and it is a hymn rejoicing in the Incarnation. Listen:

> *who, though he was in the form of God,*
> *did not count equality with God,*
> *as something to be exploited,*
> *but emptied himself,*
> *taking the form of a slave,*
> *being born in human likeness.*
> *And being found in human form,*
> *he humbled himself*
> *and became obedient to the point of death –*
> *even death on a cross.*

This is what we celebrate at Christmas; the love of a God who could have forced our loyalty and obedience through a simple act of the divine will; who could have enticed us to give our worship and admiration through displays of splendor and magnificence; but who instead chose to come and live among us, to crawl into our tent, to move into our neighborhood, to let go of all privilege and power; and come into our midst as one of us, as one of the lowest of the low; a tiny baby, born of peasant parents in a stable with a feeding trough for a bed.

Our God did this so that we would fall in love with the holy, so that we would see and know God's love as real, and so that our love for God would be real and not forced.

In the midst of all the noise and lights and distractions of the season, let us turn our attention to the main event and rejoice with quiet and loving hearts; "the Word became flesh and lived among us."

To show us the quietly tender love of God.

The Epiphany of the Lord

Sermon
by the Rev. Dr. Delmer L. Chilton

Texts: Isaiah 60:1-6, Ephesians 3:1-12, Matthew 2:1-12

The old farm house where I grew up had an old dirt basement underneath the kitchen, more like what people in other parts of the country refer to as a root cellar. You had to go outside to get to it, going through an entrance that always reminded me of the storm shelter in THE WIZARD OF OZ.

For much of the year we used it to store potatoes and yams and apples. They were in old wooden crates on a low table against the back wall, covered with burlap sacks.

Two or three times a week, Mama would send me to the basement to get something for her. I knew that old basement so well that I never turned on the light; I just walked straight into the darkness to the appropriate box and scooped up whatever it was that Mama wanted.

One year I got a flashlight for Christmas. For a few days I did nothing but fiddle with that flashlight. I did Morse Code with Cousin Bob next door, I tried to scare my little sister with the flashlight in the mouth trick, I tired reflecting light off household mirrors into people's eyes to annoy them; the usual 9 year old boy stuff.

Well, when my mother sent me to the basement for potatoes I of course took my flashlight. I stepped into the basement and turned it on . . . . and immediately wished I hadn't. In the sudden glare of my flashlight, I saw several rats and bugs and a snake or two scurry back into their hiding places.

I shuddered to think of all the times I had been down there in the dark and all those icky things were all around me and because it was dark I didn't see them.

In this case the shining of the light was not very comforting to me, instead is scared me greatly.

During Epiphany we celebrate the coming of the light of Christ into the world.

We celebrate it as a good thing, which it is. We celebrate it as a joyous thing, which it is. We celebrate it as a life giving thing, which it is.

But all too often, we celebrate it as an easy thing, a gentle thing, a non-threatening thing; which it most decidedly is not.

The coming of the light of Christ into the world is a hard, good thing. The coming of the light of Christ into the world is a severe mercy.

The coming of the light of Christ into the world brings life, but it also brings death.

Today's Gospel lesson tells the familiar story of the Magi, the Wise Men, following the star to the manger, where they find the true light, which is Christ our Lord.

Most of the text tells the story of their encounter with King Herod. In the midst of this seemingly pleasant tale, there is only one hint of darkness, when the travelers are "warned in a dream" (vs.12) not to return and report to King Herod.

This hint of darkness reminds us of the rest of the story; the fact that Herod was a bad king and a bad man. He was such a bad man that he killed all the baby boys in Bethlehem in hopes of killing the prophesied real king of the Jews.

This is usually referred to as the Slaughter of the Innocents and we don't talk much about it much, do we? It's a real downer, an ugly, dark story. Too dark and too ugly to bring up during the joyous and happy season of Christmas.

Most of us are like I was as a little boy going down into the basement in the dark. We are perfectly happy as along as we are blissfully unaware of the dangers lurking there.

When the light of Christ shines unblinkingly into the dark places of our lives, most of us are not very happy about what we see. None of us likes to have sins and shortcomings pointed out; not by God or anyone else.

But that is exactly what the light of Christ does; it shines upon our lives and shows us who we really are. It examines us in the unblinking light of God's holiness and we all blink our eyes and shudder to see the vermin of our inner selves revealed.

I have a friend who has 5 of the 7 early warning signs of melanoma. In order to keep things in check, he sees a doctor every six months for a thorough check-up.

He stands completely naked under an extremely bright light while the doctor looks over every inch of his body. It is a harsh light, a light that chows his every blemish and imperfection.

It is also a life giving light, for it reveals what needs to tended to and healed.

That is what the light of Christ is like. It is both hard and soft. It deals in both life and death. It shows both the presence of evil and the hope and way of salvation.

It was because of the darkness that Christ came into the world. There was darkness then; there is darkness now. War, injustice, cruelty, illness, uncertainty and the loss of hope are still rampant in the world.

And the light of Christ shines on, in us and through us. We are now the light of Christ in the world.

We are called to shine the light of God's love into the world's dark places. We are called to point out the ugliness of evil, and we are called to point to the eternal loveliness of Christ.

We are called to fill the world with the penetrating and healing light of Christ.

ARISE SHINE, FOR YOUR LIGHT HAS COME! (Isaiah 60:1)

AMEN AND AMEN.

The Baptism of the Lord (First Sunday after the Epiphany)

Genesis 1:1-5

There are, of course, a number of opportunities to address "beginnings" on this Sunday. We are still newly arrived at the beginning of the year. Genesis, the book of beginnings, opens with the beginning of our world. There is water here, though the dark and formless void seems more inhospitable and un-tamable than it does inviting and life-giving.

Baptism — the presence of water — will mark the beginning of both the ministries of John and of Jesus. Note also the presence of the Spirit at each of these beginnings; what "beginning" might the Spirit seek to make in the lives of the church this year?

Psalm 29

The "voice of the Lord" — a demonstrable, if somewhat unexplainable sense of presence — manifests in a number of unusual ways, according to the psalmist. Of course, there is water (think of the vast expanse of the ocean, as well as the roar experienced when standing near a waterfall.)

But there is also the cedar-ripping, oak-baring power of a storm in the forest, and the skipping/jumping/prancing euphoria of calves and young oxen loosed in the field. There is fire — a brilliant but dangerous display. There is the earthquake. As Elijah would learn, there is silence, as well (see 1 Kings 19:11-13, though not explicitly mentioned here.)

Where do you hear the voice of the Lord?

Acts 19:1-7

I've never known exactly what to make of this encounter of Paul with the Ephesians — except to note that, again, we have the presence of the Spirit of God noted in association with baptism and the message of Jesus. (Oh, and there's some business with laying on of hands, speaking in tongues and prophesying, as well — but, who wants any of that in our worship services?)

Mark 1:4-11

Baptism — repentance — fresh start — new things — Spirit of God — the Beloved — well pleased.

'Nuff said.

Sermon

"What Difference Does It Make?"

When I was a kid, if you were shy or failed to answer an adult's question, they would usually say, "What's the matter, cat got your tongue?"

As we think about the Baptism of Our Lord today, perhaps we could ask ourselves, "Has the cat got our baptism?"

What I mean to say is: "How impact has baptism had on my life?" "What difference did a few drops of water and some words make?"

In any discussion of baptism, the thing most people think they "know" is really the least important.

People "know" that you have to be baptized to get rid of original sin. Some people spend a lot of energy arguing there is no such thing as Original sin, and others worry about babies who die going to Hell if they haven't been baptized, and all of it is mostly beside the point.

This serious misunderstanding of the sacrament turns it into bot of divine Hocus-Pocus; of human beings casting spells that require God to act in a certain way, in this case, allowing the Baptized into heaven.

It is because of this understanding of baptism that people sometimes ask, "Why was Jesus baptized, since he was a sinless, perfect being, he had no sins which needed forgiving?"

This is an upside down and turned around picture of God's love. We try to earn it, or we feel unworthy of it. We try to figure out what we must do to deserve it; we try to pay for it.
This reminds me of a story I have told before, the story of Harvey Pinnick. Harvey, back in the 1920's, bought a little red spiral notebook and began jotting down his observations about golf and life. He never showed the book to anyone but his son.

In 1991, Harvey gave the book to a writer he knew and asked him if he thought it was worth publishing. The writer showed the book to an editor at Simon and Schuster Publishers. They called and spoke to Harvey's wife, saying they had decided to publish with an advance of $90,000.

Several days passed and Harvey Pinnick had not responded to the message.

Finally, Harvey spoke to his writer friend and said that with all his medical bills he just didn't see how he could come up with the $90,000 to get the book published. The writer had to explain to Harvey that he didn't pay Simon and Schuster; Simon and Schuster paid him!

All too often, we're like Harvey Pinnick. We misunderstand the message of the Gospel. We think we have to do things to make God love us when the message of our baptism is just the opposite; God loves us just the way we are.

Baptism is a message to us that our sins are forgiven; sins: past, present and future. Baptism does not forgive our sins; God forgives our sins. Baptism tells us that our sins are forgiven.

Yes, God loves us just the way we are. God also loves us too much to let us stay that way. Forgiveness of sins is not all that is going on in Baptism.

Look at our second lesson, the reading from Acts. At first glance, it looks like a bit of theological silliness; baptized in name of Jesus only, so what?

Well, if baptism is in the name of Jesus only, then it touches on forgiveness of sin and a commitment to follow Jesus, but it leaves out the most important part, the gift of the Holy Spirit. But, with the giving of the Holy Spirit, we are in a dynamic, organic, growing, pulsating relationship with God almighty.

We become enmeshed with God. God is in us, we are in God, we are the Body of Christ, we are the temple of the

Holy Spirit, we are NOT far off and distant from God, simply seeking to keep God from sending us to Hell through magical religious rites and our accumulated list of Good Works.

NO! We are part of the Divine Presence in the world. God has made God's dwelling to be within us.

Writing in Christianity Today, Pastor Paul Bocca talks about how some people find a genuinely Christian life boring. Going to church, doing the liturgy, reading the lessons, hearing the sermons, doing the rituals, serving on committees, etc. etc.

It's boring! This is why so many find their way to TV ministries and huge mega-churches that are entertaining and exciting.

Pastor Bocca then turns this boring accusation upside down – by admitting it, and then reminding us of another meaning for the word boring.

He says Christianity is boring. It is like the slow movement of a drill; slowly, laboriously digging beneath the surface of our lives. The continuing cycle of Sunday after Sunday, season after season, year after year, the Christian message and life in community bores ever deeper and deeper into our souls, until, we begin to realize the truth of the words spoken over us in baptism.

That we are a beloved child of God, we are marked with the cross of Christ forever, we are filled with the Holy Spirit, we are called to follow Christ, we are to love one another unconditionally, we are forgiven and called to forgive others, we are ambassadors for Christ.

This boring life of faith is begun at baptism, and is not completed until the day we die. We live each day in remembrance of our baptism, in remembrance of the fact that God loves us with a love so deep, so wide, so complete that nothing can separate us from that love.

And when we remember that, we will take our baptism back from the cat, we will loose our tongues to sing God's praises and free our hands to do God's works in the world.

Amen and amen.

The Second Sunday after the Epiphany

1 Samuel 3:1-10, (11-20)

As is the case in so much of the Hebrew scripture, we have some skillful storytelling in this account of God's appearance to Samuel. There are a number of "visual" clues as to what is happening:

God's words are rare, there are very few who have "visions"
Eli, the priest of God, suffers from failing eyesight
the lamp of God in the temple is dimming, as well, though it has not yet gone out.

All of which might well lead us to excuse poor, young Samuel from understanding on the first try — or the second — that God wanted his attention. Third time was a charm, with the help of the old man.

Does God ever have to try again and again to get our attention? Who is present to help us listen?

Psalm 139:1-6, 13-18

It's a fairly common occurrence when I speak with someone in the parish about accepting a place of responsibility or service: "Oh, Pastor, I don't think I'm qualified for that! Surely there's someone else who could do a better job than me!"

Whether motivated by false humility or genuine concern, we need to be pretty careful when it comes to being "called" by God for faith and service. Psalm 139 makes a strong theological assertion — God KNOWS us! God has searched us (a term of intense scrutiny) and has peered into every possible nook and cranny of our existence. And God still finds us to be "fearfully and wonderfully made."

God's work is good work. We must always remember that our lives are the handiwork of the Creator, and that God's calling and gifting are sufficient for any task God would have us undertake.

1 Corinthians 6:12-20

"Whatever, I do what I want!" might well be the contemporary equivalent of the argument Paul is seeking to broach with the Corinthians. (if you are unfamiliar with the idiom, you can check it out in the Dictionary of Urban Slang.)

As those who belong to Christ, can we do whatever we want? In a sense, Paul says, "Yes, we can" — and that's not a campaign slogan! But that is not to say that we should do whatever we want.

The issue here is not keeping a checklist of naughty and nice ways for Christians to occupy our time; rather, what is it (or, more properly, who is it) that rules or controls our lives? To make Jesus Lord — to say yes to God's will and way — means to say no, sometimes. (The contrary is true, I am sure.)

Our bodies, minds, and spirits belong to God; Christ is Lord in every inch of our existence.

John 1:43-51

Everybody needs a good, healthy skeptic in their lives. Jesus called Nathanael, whose name means "gift of God." Interesting, isn't it, that Jesus welcomed Nathanael's searching honesty into his intimate coterie of disciples?

We often focus on more well-known followers of the Lord, like Peter or Paul and the particular gifts (and foibles) they had to offer. But, Nathanael is an excellent case in point: Jesus really does want and need ALL of us in his church!

One of my favorite rejoinders when I meet someone who says, "I'm just not so sure I believe in all that God stuff" is "Great! You're just the person I'm looking for — we really need you here!"

Sermon

"The Voice of God"

I have been deeply confused over the concept of hearing the voice of God ever since an incident that happened when I was a little boy.

I grew up next door to my Grandparents and ate breakfast with them 3 or 4 times a week, which was good, because Aunt Mildred lived with them and was a great cook and made especially wonderful biscuits; but it was bad because you could not talk during breakfast because the folks, Grandpa and Grandma and Aunt Mildred, had to listen to their favorite program while they ate:

THE MOODYS OBITUARY COLUMN OF THE AIR.

It started with somber, funereal organ music, then a deep, basso profundo voice would intone...

John Doe of 334 Mockingbird Lane passed away last evening at Northern Surry Hospital. His is survived by . . . He was employed by . . . . He was a member of . . . . Funeral to be held at . . . conducted by the Rev. . . Memorials may be sent to . . . . etc.

for about 5 to 10 names, all read with great dignity by that deep, deep voice. I was about 5 or 6 at the time and concluded that the voice on the radio was the voice of God.

Who else would know all those things about a person, all those details?

And the Church we attended then put a lot of stress on the Second Coming and the Rapture and the "He Will come Like a Thief in the Night" and stuff like that.

They really talked a lot about whether or not you'd be ready to go when the Man Upstairs decided it was your turn to face the Final Judgment.

So, I decided the voice on the radio was God sending out a message: "These are the ones I took last night. Are you ready to meet your maker?"

One day, my Daddy dropped me off at Elmer's Barber Shop to get a haircut while he ran over to town to get a truckload of fertilizer.

I had just learned to read a bit and was very happily looking through the Boys Life magazines when I got scared out of my skin.

The man in the chair opened his mouth and out came that oh so familiar voice:

"Elmer, could you take a little more off around the ears?"

Oh my God, Yes MY GOD was there, right there with me in that Barber Shop.

Oh no! My time had come! He had come to take me home. It was time for me to face the Final Judgment.

And of one thing I was never more certain; I was not ready to go. So I hid in the bathroom until he left, cowering in the dark under the sink.

So, this whole audible voice of God in the night thing is a little unsettling for me.

I have never heard another audible voice that I thought to be the voice of God, and yet I believe God has called me into the Christian life and that God has called me into ordained ministry and that God has called me to various churches, and that God has called me into my present position and that God has many more calls left for me before my call to stand before the Judgment Seat.

And the words of I Samuel 3:8 have been very helpful to me in all these calls: "Then Eli perceived that the Lord was calling the boy."

God lives in community, perhaps God only lives in community, I don't know.

But I do know that I need community to live in God. I need the encouragement and correction and opportunity to love others and to let them love me.

And I especially need them to help me hear the voice of God, to perceive with me that God is calling me.

In the Gospel lesson Jesus calls Phillip and Phillip "passes on" the call to Nathanael, inviting him to come and see this Jesus of Nazareth, and the community which he has called together.

We sometimes talk about Jesus going about preaching and teaching as if he were mostly doing this all alone with a group of silly disciples/fishermen/tax collector groupies around for comic/foil purposes.

We often fail to see that Jesus came out of his wilderness experience realizing his deep need for community in the life he had been called to live out in the world. His first act was to gather such a community of love, support and companionship.

Just as Jesus needed community, so do we.

We have a tendency to want to go it alone; to fly solo. Too often our religion has a "me and Jesus," feel to it. If we have no one to talk to, to pray with, to listen to about the activity of God in the world and it our lives we might not hear or understand God's call to us, and we could get confused about who's calling and end up hiding from the wrong voice.

God's call to us today comes to us in community and calls us to community, to the community of Christ, the people of God.

Most of us will never hear an auditory voice calling our name in the middle of the night, but God has called each and every one of us.

The call comes to us like it came to Nathanael. Someone has been our Philip, seeking us out and inviting us to come and see, to come and be a part of those who seek to follow Jesus.

And all of us are called to be a Philip for someone else. We are called to seek out and find those persons who are trying to go it alone and invite them to join with us in the company of Jesus.

It's really not all that hard; just ask someone to come and see the thing that which made all the difference in your life. God will do the rest.

Amen and amen.

The Third Sunday after the Epiphany

Jonah 3:1-5, 10

"Does God ever change His mind?"

I realize that question is not formed with strict adherence to inclusive language, but I'm trying to get at the passage from Jonah here (which frames God as changing "his" mind — and relieves us of all sorts of pressure to kowtow to the urge to crack any jokes about who changes their mind more often, males or females.)

Anyhow, I have participated in one or two theological brouhahas over the implication behind the question: does God ever change his mind? Can God change his mind? Well, it would certainly seem that that would be the prerogative of the Divine; what good is it to be God if you can't do what you want to do?

Does God change God's mind? Hmmm, there are those that would argue that since God is perfect, once God makes up God's mind and decides on "God's will" for a given situation, then there is no need for God to change God's mind so — no, God doesn't change his mind.

All of that is to say that we can open ourselves up to some real feats of doctrinal derring-do and sleight of hand if we're not careful. I don't want to step in too quickly and attempt to speak for God, especially where God's grace is concerned.

Bet'cha the Ninevites are glad that God can change his mind!

Psalm 62:5-12

Good thing God is a rock.

Well, not literally...but you know what I mean. If I am trying to understand God's steadfastness and stability, it might help for me to consider the strength of a substantial boulder. I traveled across the western United States this past summer, and saw lots of "rocks" scattered about in various plains, canyons and arroyos. My impression of most of them was, "Dang, I bet that rock has been there for a long, long time."

They had withstood the tests of wind, water and time. Some of them had survived earthquakes, volcanoes and the like. At this point, they are not about to be shaken from their stance; they make a strong foundation.

God is like that, the psalmist says. God is a refuge, a shelter; you can put your trust in God. God has been tested and has proved faithful, again and again.

1 Corinthians 7:29-31

The world is just not what it used to be. So says the Apostle. Actually, I suppose Paul's message to the Corinthians is that the world never has been what we sometimes think it is!

Who, or what, do we trust with our lives? What truly is most precious? Time is short, no matter what your eschatological disposition. "The end of the world" is closer today than it was yesterday.

Mark 1:14-20

Jesus was awfully time conscious, himself. Echoing John the Baptizer's message of repentance, Jesus added the even greater sense of urgency: "The time is fulfilled,. the kingdom of God has come near...."

What can a sense of urgency do for our faith, in a positive manner of speaking? Or are we to assume that 2012 will just be "business as usual?"

Sermon

"Now Is the Time"

When I was about twelve years old, I found an old Royal manual typewriter in the closet under the steps.

It belonged to my mother, who had bought it when she was in High School.

Since at that time William Faulkner and Walker Percy were my heroes and I intended to grow up to be a great Southern novelist, I knew I need to learn three things: how to smoke, how to drink and how to type. My mother could know about and help me with only one of those ambitions.

So, she taught me to type using the phrase they taught her at Stuart Virginia High during WWII:

Now is the time for all good men to come to the aid of their country.

I sat at the kitchen table and over and over again typed it out, "Now is the time. . ." Now, 45 years later, I still type that out when testing a computer keyboard.

"Now is the time. . . "

I thought of that line as I read our scripture lessons for today. Each of them is about urgency, immediacy, the press of time.

Jonah preached to the Ninevites and his message was "Now is the time to repent." Paul in Corinthians says "Now is the time to get serious about God." Jesus says to Simon and Andrew, James and John, "Now is the time to follow me."

Now, now, now.

Jonah – "In forty days it'll be too late!"
Paul – "The appointed time has grown short."
Mark – "And immediately they left their nets and followed."

Now, I confess that this is a difficult message for me to preach. Not because I don't understand it or believe it, but rather because I am one of the world's greatest procrastinators.

My wife, "Will you take the recycling to the curb?" Me, "Sure, no problem." Hours later. "I thought you said you were going to take the recycling to the curb."

Me – "I am." Her – "Well?" Me – "Oh, you meant now?"
That line, "Oh, you meant now," is the procrastinators' mantra, our motto, our personal and communal creed.

It allows us a somewhat graceful escape by implying that we simply didn't understand the urgency of the request.

The meaning of today's scripture lessons is this: God means now!

We in the church are very good at ecclesiastical procrastination. God says, "Come and follow me."

We say, "Sure, no problem."

Presently God comes back and says, "I thought you were going to follow me." And what do we say? "Oh, you meant now?"

God says, "I want you to spread the Good news of my love." And we say, "Sure, no problem." Later, God returns, tapping an impatient divine foot and saying, "well?'"

And we say, "Oh, you meant now?"

In the all the areas of our spiritual and churchly lives, God has called us to act; to pray, to witness, to share our resources.

We are called to feed the poor, to clothe the naked, house the homeless, to heal the sick, to stand with the oppressed and suffering.

And we answer all those callings with a resounding yes. But God continually has to come back to us, reminding us, "Yes, I meant now!"

Now is the time for all people to come to the aid of God's reign. Now is the time for us to take up our cross and follow Jesus.

Now is the time to fully commit ourselves to the Good News of Jesus Christ. For, if not now – when?

Amen.

The Fourth Sunday after the Epiphany

Deuteronomy 18:15-20

The old saw, from George Carlin originally, is that "atheism is a non-prophet institution."

Certainly, the role of the prophet in Israel's religion is a central one. We are urged to listen and pay attention to the words of a true prophet. (What that constitutes is sometimes a bit up for grabs.)

But the prophet is bound pretty seriously by his or her claim to speak a word from God, as well. Verse 20 says that claiming to speak for God — when actually you are not — is worthy of death. Might want to think about that, preachers, the next time you enter your pulpit!

Psalm 111

Half-hearted. Lukewarm. Tepid. Unenthusiastic.

These are not words that describe any organization or effort that most of us would want to be a part of, do they? In fact, if we find ourselves in the throes of lethargy and boredom while attending a meeting or event, we generally will go to great lengths to find a reason to excuse ourselves and move on to something more productive — or at least more interesting.

The psalmist reminds us that worship is to be "wholehearted." This is the greatest enterprise in heaven or on earth. Come on people of God, let's give it all we've got! Or, our audience (God) might just look for an excuse to head on out somewhere else!

1 Corinthians 8:1-13

Knowledge and authority — and their proper use — are part of the theme running through today's readings. For each of us as Christ's followers, there are some things that we "know," Paul writes.

I "know" that a particular behavior or action is "okay" for me; it does not cause me any harm in my faithful walk with Christ. Someone else, however, may have a concern about that action. I need to have some level of consideration for what they "don't know" as compared to what I do.

We could probably construct a long list of such questionable actions, depending on our culture, the time period, our particular theological leanings, etc. For the Corinthians, it as all about idol meat. Growing up in a small, rural West Tennessee town in the 1960's-70's, for me it was "dancing and drinking." (Some thought good Christians could do those things in moderation; others thought it must surely be a sin!)

So, what do you know? And even more importantly, how does what you know help either to advance or to limit the purposes of God and God's reign in the lives of those around you?

Mark 1:21-28

Jesus never had to pull an Eric Cartman ("You will respect my authori-tah!")

All he had to do was what he was sent to do — teach and preach the good news of God's grace — and people sensed the authority in his words.

We are often taught or coached that we must convince people to have faith in Christ, or to hold a particular interpretation when it comes to particular doctrines or theological interpretations. Some of our traditions may even require obedience to authority represented in a bishop, superintendent or other ecclesiastical office.

Regardless, there is an authenticity that comes from representing God openly, honestly and truthfully (see commentary on Deut. 18, above.) Whether or not one's message on behalf of God is ever accepted, the power of it will be plain to see when it is offered in the spirit of Christ.

Sermon

"The Voice of Authority"

Back in the early 1990's former President Jimmy Carter was on the David Letterman show. He told a story about going on a speaking tour of Japan.

He said he told a little joke and, after the interpreter had finished translating, the room erupted in laughter. Carter was both surprised and pleased.

After the speech an old friend of Carter's who spoke Japanese told him why everyone had laughed so loudly.

The interpreter had said, "President Carter has told a very funny story. Everyone should laugh now."

Mark's Gospel says that Jesus "taught as one having authority, not as the scribes."

In this case, the scribes were like President Carter's interpreter, telling people how they should feel and respond rather than making clear what God had said..

Most people have gotten accustomed to getting our truth from interpreters who tell us how we should feel, how we should respond.

From parents to pastors to politicians; from teachers to TV talking heads; our ears are bombarded by the voices of interpreters telling us how we should feel, how we should respond, to everything from eating our veggies to the latest uptick in the stock market.

And most of us, most of the time, have learned to listen to our interpreters with a grain of salt, sort of half-listening to what is said as they drone on in monotonous, "should"ing mode.
Which is what makes an authentic and true voice so startling. A voice like the voice of Jesus, who "taught them as one having authority, and not as the scribes (the interpreters)" (vs. 22)

When Jesus preached at Capernaum, the text says the people were astounded and amazed. They didn't know what to do, nobody was telling them how to feel or what to do, whether to laugh or not.

Genuine freedom is a very frightening thing. And emotional freedom is the most frightening freedom of all, as the casting out of the unclean spirit shows.

Without debating spirits and demons and mental illness and emotional compulsion and all that; can we say that the unclean spirit is that which is in all of us that resists genuine freedom and responsibility in our lives?

Upon hearing the voice of authority, a voice declaring our freedom; our unclean spirits immediately resist because our unclean spirits recognize in that voice of freedom the call to change.

Indeed, the unclean spirit is correct when it accuses Jesus of having come on a mission of destruction, "Have you come to destroy us?"

Jesus does indeed come into the world and into our lives with an agenda of anarchy.

Jesus came to tear down any and all walls of separation that keep God's people apart from one another.

Jesus came to erase the structures of slavery to sin which keep us in bondage to our own badness.

Jesus came to wipe out the diseases of the soul that keep us from knowing God's love and hold us back from loving one another.

Yes, Jesus came to destroy. But, he came to destroy in order to rebuild, to reconstruct, to recreate.

Jesus came to remake us in the image of God. To make of us new creatures in Christ. It is no wonder that unclean spirits, past and present, are afraid.

They know that the coming of Christ spells the end of their reign of fear in the human heart.
In The Lion, The Witch and the Wardrobe, the children are somewhat afraid when they learn that the savior of the Narnians is Aslan, a lion.

"Is he safe?' they ask, "Safe!" the beaver responds, "Of course not. He's a lion. But he's good."

Just so, Jesus is not safe; he did indeed come to destroy.

But he is good, because he also came to remake us into the wonderful and loving human beings God made us to be in the first place.

And it is no wonder that the people were both astounded and amazed.

In the clear, un-interpreted, un-translated, rural accented voice of Jesus they heard a call to freedom, a call to shuck off all the shoulds they had heard all their lives.

In that voice, they heard a call to respond to the love of the one who loved them.

In that voice, they heard a call to leave fear behind and to step out in freedom to do God's work in God's way in the world.

In that voice, they heard a call to love the unlovely, to feed the hungry, to clothe the naked, to house the homeless, to cry out against unclean spirits of war and oppression, injustice and indignity wherever they have a stranglehold on human lives.

In that voice they heard the voice of God say, "I love you, come follow me."

Amen and amen.

The Fifth Sunday after the Epiphany
Isaiah 40:21-31

Verses 28-31 of today's reading are classic descriptions of God's being and power. This is the Creator of the "ends" of the earth (God has already been to the boundary of the universe that we are striving to glimpse with space telescopes like the Hubble and the Webb.) This God never grows weary — and never runs out of computing power, either!

For an interesting overview of gigabytes, terabytes, exabytes and beyond, you can check out this article from Forbes : http://www.forbes.com/sites/oracle/2013/06/21/as-big-data-explodes-are-you-ready-for-yottabytes/.

I suppose God's understanding, being "unsearchable" or limitless, must surely exceed the current largest measure of computer capacity, the yottabyte (1.209×1024)

All of that said, notice that God's inexhaustible power is made available, not only to those who wish to soar with the eagles or run with boundless energy — but also to those who need help just getting up and walking for a few more steps along the way. That's God with us!

Psalm 147:1-11, 20c

Some of God's favorite things (apparently):

- stars (knows how many there are!)
- young animals (provides grass for them)
- clouds and rain

- the brokenhearted
- the poor
- the wounded
- people who both fear God (reverence, respect) and hope in God

1 Corinthians 9:16-2

Paul's "all things to all people" approach sounds wishy-washy to some. It's really kind of hard for me to imagine Paul as either wishy or washy, but be that as it may — I believe this passage speaks of some opportunity for understanding those who are "not like me."

I am definitely not Jewish — I'm not black — I'm not female — I'm not Muslim. In fact, there are just a whole boatload of things that I am not, so there is a whole boatload of perspective that I may need to try to gain if I am to be a true "preacher" of the gospel of Christ.

An old gospel song came up in conversation in a small group that I participate in this week; I still love the tagline after all these years: "Don't tell me what a friend I have in Jesus, till you show me what a friend I have in you."

Mark 1:29-39

Jesus had a fairly singular focus: "Let us go on to the neighboring towns, so that I may proclaim the message there also; for that is what I came out to do."

But he stopped long enough to help out Peter's mother-in-law and a passel of other sick folks. Never too busy to do a good turn. Good example for pastors and busy disciples of the Lord, don't you think?

Sermon

"Busy People"

"In the morning, while it was still very dark, he got up and went out to a deserted place, and there he prayed." (verse 35)

I have a church cartoon file. In it there is an old cartoon from Leadership Magazine. It shows a pastor down on his knees in his office, Bible or prayer book open on the chair in front of him.

Secretary sticks her head in the door, looks at him and says," Good, you're not busy."

"And Simon and his companions hunted for him. When they found him, they said to him, "Everyone is searching for you." (verses 36-37)

Which is just another way to say, "Good, you're not busy."

That's pretty much what happened to Jesus in today's Gospel reading. The story takes place early in Jesus' ministry. He has been baptized and then tempted in the wilderness.

He has returned to the area and begun gathering disciples and doing some teaching in the synagogue, where he healed a man with "unclean spirits."

And today, they leave worship and go to Simon's house for dinner. While there Jesus learns that Simon's mother-in-law is not well and he very matter-of-factly heals her.

Word of both healings spreads and instead of a restful Sabbath afternoon, Jesus spends the day healing sickness and casting out demons. A very full work load for anybody, even the Son of God.

So, early the next morning Jesus sets out to find some "me time." Or, perhaps more correctly, some "me and God time." After a day like the one he'd had, he needed to think, to pray, to just be in the presence of the holy for a little while.

But it was not to be. Here come "Simon and his companions," like a herd of zealous church secretaries. When they find him sitting quietly alone they say, "Good, you're not busy. Everybody is searching."

They probably expected Jesus to jump up and say, "My goodness, where did the time go? Boy, I've got to get back to town and get on those healings and exorcisms right away. Thanks for coming to get me."

But that's not what he said. And that's not what he did.

Instead, Jesus got up, stretched and said, "Let's go to the next town, so I can preach the message there too. After all, that's what I'm here for."

Or as Mark puts it, ". . . so that I may proclaim the message there also; for that is what I came out to do."

What is this message that Jesus has come out to proclaim?

It is a promise and an invitation; a promise that God has not forgotten or abandoned the world, and it is an invitation to become a participant in God's work in the world.

One of the most important keys to reading Mark's gospel is to realize that all the healings and exorcisms show us not only who Jesus is, but they also show us who God is and who we are and who we are called to be.

The healings and casting our of demons show Jesus to be a healer and proclaimer sent from God, carrying on God's work in the world.

They also reveal clearly that our God is a God who is present and not far off, a God of love and compassion, a God who is active in the world and in our lives.

These healings also revel to us who we are.

We are the people whom God loves; loves enough to touch and heal and care for.

And, we are people invited by God to join in the divine mission and ministry of healing and reconciliation in the world.

And it is in the context of this life of service to God and the world that going off alone to pray makes sense, for Jesus and for us.

Every few months, there is another article in the religious press about why a lot of people have left the church. More recently I have seen articles in USA Today, the New York Times, even the Wall Street Journal.

In the midst of most of these articles you will find the phrase, "spiritual but not religious." Often you will also find, "They like Jesus, just not the church."

They, depending on the authors intent, are either "young people," or "modern people," or "urban people," or "working-class people;" some socio-economic demographic or the other.

Anyway, this "spiritual without being religious," has led to a notion that spirituality and prayer being mainly personal and private, for one's own good and benefit.

The "value" of God and Jesus and the Church in our increasingly materialistic and consumerist culture is calculated purely on their effectiveness in "making my life better."

This is why you have folk moving from church to church or abandoning the concept of church all together while saying, "Well, I just wasn't getting fed; I wasn't getting anything out of it."

Listen up people, it's not about you.

It's not about me, or any other clergy person. It's not about the church board or the youth program or the Sunday School or whatever.

It's about God and it's about the world and it's about the people in the world.

It's about joining Jesus in his mission to proclaim the Good News of God's love and grace to all the people in the world.

And that is hard work and you can't do it 24/7 and you need friends and you need God to be able to pull it off.

Jesus went to synagogue, Jesus had a small group, Jesus spent time alone, Jesus proclaimed the kingdom, Jesus did healing.

It is only as a part of this sort of rhythmic cycle that the personal time with God fits, it cannot stand on its own.

For us to answer God's call to follow Jesus, we need public time gathered around Word and Table, we need the support of and conversation with like-minded folk, we need private prayer and meditation and we need to be out there, sharing God's love in word and deed with God's suffering children.

We are called to a life of prayer and service, living within God's community so that we will be strengthened and empowered to love and serve and heal and save the world.

We are continually called into God's presence so that we may be sent back out into God's world, proclaiming God's love, healing God's people, being genuinely busy doing what we too have come out to do.

AMEN and AMEN.

The Sixth Sunday after the Epiphany

2 Kings 5:1-14

The mighty and the lowly are often juxtaposed in scripture. Mountains are made low, valleys are exalted; rich men are cast down, beggars are lifted up. Ignorant fishermen are occasionally called to preach, just as learned rabbis are by-the-by given "thorns in the flesh" as they seek to minister.

Naaman, as Dr. Chilton reminds us (see sermon below), was a great man by any society's measure. Super successful, virile alpha-male, probably even photogenic in his prime (he would be a great presidential candidate in our time, I suppose!)

But he was afflicted with a disease that was the scourge of the lowly. The great warrior was a leper. He needed some serious help from the great prophet of Yahweh, and so sets out to (eventually) find Elisha.

Interesting to note that he might never have been cured if it were not for the advice of a captive slave girl (another mighty/lowly juxtaposition in vv. 2-3.)

Though Elisha wielded great and impressive powers in his own right, there is no spectacular miracle of healing to be performed. He doesn't even meet Naaman in person, but rather sends a messenger. "Go wash seven times in the Jordan River — that'll do it."

Naaman is incensed at such a simplistic prescription — he doesn't even consider the Jordan to be a real river! It is his own servants who convince him to give it a try; seven dips and it's done. Naaman is healed.

In what ways might God be seeking to use the lowly things of our lives to accomplish a mighty purpose? Do we complain or obey?

Psalm 30

The psalm text has language that echoes the experience of Naaman; the Lord has "drawn up" his servant. God "brings up" from Sheol.

For the burdens of mourning and sadness, God offers dancing and gladness. Good swap anytime you can get it!

I love v.12 and its association with Fanny Crosby's gospel song text, Redeemed: "I sing for I cannot be silent, [God's] love is the theme of my song!" (Learn more about the song here)

1 Corinthians 9:24-27

We live in a success-oriented society — "everybody likes a winner!" Of course, we also live in an age when "every player gets a trophy" — a practice that is decried by some. I guess the flip side of everybody likes a winner is that we need a lot of losers.

I don't think the apostle is trying to say that, in Christ, some of us (or just one of us) is going to be the "winner" in the heavenly sweepstakes, and that all the rest of us will be losers. I also don't think that this is a case of every player gets a trophy, either.

Regardless of one's soteriology, it seems that Paul's point here is that living the Christ life is worth the struggle; none of us should "run aimlessly."

Imagine Usain Bolt (check out http://usainbolt.com if you don't know who Bolt is) taking off at the crack of the starter's pistol and trotting forward a few steps, then veering off and running toward the stands, stopping to chat and grab a little popcorn…you get the idea.

"Run, Christian, run!" might be an acceptable paraphrase?

Mark 1:40-45

"If you choose…" is the challenge and approach of the leper in today's gospel story. An interesting and novel approach to prayer, perhaps. In this instance, Jesus is moved with compassion and does choose to bring healing.

Jesus seems willing because the leper seems willing. There's an important idea here about the way we cooperate with the power of God, I think.

Of course, there are still some unanswered questions in this account, as well. Are there times that Jesus does not choose to make one whole? Are there people who pray, seemingly willing for God's power to be displayed, and yet no apparent healing occurs?

Later in the gospel story, it is Jesus himself who will be faced with something of a dilemma concerning God's choice at the cross- "Abba! Father! All things are possible for You; remove this cup from Me; yet not what I will, but what You will." (see Mark 14:36)

Submission; acceptance; trust. God's mighty power at work in the lowest (and lowliest) places of our lives. My, oh my, we preachers have a lot to work with here!

Sermon

"Healed by God's Love"

Naaman was a great man. The Bible calls him a "great warrior," and says he was "in high favor with" the King of Aram, a neighboring kingdom to Israel.

Naaman also had a problem, a weakness. He had a skin disease. The Bible calls it leprosy, but it could have been anything along the lines of eczema or psoriasis.

As the story unfolds, an Israelite girl who had been captured in war becomes a servant girl in Naaman's household. She tells Naaman's wife about a prophet and faith-healer over in Israel.

The wife tells Naaman and Naaman tells the king.

The King values Naaman so highly that he sends Naaman to the King of Israel with a letter of request and lots of money and gifts.

Naaman comes before the King and presents his letter. Here's what the letter said,

"When this letter reaches you, know that I have sent to you my servant Naaman, that YOU may cure him of his leprosy."

When he reads the letter the Israelite king panics. "What kind of trick is this?" he thinks. "He sends his great warrior in here and demands that I cure him of leprosy, what's he trying to do, start a war? I'm not a healer, I can't cure anybody!"

The servant girl said that a prophet in Israel could heal Naaman but somewhere along the way it turned into a request for the king to cure. The king of Aram assumed the other king had all the power in his own kingdom. And notice how quickly the king of Israel assumed that the other king was up to no good. It does not seem that much has changed in the world of politics in 3000 or so years.

If Elisha the prophet had not stepped in at this point an attempt to do a good deed for a friend could have been turned into an excuse for war.

But, Elisha did step in. He invited Naaman and his entourage to come to his house for healing.

However, the misunderstandings weren't over yet. Naaman shows up at Elisha's house, fully expecting a grand welcome.

I suspect he also had a preconceived notion as to how things were supposed to go when one goes to a faith-healer. He was looking for ceremony and pyrotechnics and grand gestures invoking the power of the gods.

Instead, Elisha sent out a servant with a short and somewhat strange message:
"Go wash in the Jordan seven times and your flesh will be restored and you shall be clean."

That was all. That was it. No incantations. No "magic salve." No "balm from Gilead." No mumbo, no jumbo.

Just "Go. Wash. Restored. Clean."

Now it was Naaman's turn to get a bit reactive.

The prophet had seriously disappointed him. No royal welcome, no flashy ceremony. And wash in the Jordan? That's just a piddly little creek compared to the great rivers of Damascus, my home town! Why can't I wash there? This is ridiculousness. I've never been so insulted in all my life!

So, like a little boy on a playground who didn't get his way, Naaman grabs up his stuff and stomps off toward home.

Once again the common folk, the servants, come to the rescue. They approach him, call him down and talk a little common sense into him.

"Look, if the prophet had asked you to perform some great feat like climbing a high mountain or slaying a great monster, you would have done it. Your problem is all he did was tell you "wash and be clean." Can you not do this simple thing?

Naaman calmed down and listened to his servants and went to the Jordan and washed three times. And yes, his skin was restored. He was cleansed and he was healed.

And you know what. In the end, Naaman did do a great thing, or at least a thing that was difficult for him. Naaman humbled himself in obedience to God and God's word.

Naaman put aside his pride and his expectations and his preconceived notions and his resistance to simplicity and made a decision to trust.

Naaman didn't trust God, but because he didn't know or believe in the God of Israel. Naaman didn't trust Elisha, because Elisha didn't act like the religious leaders he was used to. But Naaman did trust his own servants and with that tiny sliver of trust, of faith, he was healed.

All of us could use a little healing, most likely.

All of us have places of brokenness and weakness. No matter how great or powerful or rich or successful we may be, all of us have blemishes, things that weaken us, part of ourselves we don't want other to see. All of us need to be healed in some way at some time in our lives.

And all of us, like Naaman, need to learn to trust.

We need the opportunity to find a place that is safe enough that we can let go of our pride and our pain long enough to let the gentle healing power of God's love wash over us. We need to remember that we are all called to a life of servanthood.

Remember, Naaman didn't trust God, Naaman didn't trust the official religious person Elisha, but he did trust those who served him.

We are servants of God and servants to each other. Many times we will be the only voice of hope and love another person in our life will be able to hear.

We are called take responsibility for speaking gently and in love to those around us, constantly reminding them of the simple power of God's love.

We are called today, as individuals and as a community of faith, to allow ourselves to be healed by God's love. It is not an easy thing to do. Many things can stand in our way. Let us be like Naaman and let go of those things.

Gathering whatever sliver of faith we can muster, let us give ourselves into the simple love of God, trusting that it will change our lives forever.

Amen and amen.

Transfiguration Sunday (Last Sunday before Lent)

2 Kings 2:1-12

It's a bit of an odd story — but, of course, it's important, not only for the gospel reading for today, but in its own right, as well.

Elijah has had a long and varied ministry. Like most of us called to serve God, he has been more faithful some days than others. But, no one doubts that Elijah has pretty much been "THE MAN" when it comes to prophesying God's word in Israel. Ever since he flamed the prophets of Baal on Mt. Carmel (and subsequently went into pouting mode,) God has led Elijah through the depths and to the heights of ministry.

Now, it's Elisha's turn; we can certainly say that Elijah's successor has determination and perseverance. Elijah tries three times to "give him the slip," but Elisha will have none of it. All he wants is to be twice as successful at following God as Elijah has been. I don't think he's begin cocky — he really, really wants it!

His predecessor can't guarantee it, but because Elisha is willing to stick with it — God blesses him. Nice parable for us.

Psalm 50:1-6

Psalm 50 is a nice worship piece for this Sunday, with its images of fire, light, and shining forth.

2 Corinthians 4:3-6

Our "natural" hearts and minds are veiled; we cannot see spiritual things clearly. But, the presence of God causes light to shine out of darkness (a connection to the primal creation story) and reveals Christ to us and in us.

Mark 9:2-9

Fire on the mountain, as it were; the Transfiguration is always an exciting story. Mark's terse treatment, if anything, highlights and accentuates the action.

I like it that it was a SUDDEN realization that there was no one to go down the mountain with them but Jesus. Wherever we go, Christ is there.

Sermon

"Where God Has Sent Us"

Imagine the Peanuts Cartoon: Linus and Charlie Brown are lying on their backs on the pitcher's mound, staring up at the clouds in the sky. Charlie Brown says, "Linus, do you ever see anything in the clouds?"

Linus: "Well, yes Charlie Brown, I do. For instance, that one over there bears a striking resemblance to Michelangelo's depiction of the Creation on the ceiling of the Sistine Chapel. And that one, there over the school, looks like a map of Scandinavia, see; there's Denmark and Sweden. And that one there looks like a helix. Do you ever see anything Charlie Brown?"

Charlie Brown: "Well, I was going to say a Ducky and a horsey but I changed my mind."

Every time I am confronted with a Biblical story like the Transfiguration, I feel a bit like Charlie Brown; compared to the religious experiences of others the things I have seen are simple and plain. My personal religious experience contains no bright flashes or red-hot emotions, no defining moments of transcending clarity, no poetic, mystical exuberance.

No, my religious experience tends toward the mundane and the ordinary; reading the Bible, family prayers, church on Sunday, familiar hymns. I have no frame of reference with which to begin to try to understand what happened to Jesus and his Disciples on top of that mountain.

The experience is completely and totally foreign to me. And yet, there is something within it that tugs at my heart, that pulls at my soul, that preys on my mind.

There are two ways to approach a story like this: one is the rational, analytical, scientific approach. The other is as a child, with eyes attuned to seeing mystery and magic.

Soren Kirkegaard told a parable about this:

There were two young people, one a German girl, the other an English boy. They met on the beach in France; they conversed in high school French. After returning to their respective homes, the girl wrote the boy a passionate letter in German, which he did not know.

First, he laboriously translated it, using grammar books and dictionaries and lexicons. But, he did not stop there. He put aside the intellectual work and read the letter for what it was; a love letter from a girl; a love letter aimed at his heart, not at his head.

So it is holy stories, with the Bible. While we must not turn off our brains in looking at a story like this, we cannot stop at the rational level, we must remember to read the Bible for the other thing that it is; a letter of love aimed at the heart. Matthew wrote this story to touch our hearts, to let us know something important about the love of God for us.

I learned to read using Dick and Jane books. Some things have stayed with me. "See Dick. See Dick go. Hear Jane. Hear Jane talk. Go Dick go. Go see Jane. Etc."

One way of looking at, listening to, hearing the story of the Transfiguration is through the mind of a child, through the simple words of See – Hear – Go.

What did they see? We must remember that this was a vision, a thing seen! So the important question is not what actually happened, what factually occurred. The important question is what did the disciples report that they saw; what was revealed to them?

So, again what did they see? They saw light and clouds which are ancient symbols of God's presence; remember the Exodus through the desert, God lead the Children of Israel with a cloud by day and a fire, a light, by night. The disciples saw God's presence and guidance, a cloud and a fire, on Jesus.

They saw Moses and Elijah. In Jewish tradition Moses represented the Law and Elijah stood for the Prophets. In Jewish Tradition, both Moses and Elijah were to return before the Messiah, the appearance of Moses and Elijah signaled to the disciples that Jesus was the Messiah.

Moses and Elijah give Jesus their blessing and then the disciples see Jesus' alone: this shows that Jesus completes, fulfills, the Law and the Prophets.

What did they hear? They heard divine speech silence human speech: vs. 5 – "while he was still speaking." They heard a command to listen to Jesus: vs. 5 – "listen to him." They heard from Jesus the Gospel: vs. 7 – "get up and do not be afraid!"

Through the eyes of Peter, James and John we have seen the vision, we have heard the voices. How are we called to respond? Where are we to go?

First, we are called to the mountain. Not to blinding lights and booming voices but to time apart with Christ. We are called to look at Christ with awe and hope and love, we are called to listen to his commands to love one another with body, mind and soul.

Then, we are called off the mountain and back into life. Like Peter, we want to stay on a spiritual high but we can't stay, we have to go back down to where life is lived for real.

For it is down here, and out there, in our homes and schools and jobs and communities in the mundane, ordinary, "so-called" real world that real faith is lived out. That is where we live our faith, that is where we shine the light of Christ, because that is where that it is needed most.

And that is where God has sent us.

The Seventh Sunday after the Epiphany

A Lectionary Lab Bonus Sermon
(for those who may not be celebrating the Transfiguration of the Lord on the Seventh Sunday after the Epiphany)

by the Rev. Dr. Delmer L. Chilton

Alex Haley, the author of Roots, was not an overnight success. He grew up on a farm in West Tennessee then spent many years in the merchant marine. After he was discharged he turned to writing penny-a-word short stories for pulp magazines under many pen names.

He worked in relative obscurity until first his biography of Malcolm X and then roots made him both rich and famous.

In his office Haley had a framed photograph of a turtle sitting on top of a fencepost. When asked about it, Haley would explain; if you see a turtle on a fence post you know he didn't get there by himself. He had some help. Whenever I start thinking about what a great job I've done, I look at the turtle and remember how I got here. I had help.

Today's Gospel lesson is about a man who got well. He didn't do it alone, he had help; help from Jesus and help from his friends.

As the story opens Jesus has returned to Capernaum, where he was "at home," the Bible says.
We're not sure if that means he was a home-owner and they were in his house or if he lived in someone else's home. Either way, people had heard about his healings out on the

road and they knew where to find him and flocked to his house.

There was a crowd, a crowd so large and tightly packed that one person in search of healing could not force his way in. So he and his friends hit upon a clever idea.

They went up on the roof and cut a hole in the ceiling and lowered him into the room where Jesus' was. This was not as difficult as one might think. There was almost certainly a set of stairs on the outside of the house leading to the roof. The roof itself was probably flat because families used the roofs the way we use patios; as a cool place to eat and sometimes sleep during warm weather.

The roof was formed by thick beams three or four feet apart, first covered with tree branches and then several feet of dirt. This is why the text says they "dug through it." Though this was not a welcome act of destruction, it was one that could be easily and inexpensively repaired.

So they lowered the man down into the room so that he could be healed by Jesus. Then comes the most fascinating line in the story; "When Jesus saw their faith, he said to the paralytic, "Son, your sins are forgiven."

Did you catch that? Mark says Jesus saw the faith of the friends and healed the man. This was indeed a turtle on a fence post, for he was completely dependent on his friends. As are we all.

Several years ago I knew a man who was a prominent church leader; a pastor, a professor, eventually a bishop. He was a man of strong faith.

But his faith grew very cold when his wife died of cancer at a relatively young age. A few years later he wrote about his very personal dark night of the soul. He said he could no longer believe in God, he felt no love, no hope, no faith, no anything. He went through the motions in his job, but his insides were dead.

He wrote of going to church and being unable to pray. He went, he said, and sat when everyone else sat and stood when everyone else stood, he read the prayers, he sung the hymns, but he felt nothing. Nothing at all.

The worst time was during the prayer of the church. He could not pray, he could not believe that anyone was listening. He knelt, he said the appropriate responses, but nothing was happening, it felt so unreal.

Often he asked himself, "Why do I go? Why go through the motions?" And the only answer he could come up with was that he needed to be there with those people who did believe and who did care, about God and about him.

Eventually this man's faith grew back again. He said it was a long, slow process of hanging on. And the most important factor in being able to hang on was the people who prayed for him.

He said, "I don't mean the people who prayed to God mentioning my name and my need and asking God to help me. I mean the people who, week after week in church, prayed the Prayer of the Church while I sat among them unable to pray. They prayed for me, in my stead, in my place, because I was unable to do it for myself.

In those days, he was a turtle on a fencepost, carried by the faith of his friends when he was unable to lift himself. The faith of the church became his faith when his faith was paralyzed.

We are all called to be friends to one another.

We are called to carry each other into the presence of Christ.

We are called to pray for one another.

We are called to have faith in and for each other.

We are called to carry each other before the presence of the Christ, where our sins are forgiven and we are truly healed.

Amen and amen.

Eighth Sunday after the Epiphany (see Proper 3 – Season after Pentecost)

Depending upon the date of Easter each year, the liturgical calendar and the lectionary readings shift with regard to the length of Epiphany and the Season after Pentecost.

The same readings serve the same Sundays, but the Sundays are sometimes called by different names. Hence, you will find the readings listed below either as the Eighth and Ninth Sundays after the Epiphany, or as part of the Proper series beginning after Pentecost. We're only printing them once, so please flip away to your delight, depending on what you need this year!

Ninth Sunday after the Epiphany (see Proper 4 – Season after Pentecost)

Ash Wednesday

A Bonus Sermon for Ash Wednesday

Matthew 6:1-6, 16-21

A few years ago I was pastor in a church that was in the midst of a renovation. On the hall where I had my office there was a temporary wall with plywood door. On the door was a sign "Danger. Do not enter."

And every Sunday after worship I returned to my office and observed the tell-tale dusty footprints on the hall carpet. People simply couldn't resist going into the education wing to check out the progress.

Remember that you are dust and to dust you shall return.

Like dusty footprints in the hall we leave behind us traces of our humanity, signs of limitedness and imperfection for all the world to see.

We are human and prone to failure.

We are human, and unable to make of ourselves anything else.

Dust reminds us of the messes we make in life, the messes we sometimes make of life.

No matter how hard we try not to we leave bits of dust, of mess, behind us wherever we go.

That is why the Ash Wednesday liturgy has within the long confession. It is an invitation for us to own up to the inevitable messiness of our lives.

But, it is important for us to remember that confession always ends with absolution, with a declaration of forgiveness, with a word of grace and wholeness.

Remember that you are dust and to dust you shall return.

These words themselves contain both confession and absolution, law and gospel in equal measure.

They echo the story in Genesis in which God took a lump of clay, a bit of dust, and breathed life into it, into us.

We are dust, but we are very special dust, we are dust filled with the breath, the spirit, the very life of the creator God.

And when we die, we in all our dirty dustiness will return to our maker, to God.

Far from being rejected for our dustiness, we will be gathered back to the one who gave our dust, who gave us, our very lives.
In the meantime, between birth and death, between dust and dust, we live in the world as imperfect human beings, as fractured angels, as what Luther called being a saint and sinner at the same time.

All too often we see ourselves and our God at one end or the other of the holiness spectrum.

Either we see God as a stern and unbending judge and ourselves as miserable sinners or we see God as an indulgent grandparent who excuses our every mistake on the strength of great love and ourselves as sweet, harmless, and innocent little saints.

And the truth lies somewhere in the vast empty space in the middle, both for God and for us.

Yes, God is righteous and holy. Yes, God does hate sin and demands justice and obedience. Yes, we do often fail to measure up.

And yes, God does love us with a complete and unconditional love, a love that casts our sin deep into the sea, as far from us as the east is from the west.

And the problem is we can't find a nice middling image for God, halfway between these two extremes; there is no middle position, God is not either/or; God is both/and.

God is both judge and savior just as we are both saint and sinner.

Remember that you are dust and to dust you shall return.

We are dust beneath God's holy feet and we are dust that has had holiness breathed into it.

The God who condemns is also the God who saves, both, at the same time.

Our Lenten journey is a journey to the cross, to the place where the ultimate mystery of God's eternal love is revealed.

The cross is the place where God's judgment of sin and God's forgiveness of sin merge into the form of the crucified Christ.

Luther said that there is only one place we can look and be certain that we are seeing God.

There is only one place where God's terrible justice and God's steadfast love can be clearly seen together. That place is Christ upon the cross.

So, please, please, remember that you are dust,

And please, please remember, to dust you shall return.

Amen and amen.

The First Sunday in Lent

Genesis 9:8-17

Lent begins with a covenant.

God made a promise (a solemn agreement, if you will) to Noah that God's vindictive judgment would never again occur by means of a flood. The rainbow becomes a symbol of life through this covenant. It is a sign of hope for "all flesh," as well — God's love for the world is just that. God's love for the world.

Might Lent be an opportunity for us to review our own covenant with creation? How shall I treat the world that God has made, and which I am privileged to occupy?

Psalm 25:1-10

Psalm 25 makes an excellent prayer guide for Lent: "Make me to know your ways, O LORD; teach me your paths." (v.4)

Walking the path — participating in the journey — taking time to prepare our hearts and lives. Perhaps these metaphors for this season of the church's life are a bit overworn; however, listening and watching for God's guidance ARE age-old practices that can and should be renewed — not just in Lent, but throughout our lives.

1 Peter 3:18-22

We follow Jesus.

That's our "job description" as disciples. Everywhere Jesus goes, his disciples follow. (For Peter and the gang, that got a little tough in the garden, outside the judgment hall, and at the cross.) What it means for us to follow Christ in his suffering and death is the subject of much consideration for us these next few weeks.

But, one thing is certain: when we follow Christ in suffering and death (here, "death in the flesh,") we are, like Christ, made "alive in the spirit."

Baptism is connected to this supreme action of God in our lives by Christ; it is his acting, his living and dying, which saves us. As Christ was obedient to God in all things, including his own baptism (see the gospel reading for today,) so for us obedience in baptism is an act of following Christ. We are his disciples when we believe and are baptized.

Mark 1:9-15

Belief. Temptation. Ah, the twin experiences of the life of faith!

It would be nice, we are sometimes prone to think, if we weren't faced with so much temptation as we attempt to live for Christ. We truly believe…and we don't really mean to mess up when tempted to do so. We feel guilty because of our continuing propensity to sin.

We may be unsure, at times, of our own worth before God. Why, oh why, do we have to face such trials? Why couldn't God just remove them from our lives?

The wilderness experience of Jesus — coming as it does on the heels of his own "profession of faith" with John at the

Jordan — is a time of preparation. It is signification of things yet to come. Whatever it was that Jesus faced for 40 days in the desert, it was nothing like the trial he would face as he approached the cross.

Perhaps the wild place — the barren, lonely place — is the time we need to be assured of the presence of God, the constant Love of God for our lives. Perhaps this is where we most effectively learn to pray, "lead us not into temptation, but deliver us from the evil one."

Is our own time of trial a preparation for what we have yet to face? Can we learn the deep truth of all that it means to be the Beloved of God?

Sermon

"Just the Facts"

When I was a kid I used to watch a detective show with my father. It was called "Dragnet," and I always liked to see Sgt. Joe Friday begin to get impatient and then say to a witness, "Just the facts. Ma'am, just the facts."

Marks' gospel is the "just the facts" version of the Jesus story. He covers the entire, "Jesus tempted in the desert by the devil," in just thirty-three words; "And the Spirit immediately drove him out into the wilderness. He was in the wilderness forty days, tempted by Satan; and he was with the wild beasts; and the angels waited on him."

It took Luke 250 words to cover the same ground.

But, in spite of his brevity, or perhaps because of it, Mark gets his story told, and told effectively. There is no time to waste on literary ornamentation or theological speculation.

This is important. Time is of the essence. The Messiah has come, and you, me, we, everybody has to decide and decide now, what to do about it.

Eugene Peterson in his Message translation of the New Testament, modernizes the last line like this: "Time's up! God's Kingdom is here. Change your life and believe the message!"

It the "time's up" that grabbed me. I am an inveterate procrastinator. I wait until the last minute on almost everything. In college, I pulled all-nighters to write term papers. When I first became a pastor, I wrote sermons on Saturday night, (and some on Sunday morning!) For years, I have done the family taxes on April 15, driving around late at night, looking for an open Post Office.

So the words, "Time's UP!" sent a chill down my spine. And I think that one of the things that ails me and all of us in the life of the church is that we have very little sense of urgency about the gospel. After all, it's been 2000 years and Jesus hasn't come back yet, so why worry?

But really, a better question is what are we waiting for? A sign from heaven? Already had one and his name is Jesus.

What are we waiting for? Clear instructions on what to do? Already got those. Love God with heart, mind and soul and the second is just like it, love your neighbor as yourself.

What are we waiting for? Don't have enough time? We've got all the time we need; from this moment until the day we die, and then - really and for sure, it will be "Time's Up!"

"The right time has come, and the Kingdom of God is near! Turn away from your sins and believe the Good News." (The Good News Bible)

Amen and Amen.

The Second Sunday in Lent

Genesis 17:1-7, 15-16

The idea of "covenant" continues from last week; God's covenant with Noah symbolized life and hope — cessation from destruction. Now, God Almighty asks Abraham to walk before him and to exercise faith ("be blameless.") Not to be perfect, really, because Abraham (like Noah before him and countless others after him) certainly has his moments of weakness.

But it's the intention that matters; Abram's submission to God is shown as he "falls on his face" (recognizing the superiority of the other.) The covenant is one of blessing, of multiplied goodwill and prosperity. Abram is promised many descendants — and he knew as well as anyone that that is some promise to a 99-year old man!

This God is a God of awesome promises and spectacular fulfillment. Can God really be trusted to do what God says?

Psalm 22:23-31

God's work is multi-generational. Always has been, always will be. God's promises are to Jacob and his offspring, but God's work is intended for the benefit of all nations (I love the phrase "all the families of the nations shall worship before him" in v.27.)

Notice that we are included in the psalmist's invocation: "future generations will be told about the Lord, and proclaim his deliverance to a people yet unborn." (vv. 30-31) Pretty cool, huh?

Romans 4:13-25

The apostle goes right to the heart of the matter, recognizing that it must have been something of a struggle for Abram to believe that two old people like Sarai and himself could become parents — indeed, that he would truly become "the father of many nations." But, Abram found a way to believe.

Abram "faithed" it out. It was definitely a process, as Paul notes that he "grew strong in his faith as he gave glory to God." (v.20) Nobody automatically starts strong in their faith. It has to grow on you. Or maybe in you, or all around you.

What ways can we "give glory to God" as we continue to grow stronger in our faith?

Mark 8:31-38

Nobody likes negative talk; Johnny Mercer knew that when he penned the lyrics to his hit song, "Accentuate the Positive, Eliminate the Negative" in 1944. (It's a catchy tune, and was purportedly based on a sermon he heard his priest preach in Savannah, Georgia. Listen to Mercer's original version at

https://www.youtube.com/watch?v=f3jdbFOidds)

Peter tries to give Jesus some similar advice, but the Christ will have none of it. "Get behind me, Satan…" are not the words you hope to hear when you have a one-on-one conversation with Jesus.

The kingdom happens through denial and cross-bearing; it wasn't a particularly popular message then, nor is it now. One finds one's life by losing it. We still have a long way to go in figuring that one out, don't we?

(For Mark 9:2-9, see commentary for The Transfiguration of our Lord.)

Sermon

"Changing the Recipe"

In an old Reader's Digest at the doctor's office, I ran across this little story. A woman writes:

When my sister-in-law Ginny cooks she likes to substitute ingredients for those in the recipe.
One time I gave her the recipe for a chicken-and-walnut dish that her husband, my brother, likes, and she served it one night when I was over.

In place of walnuts, she used raw peanuts. And for chicken, she substituted beef. In fact, every major ingredient had been replaced.

"This is terrible!" my brother said after one bite. Ginny glared across the table at me and said, "Don't blame me! It's your sister's recipe!"

In today's Gospel Lesson, Jesus tries to explain to his disciples what it means for him to be the Messiah and for them to be his followers. But Peter doesn't like it. He wants to change the recipe, the formula, the instructions.

All this suffering and dying business doesn't fit his understanding of what a Messiah is, and it REALLY doesn't fit his understanding of what he wants to do with his life in God's service and Jesus' footsteps.

Starting our Gospel lesson with verse 31 is a bit jarring; we begin in the middle of the story. It's like walking into a party just as everyone gets deadly silent and a woman screams at her husband "That's what you think!" and stomps off upstairs and locks herself in the bedroom. You're left looking around at everyone asking, "What? What was that about?"

In order to understand this text, you really have to know what went before. Just a few verses earlier, Jesus asked his disciples: Who do people say that I am? And the disciples offered up John the Baptist, or Elijah, or one of the Prophets. Then Jesus asked, "Who do you say that I am?" Peter answers for them all when he says, "You are the Christ, the Messiah!"

This is where we come in; Jesus is explaining what it means for him to be the Christ, the Messiah. 'The Son of Man must undergo great suffering, and be rejected by the elders, the chief priests and the scribes and be killed . . ." Jesus went on to talk about being raised after three days, but Peter quit listening at the part about being killed.

Peter's brain screamed NOOOO! NOT Jesus, NOT the Messiah, NOT the Christ. That's not the way the story goes; that's not right; that's not the formula for success, we've got to change that!

So Peter grabs Jesus and takes him aside for a little private conversation. Actually the Bible says Peter rebuked him; that's a strong word. It means he fussed at Jesus for not being Holy enough, for not staying up there on the pedestal where Peter and the rest had put him and wanted him.

When Jesus yells "Get behind me Satan," he is not yelling at Peter; he is yelling at Satan. This business of avoiding the cross is a real and terrifying and lifelong temptation for Jesus. This was Jesus' lifelong spiritual battle.

In Luke's version of this story, he says that Satan left Jesus alone until a more opportune time. Well this is it. This is a good time to get under Jesus' skin with the temptation to power and privilege

Here Jesus is; surrounded by an adoring crowd that has begun to call him the Son of God, the Christ, the Messiah. He has struggled to maintain his humility by referring to himself as the Son of Man and by talking about suffering and rejection and death.

But Peter, his main man, tries to talk him out of it. Jesus recognizes the voice of Satan when he hears it. This is a moment of genuine temptation which must be resisted firmly:

"GET THEE BEHIND ME SATAN!"

This battle continues all the way to the cross. Remember in the Garden of Gethsemane, how Jesus prays and drops of blood form on his brow and he cries out, "Not my will, but thine be done?" That's the moment Jesus finally puts Satan away, the moment he completely replaces his own will and desires with the will and desires of God the Father.

After pushing Satan away, Jesus gathers the whole crowd together to teach them, and us, what it means to be disciples of Christ, followers of Jesus.

One thing's for sure; no one can accuse Jesus of false advertising, of luring followers with hip music and entertaining video displays and cool, helpful sermonettes on *Three Tips for a Happy Marriage* or *Ten Biblical Investment Strategies.*

Jesus lays it out straight and unmistakable: "If any want to become my followers let them deny themselves, take up a cross and follow me." Now, many of us, when we hear that recipe for being a Christian; that set of instructions for building a Christian life, we rebel.

Not like Peter, with a straight out rebuke and argument with Jesus. That, I think, would be more honorable than what we do. No, we're more like "Ginny," changing the recipe.

Well, he couldn't have meant for us to deny ourselves, not really. That's just, well, that's just un-American. We're supposed to have the things we want because God loves us and will bless us. He must of meant that we should read the Bible carefully for all those wonderful promises about how we can be happier and richer and a more well-rounded and well-liked person.

And take up a cross? Surely not! Surely, he didn't mean that we show give away our heard-earned money; that we should actually suffer for the good of others. Probably he meant that we should give a reasonable percentage of what we have, like the Lutherans, say 2 or 3 %. That's probably what he meant. He was just exaggerating to get his point across, like my old gym teacher.

And follow him? Gee, I don't think so. After all, Jesus ended up dead. I think he meant we should admire him, and worship him, and expect good things from him, especially when we're in trouble; but follow him? I don't know.

Yes, the change the recipe and then wonder why the Christian life isn't all it's cracked up to be. GK Chesterton said that Christianity has NOT been tried and found wanting; Christianity has been tried and found difficult and then abandoned by most.

Brothers and sisters in Christ; Jesus meant what he said. On March 20, 2000 PEOPLE magazine ran a story about Bennett Chapel Missionary Baptist Church in Center, Texas. One day the pastor's wife was praying and asking God "Why is my life so empty?"

Soon thereafter she and her husband began taking the state classes to be foster parents, and soon the idea spread throughout the church. Bennett Chapel is a tiny church, made up of working class people making a living as loggers or down at the chicken plant or at the hardwood flooring company.

They didn't have much to start with. But they decided to use what they had to make a difference in the lives of hurt, abused and unwanted children. As of the year 2000, 17 families in the church had become foster parents to 43 children in just two years.

As I think about that story, I am always struck by two things:

First, these were just ordinary people, with ordinary incomes and ordinary lives who basically did not need another child around to feed and clothe and worry about. Yet, in response to the tug of God's will, they laid aside their own wants and needs for the sake of another.

Second, a quote from the social worker that echoes our Gospel lesson's conclusion.

Social worker: "They don't view themselves as a blessing for the child. They view the child as their blessing."

Jesus: "For those who want to save their life will lose it, and those who lose their life for my sake and the sake of the Gospel will save it."

Our calling today is to lose our lives into the life of Christ, to lose our wills in the will of God to give ourselves up totally and completely to the one who gave himself up for us upon the cross.

Amen and amen.

The Third Sunday in Lent

Exodus 20:1-17

"Nope. Not gonna' do it!"

Dana Carvey made a mint on his impersonation of President George H.W. Bush (the first Bush to be POTUS) and his famous line regarding raising taxes. The monologue had, as its chief virtue, the short-but-sweet repetition of the "not gonna' do it" tag-line. It stuck in the popular culture.

Now, there is no real comparison between the Decalogue and Dana Carvey, but the strength of these "ten words" that have impacted culture for several thousand years are their brief, to-the-point presentation of the way that we should live. (Not that we always do, but we can aspire, eh?)

Other gods? No, don't do it!
Idols? Nope.
Use God's name the wrong way? Negative.
Labor on the Sabbath? What were you thinking?

Honor Mom and Dad…good.
Murder. Bad.
Adultery. Unh-unh.
Stealing…don't even think about it!
False witness — tsk, tsk, tsk!
Really, really wanting what belongs to somebody else? Bad idea!

Psalm 19

How do you say it, but not really have to say it? Lots of guys wish they could figure this question out when it comes to professing their love. We're not that good with words — at least not most of the time.

The heavens, on the other hand, are quite good at expressing the greatness of God without the need for any words or voice. All one need do to get a glimpse of the glory of God is to take a look around. The world is full of it!

1 Corinthians 1:18-25

What we do as preachers can certainly be considered foolish by some.

I mean, come on...we're going to make some sort of difference in the lives of our parishioners and congregants by what we say week after week? Get a grip!

Except that the message we seek to impart — the message of the cross of Christ and its self-giving power in the midst of our existence — THAT really does make a difference when we hear and act upon it.

Preaching, and the message that we preach, may seem foolish; but, the Apostle rightly reminds us that "God's foolishness is wiser than human wisdom, and God's weakness is stronger than human strength."

John 2:13-22

Okay, so were the sellers of cattle, sheep, and doves — and the notorious "money changers" — really doing a bad thing?

No, they were actually providing a decent and helpful service to the pilgrims who needed to travel a long way to make their Temple sacrifice. Nothing wrong with the service itself.

But…we must always be careful of allowing even good acts and intentions of encroaching on the space that belongs to God and God alone. Selling stuff "in the temple" is a whole other ball game. The temple is set apart for worship; sheep just really don't fit here! (Ahem, see the "ten rules" mentioned above.)

Are there any ways that we are filling God's temple with things that don't really deserve to be there? What encroaches on the "holy space" in our lives that belongs to God and only God?

Sermon

"What Shall We Do with Freedom?"

Samuel Wells, former Dean of the Duke Chapel and minister to Duke University, writes of something that happened 20 years ago in Romania.

"The Iron curtain was falling all over Europe, Communism was collapsing. On Christmas day of 1989 Romania's President was arrested, tried and executed.

"The country was in turmoil. No one seemed to be in charge. Reporters flooded the country, looking for anyone who could speak English.

"Finally they found someone, and in one sentence she summed up not only Romania's predicament, but the human condition: 'We have freedom,' she said, 'but we don't know what to do with it.'" (Christian Century, March 15, 2000)

A similar thing happened in Germany after the Reformation started. Turned loose from the rules and regulations of the Catholic Church, many people thought the Gospel meant that they were free to do as they pleased because God's grace was free.

Martin Luther himself was sent out to visit the churches all around Wittenberg and wrote his catechisms, Large and Small, as a response.

Referring to his visitation of the churches he wrote in the introduction, "Alas, what wretchedness I beheld. We have perfected the fine art of abusing liberty."

The Bible tells us that this was the situation of the Hebrew people when God gave the Ten Commandments.

They had just been liberated from slavery in Egypt, they had been handed a great gift of freedom, and they didn't know what to do with it. They too were perfecting the fine art of abusing liberty.

The word we often translate from Hebrew into English as law is Torah. Instruction, guidance or teaching would be better.

The Hebrew people themselves never considered the law to be onerous or a burden; rather they saw it as a gift. A gift flowing out of God's love and concern for the people who needed to learn how to live with their new freedom.

We too struggle with issues of what to do with our spiritual freedom, our religious liberty; and how to treat God's law in light of God's grace and forgiveness.

Many of us give ourselves lots of slack in regards to the Ten Commandments, believing ourselves to stack up pretty well. Which is, I think, to miss several important points.

The Ten Commandments aren't rules that God has laid down as a test to see if we're good enough to get into heaven; rather they are God's very practical guide to living a fulfilled and fulfilling life.

As such they work on several levels.

First, they are an outline for living together as ethical human beings; a picture of the kind of life God wishes for us. It is perfection we will not reach, but that is no excuse for not trying.
.
Second, they are a "mirror for the soul," as Luther put it, helping us see ourselves as sinners in need of God's grace.
I was looking them over and trying to figure out which ones I had not broken; at least not in the strictest, most literal sense.

No other Gods – Nope. No Baal or fertility cult worship going on in the Chilton household.

No graven image – Nope. No bowing down to a man-made object that's not a God.

Not taking the Lord's Name in Vain – Nope. Well, I do have a barn-yard vocabulary but I draw the line at G– D—.

Remember Sabbath Day – Nope. Always go to church on Sunday, seldom do manual labor or other such work.

Honor parents – Nope. Birthday cards, weekly phone calls, Christmas gifts. Done.

You shall not kill – Nope. Never even been in a fight since 7th grade.

You shall not steal – Nope. Unless you count sneaking fries off my wife's plate when she's not looking.

You shall not bear false witness – Nope. Like Daddy said, always tell the truth. That way you don't have to remember what you said.

You shall not covet, neighbor's house, wife, slaves or his ox or his ass – Nope. Good on all of them.

Looks like I'm in the clear. Based on this record, I didn't need Jesus to die for me. I've got the being good thing covered.

On the other hand, if "Other Gods" means things which get more of my attention and loyalty than THE GOD, then I'm probably guilty.

And if "Graven Images" implies earthly things to which I have devoted a great deal of time and energy and which are the most important things in my home, well . . .

Suppose taking "the Lord's name in vain" means using religion for less than holy reasons, oops!

And the Sabbath could be about creating enough silence and space in my life to allow God to seep in and nurture and lead and refresh me. Oh my!

Honoring father and mother may have something to say about how I deal with those who have taken on the responsibility for leadership; have I been responsive and cooperative? Dang!

Well, I really haven't killed anyone; but I haven't prevented or protested a lot of the violence which goes on in my name, funded by my dollars.

Adultery? Well there is that "lust in the heart" thing Jesus talked about. You shall not steal? What was it Augustine said, "Anything you have more than you need is stolen from the poor." Ouch!

False Witness? Well, I do not lie, but I can "spin" the truth like a whirling dervish.

Okay, okay; but I still haven't coveted anybody's donkey and nobody can say that I did!

The law may be a good teacher but most of us are, in one way or another, bad students.

No matter how hard we try we fail more often than we succeed in our attempts to live up to its requirements.
Lent is a time when we are called to examine our hearts and our lives and to repent and return to the LORD.

It is time when, like Jesus chasing the money-changers out of the temple, we are called to gird up our loins and chase the evil-doing and misdirection out of our lives.

A look at our lives in the light of the Ten Commandments shows us why what Paul in First Corinthians calls "the foolishness of the cross" was necessary.

It is also a time when we are reminded that there is palace where we can let go the burden of trying to live up to laws and expectations.

A place where God's grace is freely given and where we freely accept it and live in it.

A place where our freedom is made complete.

That place is the foolish stumbling block of the cross; where our need and God's love come together.

Amen and amen.

The Fourth Sunday in Lent

Numbers 21:4-9

A curious thing about poison — it not only is a substance which can sicken and kill, but is often also the means of producing the antidote which becomes a cure. Of course, it must first be injected into a subject who is capable of producing antibodies, becoming affected and quite likely sickened in the process. (For a review of how snakebite antivenom is prepared, here's a nice episode of the internet series, Sci Show—found only here at The Lectionary Lab!)

https://www.youtube.com/watch?v=0yqVow4J4oA

Consider the imagery of sin as poison; consider as well the One who is willing to be afflicted with sin on our behalf in order to produce the ultimate antidote — life from death.

Psalm 107:1-3, 17-22

The psalm supports the first reading, though the names have been changed [or omitted] to protect the guilty. The key thought here is not to cast further blame on the wandering Israelites for their complaining and lack of faith, but rather to focus on God's action when God's people cry out in their trouble (v.19) –"he saved them from their distress."

There is help; there is a Savior.

Ephesians 2:1-10

The bottom line for all of us who live as human beings in this world is simple: we have a sin problem and God has a sin solution. It is high time that the ones with a problem and the One with a solution should meet.

John 3:14-21

The word of grace is always set against the backdrop of sin and its judgment. Notice that it is sin that is judged by God; the wrath of God is always directed against the power of evil. Sinners (which includes all of us, naturally) are affected by sin and are touched by the judgment of God so far as sin remains in our lives.

But God's purpose is not now, nor has it ever been, simply to punish sinners. God's eternal purpose is to bring light into the darkness and forgiveness into the midst of a sin-affected world. The simple, beautiful doorway to God's grace is belief — trust — in the Beloved One we know as God's only Son.

Sermon

"The Gospel According to Aunt Mildred"

I have concluded that almost everyone has a relative like my late Aunt Mildred.

She was my Daddy's sister, she lived with her parents until they died, then she married her longtime suitor. She never had children, which, some of us think, was something of a blessing for those unborn.

Having no children, she doted on her nieces and nephews and sent us birthday cards with sticks of gum in them until we were well into our 30's and 40's. She also wrong long, disjointed letters all over those cards; front, back, and then folded them out and wrote on the inside.

One time, in the midst of all the news about Uncle LW's impending hernia surgery and what they had for lunch at the Derby and what they had to pay for it and what was wrong with it, and how Myrtle feels about her son's job change (now if I can only figure out who Myrtle is) and a long digression on the ugly dress Cousin somebody wore to Grandpa Watson funeral in 1960 and a guess at how much rain they had last week based on the amount in the coffee can on the stump in the backyard, there was buried this line: "I paid the premium on your Combine Accident Insurance last week."

Believe it or not, that was the first thing in that letter that I did not understand at all. What? What is Combine Accident Insurance? A combine is a piece of farm equipment I haven't been near since I was twenty years old. And, I'm sure it's not about farm equipment anyway and what kind of insurance is it and why is Aunt Mildred paying the premium? In the midst of this muddle I did what all southern boys who have been raised right do. I called my mother.

She said, "Oh Lord, you know your Aunt Mildred, bless her heart. She takes out these policies on all you children all the time. She's scared to death somebody she knows will wind up in the hospital unable to pay their bills. She's got policies on all 5 of you children, plus LW's nieces and nephews too. I tell her you all have got jobs and insurance but she just says it might not be enough, you can't ever have too much insurance."

I said, "Mama, what should I do? She's wasting her money!"

"Oh honey, there's nothing you can do. She's convinced that this Combine Accident Insurance is the greatest thing in the world and nobody can change her mind. If you ever have an accident, would you please her know. Nothing would make her happier than to file a claim on you."

Though it did make me feel strange to learn that the best way to make Aunt Mildred happy was to get hurt, I decided that Mama was right and wrote Aunt Mildred a thank-you note and let it go.

What struck me most deeply in this episode was the realization that for all those years Aunt Mildred had been spending that money on me. She didn't ask me, she didn't tell me, she didn't expect anything from me. She did it because she loved me and cared about me, because she thought it was a good thing to do for me.

In the midst of all this I felt twinges of guilt. " Geez," I thought," I don't even read her letters and she does that for me." And, putting aside all the practical reasons why this was a silly thing to do, I did realize it was a sign of her love and that there was something very tender and sweet and humbling about her doing that for me. I was touched, I really was.

A few years ago these texts came up and a pastor friend asked me if I was going to tackle the bronze serpent in the First Reading. I said no, I thought I'd stick with Ephesians and John 3:16 and he said, "Well, that's safe. It would be hard to mess that up."

I laughed and agreed it would indeed be real hard to "mess up" such a clear Gospel message. But then I thought, as hard as it is, that is exactly what we do. For various reasons and in various ways we regularly mess up the message of God's gift of grace.

We "mess up" the gift of God's grace by not taking it seriously enough. We say, "Yeah, yeah, yeah I know all about that salvation business. Yeah, yeah, Jesus died on the cross, good. But what has he done for me lately? How can this Christ business improve my life now?"

I recently heard a story about a company that was having a hard, hard time. The owner called in all the employees and told them that things were bad but that he believed they would soon get better.
He told them that he had decided that instead of laying everyone off, he was going to keep them on full payroll; all they had to do was come in on Wednesdays and do maintenance on the machinery and clean up the place.

There were sighs of relief and smiles all around the room and then somebody asked, "Do we have to come in every Wednesday?"

That's us. In the face of the stupendous, gigantic gift that is God's grace, we want to know the details. Do I have to go every Sunday? Do I have to pray every day? Do I have to give a part of everything I earn?

Just like I failed to take the depths of Aunt Mildred's love seriously. Sure, she was a little eccentric and capable of incredible silliness. She was laughable.

And she loved me, and she loved my brothers and sisters. She loved us with a love we did not deserve nor adequately appreciate. We certainly did not earn it, we seldom responded to it, we never understood it.

This is a parable of our relationship with God. God loves us in spite of ourselves, God loves us more than we deserve, God loves us in ways we do not understand, God loves us in reckless, extravagant, spendthrift ways. God does things for us, like dying on the cross, which seem to others to be silly, foolish even.

And yet it is that silly, foolish, incomprehensible love which is the Gospel, the message of the gift of God's grace.

And the most silly, most foolish and most totally incomprehensible thing about it is this: in spite of our unworthiness and unresponsiveness and inability to understand it, God just keeps on loving us, just keeps on giving us the gifts of divine grace.

"For God so loved the world that he gave. . . ."' John 3:16

Amen.

The Fifth Sunday in Lent

Jeremiah 31:31-34

It has always been a comforting thought to think of God, as a Heavenly Parent, holding me by the hand. Good image; strong image.

But, evidently, as a wayward child, I can decide to withdraw my hand from the protective grip of God. So, God has designed, so says Jeremiah, a new way to hold me: God has placed God's "law" inside of me. God's word, God's law is — to the Hebrew understanding — the very presence and assurance of "God Himself."

So, when I consider that God has now placed God's law in my heart, that is pretty much the same as saying God has taken up residence there. No longer is it necessary for anyone to "tell me" what I need to know about God. I simply look within my own heart — God's home.

Psalm 51:1-12

Sin is a sticky thing; like peanut butter on the roof of your mouth, or an annoying piece of lint that you just can't flick off of your shirt — it keeps coming back and coming back at you, no matter how hard you try to get rid of it!

Only God can get rid of sin and the images it burns into our minds and into our souls. One of the favorite attacks of "the evil one" is to remind us over and over of the ways we have messed up, that we are inferior, that we are undeserving of love because "we've been bad."

I'm so glad that one of the favorite techniques of the Holy One is to blot out our transgressions with the abundant mercy of God. God sustains joy; the Lord sustains us spiritually.

Psalm 119:9-16

In keeping with Jeremiah, "the word" of God here symbolizes God's very presence. Therefore, how does any one of us — young or old — keep our way pure? By hiding, or treasuring, God's word in our hearts.

Keep the things God says -what God really wants you to know — close by you all the time. Keep 'em in mind; be ready to pull them out of your pocket. You'll be surprised just how handy they will turn out to be!

Hebrews 5:5-10

For now, don't worry too much about Melchizedek, who he is, or what he does (though if you have a hankering, you'll find his story in Genesis 14.)

The real emphasis here is on what Jesus does — the Great High Priest — who, even though he had every right as the Son of God, instead learned about obedience (a term used for a servant, not a son) and suffering — and thus received glory from God. He did not seize it or assume it for himself.

The glory of God, in Jesus, is also shared with us; we receive eternal salvation because of what Jesus has done.
John 12:20-33

The appearance of the Greeks who sought after Jesus has always been something of a reminder to me that we never know who is going to be intrigued with our message about the Christ. These guys seem to come "from left field," so to speak, and Philip seems a little puzzled as to what to do with them.

Ever have someone like that come to your church? We all say we want to reach "new people" — but then you get somebody who is really from beyond the edge of your normal constituency, and you find yourself asking the internal question, "How in the Sam Hill did they get here?"

To Jesus, it seemed to represent an important development; it is almost as if he says, "Okay, boys; if the Greeks are showing up, then it's just about time to kick this thing into high gear."

Does he know that means the stuff is about to hit the fan? He seems to intimate that with his prayer about being troubled and asking God to save him from this hour.

Certainly, this is the human Jesus that Dr. Chilton leads us to consider in the sermon below; what God had for him to do was hard and he had to find himself somewhat reluctant, at times, to carry it forward.

And, yet, the Savior is willing to play the part of the kernel of wheat falling to the ground — there is new life yet to come even in the midst of an impending burial.

Sermon

"It's the Way of the Cross"

Psychiatrist and Christian writer M. Scott Peck tells of treating a woman who had been involved in a variety of cults.

Peck says, "I asked her one day, 'Tell me about Jesus . . . how he died?'

'He was crucified.' She answered. Something, perhaps the fact that she did everything she could to avoid pain, propelled me to ask, 'Did it hurt?'

'Oh no!' she responded . . . . . I persisted 'How could it not hurt?'

'Oh,' she replied happily, 'He was just so highly developed in his Christ Consciousness that he was able to project himself into his astral body and take off from there.'"

Well, I suppose that's one theory.

A Unitarian friend of mine continually reminds me that there is danger in thinking of thinking of Jesus as both divine and human.

He says that if we think that Jesus was divine, we may begin to excuse ourselves from the call to follow him to the cross.

We think, "Well, Jesus was God, so he could do those things and it didn't really hurt him. At least it didn't hurt him the way it would hurt me. So really, I'll worship him, but following him is a bit too dangerous."

Unless we take the human pain and suffering of Jesus seriously, we may fail to take seriously our own call to face pain and suffering for the sake of the Kingdom of God.

In our Gospel lesson Jesus reminds us that our calling as Christians is to follow him, and that following him includes following him to the cross, not as spectators but as participants in suffering for the sake of the world.

Hebrews gives us an intensely human portrait of Jesus; one filled with mental anguish, the dread of anticipated suffering, pleading for mercy and, finally, resignation to his fate.
The Greek word here is sarx. It means meat; bones and blood and muscle. It is a declaration of Jesus' very real humanity.

The verse continues, "Jesus offered up prayers and supplications, with loud cries and tears,"

Many rabbis taught that there were three levels of prayer:
Prayers – verbal or silent, thought out and controlled
Loud cries – shouting at God in anger or anguish.
Tears – pure emotion and pain.

Hebrews shows us Jesus engaged in all three but most especially loud cries and tears, pouring out his fear and pain to God. One who feels no pain and no fear, one who is not "human," does not weep and cry before God.

Verse 7 continues: "to the one who was able to save him from death, and he was heard."

Jesus knew that the path he was on lead to death, to the cross. Jesus also knew that God could save him from this end. And Jesus was not afraid to let his fears and feelings be known, to God and to others.
What agony he must have felt. You could save me if you would, but you won't! Why won't you? Why won't you? My God, my God, why have you forsaken me?

Now, Hebrews 5:7 says he was heard – – – and yet, he died. Died in agony upon the cross. What kind of hearing is that?

When I was about 12 or 13 I was in the Boy Scouts. One night at Scouts we were running a race and I tripped. I fell face down in gravel on the side of the road. I lodged a piece of gravel under the skin on my forehead.

The rural medical clinic was a mile or so down the road from our meeting place. The Doctor and my father were both assistant Scoutmasters so they gathered me up and took me to the clinic.

The doctor was good but his bedside manner was a bit on the brusque side. As I lie there on that cold, hard metal table he came at me with a huge needle to numb my forehead. I am still not very fond of needles, but then I was deathly afraid of them.

I looked over at my Daddy and began to cry out, "Daddy, Daddy, daddy, please Daddy. Don't let him hurt me, please Daddy. Daddy, Daddy, Daddy."

The doctor threw a leg over me to hold me down, put his left arm down on my chest and proceeded to inject the needle. All the while I continued to cry and beg and plead for my Daddy to make him stop. And just as the needle entered I saw my Daddy's hands, knuckles white as he clutched my jacket. I looked up and saw a tear in the corner of his eye. It was the only time I ever, ever saw him cry.

Daddy, Daddy, Daddy. I was heard, oh yes, I was heard. And I was denied.

Hebrews 5: 8 "Although he was a son, he learned obedience through what he suffered, and having been made perfect, he became the source of eternal salvation for all who obey him."

Here is a great mystery of the faith. Wherever are, God in Christ has been; fully, completely, totally.
Think about the most scared, lonely, and troubled you have ever been.

And Jesus has been there.
Think about the moments when you have felt ignored and abandoned by God. And Jesus has been there.

Think about all the times when you just did not know if you could make it. And Jesus has been there.
The Promise of the Gospel is not that if you are a Christian life will be easy.

The Gospel is not about ways to make your life, your marriage, your career, your children or anything else work out in a way pleasing to yourself.

The Gospel is the call to follow Jesus to the cross and beyond.

To follow Jesus in serving the poor and needy.

To follow Jesus in reaching out to the despised and rejected.
To follow Jesus in standing up for those who are oppressed and ill-served by the world.

To follow Jesus in fighting against illness and evil wherever they may be found.
And sometimes following Jesus to the cross means we will suffer for our commitments, that we too will be rejected and scorned as much as those with whom we take our stand.

Christ calls us to follow him.

It is not an easy way.
It is not a painless path.
It is not likely to be smooth sailing.
It is the Way of the Cross.

And the promise of the gospel is that where God calls us to go, Jesus has already been, and as we go, Jesus is going with us.

Amen and amen.

The Sixth Sunday in Lent (Palm/Passion)

Isaiah 50:4-9a

As I consider the overwhelming passion of the Lord on this beginning of Holy Week, I am struck (and I genuinely intend no pun here) by the depth with which Isaiah's text connects us to the willing submission of Christ.

"I gave my back to those who struck me, and my cheeks to those who pulled out the beard." (v. 6) I am simply stunned at the unbegrudging audacity of Jesus in accepting the fulfillment of this passage in his life.

The haunting refrain of an old gospel hymn comes back to me at this point: "I gave my life for thee, what hast thou given for me?"

(for the powerful background on this hymn text by Frances R. Havergal, visit Hymnary.org and this link: http://www.hymnary.org/text/i_gave_my_life_for_thee)

Psalm 31:9-16

In the midst of plotters and schemers, the confidence of the Christ is ultimately in God.

Again, I am reminded that, for Jesus, the imminent threat of death was very real; the run-up to Golgotha was not some dress rehearsal or momentary discomfort. Jesus is going to die, and I suspect he knew that.

Close behind that thought must have been, "If God does not save me, I am lost." That may be the deepest truth of the Passion.

Philippians 2:5-11

This classic worship text of the early church is a reminder of the close proximity of privilege and humility, of submission and glory, of obedience and exaltation. Needless to say, it prepares us for the greatest proximal opposition of all: life out of death.

Mark 14:1-15:47

When considering this entire passage, opportunities for preaching abound. The real task is deciding what must be left unsaid in the sermon. (The story does, after all, speak for itself — and quite well, at that!)

One organizational theme that suggests itself is that of acceptance vs. rejection. In his characteristic rapid-fire manner, Mark presents several characters in rapid succession who all make decisions based on either accepting or rejecting participation in the unfolding drama of the passion:

- the woman with the alabaster box of ointment — accepts Jesus and anoints his feet
- those in attendance at the meal who complain — rejecting this seemingly pointless extravagance
- Jesus affirms the woman's action — accepts her offering and memorializes her action
- Judas Iscariot, who departs for the purpose of betrayal — rejection of Jesus and his actions
- the man with the jar of water — acceptance displayed by provision of the upper room

- Peter of the bold predictions — penultimately rejects Jesus at the crowing of the rooster
- Jesus struggling in prayer in the garden — acceptance of the difficult task before him
- the mob from the "chief priests, scribes and elders" — arrest and rejection

And so on, and so forth…you get the idea.

The theme of acceptance and rejection will continue through to Mark's stark ending of his gospel at 16:8 — basically handing the story off to we, the hearers and readers of his story.

Sermon

"I'm Gonna Quit That, Too!"

Sir Isaac Newton, the great scientist and mathematician, had a dog that he loved very much. Wherever Newton went, the dog went with him.

The story is, one time he had worked for months and months on a theory about the nature of the universe, working late into the night by candlelight, his worktable covered with papers, which were in turn covered with formulas and theorems and conclusions.

Late one night, newton got up from the table to leave the room and the dog jumped up and bumped the table, turning over the candle, which set Newton's papers on fire.

Newton returned to the room to find years of work gone up in flames.

He put out the fire, then sat on the floor and wept. The dog nuzzled up to him and licked his face and Newton hugged his dog and said, "You will never, ever know what you have done." (Ravi Zacharias, Jesus Among Other Gods, p. 36)

The story is that when Eve took the fruit from the tree and when Adam took the fruit from Eve; things fell apart. And God looked at Adam and Eve with great sadness and said, "You will never ever know what you have done."

What began in Adam and Eve continues in us.

Each of us plays out our own, personal little Garden of Eden in which we discover our capacity for doing things that tear God's creation apart.

Back when I was young and knew everything and had not had either the time or inventiveness to really mess things up in life, I didn't worry too much about the sinfulness of humanity in general and my own sinfulness in particular.

But I'm older now and I don't even like to think about the ways that I have been less than I meant or hoped to be.

I have not just failed to do good, I have on occasion done bad; and knew I was doing bad when I did it, and I did it anyway.

And I don't know why.

And I have no excuse other than the fact that I am human and that is what humans do sometimes.

I don't blame any one or any thing else; not my mama or my daddy or my environment or anything else.

It was just me and my life and an occasional fit of sorriness. And I'm sorry.

And I have a deep, deep need for a voice from outside myself who will neither condone my misdeeds nor condemn me for them.

And we meet that voice, that God, in the one "who did not regard equality with God as something to be exploited," (Phil. 2:6) but rather "emptied himself," and come to be one of us, to live with us, to die with us and for us on the cross.

My daddy's sister, Aunt Mildred, never, ever really threw anything away. When her nieces' and nephews complained to her about this, she would say, "You just never know when you might need it."

Our protests that you had to be able to find "it" in order to use "it" when you needed "it," fell on deaf ears. She was confident that she knew where all her "its" were. And I think she did.

I would ask her about a bill or a letter or a magazine and she would say something like, "It's in the back bedroom, in the left hand corner of the closet, third shoebox from the bottom, in a plastic bag." And she'd be right.

God is, I think, a bit like Aunt Mildred; if not southern then at least eccentric.

God shares her passion for saving everything and her awareness of everything she had saved.

God doesn't do the expected and normal thing and condemn useless and unholy trash to Gehenna, the fiery garbage heap outside the walls of Jerusalem.

Instead, where others may see worthlessness, God sees something worth saving, something worth hanging on to, something worth taking a risk for, something worth making a great effort for, something worth dying for.

And God knows where all that saved stuff is. God cares about that which God has saved.

And it is God's will that it all be saved, because God made it all, and God loves it all, no matter what it has done.

The Gospel is that it is because of our great need and God's great sorrow and anguish over our great need that Christ came into the world.

". . . but emptied himself, taking the form of a slave, being born in human likeness, and being found in human form, he humbled himself and became obedient unto death – even death on a cross." (Phil. 2: 7-8)

And so, the great question is not whether or not God loves us and cares about us – that question has been answered once and for all by Christ upon the cross.

The question is; are we being obedient to our call to take up our cross and follow?

The Ryman Auditorium in downtown Nashville was for a long time the home of the Grand Ole Opry. It was originally a church, built as a preaching place for a famous evangelist named Sam Jones.

The story is that Jones was holding what the holiness folks called a "quitting meeting," during which people confessed their sins and swore off drinking, and smoking and cussing and running around with people they weren't married to and such like misbehavior.

The meeting had reached an emotional high point when Jones called on one ultra-righteous woman in the congregation and asked her what she was going to quit.

She said, "I ain't been doing nothing, and I'm going to quit that too."

I'm a Lutheran, and we Lutherans learned a long time ago that there is nothing we can do to make God love us, nothing we have to do to earn our salvation.

The problem is, some of us learned that lesson too well and we do nothing in response to God's love for us.

God calls upon us today to "quit doing nothing," in response to the Gospel.

We are called to give ourselves for others as Jesus gave himself for us.
We are called to care about the hurts and pains of others as Jesus cared about our hurts and pains.

We are called to live lives of obedience to Jesus' call to us to take up a cross and follow.

Follow him into the world with hope in our hearts, with acts of love in our hands and with words of grace and promise on our lips.

Amen and amen.

Maundy Thursday/Good Friday

Texts: Exodus 12:1-4 (5-10) 11-14; I Corinthians 11:23-26; John 13:1-17; 31b-35

One day about 20 years ago I went to a Holy Week breakfast at the big downtown church in a major southern city. It was a Chrism Mass and the Bishop had called us together to renew our ordination vows and to eat together.

We drove in early, most of us from the suburban and rural outskirts. We wore our best Lutheran finery, black suits and black shirts and white collars and silver crosses. We vested in the chapel and filed into choir stalls in the chancel where the bishop preached and prayed and gave us communion and we prayed and pledged our troth and received the elements with humble hands if not totally humble hearts.

We divested ourselves of our albs and stoles and then retired to the small dining room where the Altar Guild laid before us a brunch of eggs and bacon and biscuits and cheese grits and sausage balls and fresh fruit and, and and. . . .

We sat at oak tables covered with linen table cloths and ate off good china with silverware that appeared to have a significant amount of real silver in it. And we had a wonderful time lamenting how difficult our lives were and how taxing our jobs were and what a burden Holy Week was and eventually it got time for me to leave.

Somewhere between the small dining room and the chapel where I recovered my alb and the long hallway to the parking lot I got turned around and lost and went downstairs and down a corridor and found my self spilling out into the street on the opposite side of the church from where I expected and wanted to be.

The morning sun was shining brightly in my eyes and it took me a moment to gather my wits and figure out where I was and when I came to myself I looked down the sidewalk in the direction I wanted to go and saw a long line of folk huddled on the dewy grass, trying to stay warm and dry while waiting for the food kitchen housed in the church's basement to open.

I felt very conspicuous walking along beside that row of folk, dressed in my best suit, carrying my white robe, a silver cross around my neck. I spoke to a few folk as I hurried past them to the corner. As I came to the street and turned to the left I glanced back and then I looked up and to my right. And what I saw stopped me dead in my tracks.

From where I stood, I could see in the floor to ceiling, wall-to-wall windows of the small dining room. I could see the assembled holy people of the area Lutheran churches, smiling and talking; warm, dry, and well-fed.

By simply shifting my eyes I could see a significant portion of the area's homeless population, cold, hungry, silent and appearing as alone in a group as they were by themselves.

And I wondered, "On this Tuesday in Holy Week, in this city, at this hour; which group would Jesus be eating with; the clergy or the homeless?"

Really, I wondered, "Which group should I be eating with?" Or better yet, "Shouldn't all of us be down here eating with all of them?"

Jesus says, "For I have set you an example, that you also should do as I have done." (13:15)

In our text from John's Gospel, we find the story of Jesus washing the disciples' feet. In a note in a study bible and another in a textual commentary I was reminded of the extreme lowliness of this task.

Footwashing was normally done by a slave or a servant, not the host. If the host had no slave, he would provide water and a towel, but would not wash the guest's feet himself. Indeed, it was a job that could be performed by a woman or a child or a non-Jewish slave, but no Jewish male, not even a slave could be required by a Jewish master to do this for another. (<u>*The Access Bible*</u> and <u>*The Lectionary Commentary*</u>)

The example that Jesus has set for us is not the particular one of putting on towels and washing the feet of our fellow churchgoers, (though it would be nice if we actually thought that much of one another and could naturally do that without laughing or cringing.)

No, the example here is one of indifference to one's own importance and of close and particular attention to the hurts and needs of the other to the point of self-forgetfulness in service of those needs.

On this night, this Maundy Thursday, we are called to remember a number of things.

The text from Exodus tells us of the night of the Passover, the night the Hebrew people were set free from slavery in Egypt by God's strong hand.

The meal Jesus and his disciples ate on the night of the footwashing was a Passover meal and the early church saw Jesus as the Passover lamb whose blood has protected us from the angel of death.

Our reading from I Corinthians reminds us that on the night that he washed the disciples' feet, Jesus said some things that must of seemed strange to the disciples on that night but which came to mean a lot to them after his death and resurrection.

After they had seen his body broken and his blood spilled upon the cross, his words over the bread and wine that night took on new and more vital meaning and significance.

And buried within the John story is the reason this night is called "Maundy" Thursday.

After all, what sort of word is Maundy? What does it mean? It is an old English word related to "mandate" or "command" and this night is called Maundy Thursday because it was during the Passover meal, after he had washed everyone's feet that he told them, he commanded them, "to love one another."

Vs. 34 "I give you a new commandment, that you love one another."

Well, how do you command love? To be more specific, how do you command one person to love another? To be really specific, how do you command someone to love someone else they don't even like very much, if at all?

Well, you do it like Jesus did it, and he may have been the only one who could have done it and deserved to be obeyed. You see, you do it by having loved everyone completely and totally and "to the end" (13:1)

To the end of his life?

To the end of time?

Or to the end that they will in response love one another?

Like YHWH freeing the Hebrew people from slavery in Egypt, God in Christ upon the Cross has freed us from our bondage to this world's power, summarized by Luther as "sin, death and the devil."

We have been loosed and set free by the death and resurrection of Jesus, shown forth to us in the bread and wine of communion. "For as often as you eat this bread and drink the cup, you proclaim the Lord's death until he comes." (I Corinthians 11:26)

It is because of this new freedom and the love that Jesus gives to us that we are able to love others, "Just as I have loved you, you also should love one another." (John 13:34)

Our calling this night is to remember the Lord's death, and to anticipate his resurrection.

Our calling this night is to receive the love of God in Christ into our lives, the way the disciples received Jesus' gift of washing their feet.

Our calling this night is to go out into the world renewed in our commitment to let the love of God in Christ that fills us, overflow from us into acts of kindness and generosity to others.

Amen and amen.

Resurrection of the Lord (Easter)

Sermon
by the Rev. Dr. Delmer L. Chilton

Mark 16:1-8

Some years ago a pastor in SC was invited to a baptism by one of his parishioners who was a guard at the Central Carolina Prison in Columbia.

The pastor arrived at the prison early in the morning. He was searched, IDed, interrogated, moved from waiting area to waiting area for over an hour; all to simply move him fifteen feet from outside the prison walls to the inside.

Finally the pastor met his guard friend and they walked together down long, cold corridors to the prison chapel. It was a small room, with a few rows of chairs and a platform at the front. On this day the pulpit and piano had been pushed to the side against the wall.

In the pulpit's place, flat on the floor, there was a large wooden box. In the box there was spread blue plastic sheeting that draped over the sides of the box and into the sheeting had been poured gallons and gallons of cold water.

As the small group gathered around the makeshift baptistery, at the very moment the convert stepped into the box full of water and the preacher reached over to grab his hands, lower him into the box and began to say, "I baptized thee. . . " the visiting pastor had a realization that took his breath away.

The box was a coffin; a standard, prison-issue, pine-box coffin. The man was being baptized in a casket, he was going into and coming up out of the grave.

The Funeral liturgy in my tradition's worship book contains these words at the placement of the pall as the service begins: "When we were baptized in Christ Jesus, we were baptized into his death. We were buried therefore with him by baptism into death, so that as Christ was raised by the glory of the father, we too might live a new life. For if we have been united with him in a death like his, we shall certainly be united with him in a resurrection like his." (Evangelical Lutheran Worship, p. 280)

Death and life, despair and hope, going under and rising again; those are our themes today.

When the women went to the tomb, they went in deep sadness and despair. They went into a place of coldness and death, a prions house of the soul.

They went with ho hope, no anticipation, they went reluctantly, to perform a duty, to prepare Jesus' body for burial, to put their friend into a grave.

But, when they got there they discovered that things had changed. The tomb was empty, the body was missing, there was an angel hovering about.

"Do not be alarmed," he says. Easy for him to say. "So," the angel goes on, "you're looking for Jesus? Sorry, he's not here. He's been raised. He's gone to Galilee. Go tell Peter and the others to meet him there."

The women are stunned, reeling, speechless. The no wonder the Bible tells us they fled in terror and told no one, at least for a while.

This business of rising again from the dead has never been easy for anyone to believe. It's not natural, it's not normal. It wasn't normal 2000 years ago and it's not normal now. All of us who proclaim it know it's not easy to believe.

But it is a story full of possibilities for all of us. From death to new life isn't just about going through physical death and then living happily ever after in heaven. It's about being changed, transformed, in the midst of our circumstances, here, now.

The prisoner who was baptized in a coffin didn't get to leave prison because he got religion, far from it. He still had 20 years to go on his sentence.

For him, nothing external changed at all, and yet internally, everything had begun to change completely. After the baptism he gave a "testimony" he which he said he had gone from being a dead man walking, a person already dead in spirit waiting to die; to life as a man filled with the new life of Christ living in him.

The question for us today is this? What sort of prison are we living in? What darkness grips our soul? What cold and clammy tomb is holding us back from a joyous life?

The message of Easter is this:

- You have to step into the cold waters of death in order to come out on the other side of the Jordan.
- You have to bury what's holding you back in order to embrace the new life God is giving you.

- You have to lay down in a coffin in order to stand up with joy on Easter morning.

We are invited to a changed life today; a life full of hope and opportunity, overflowing with love and freedom; filled with the joy of the Risen Christ.

Christ is risen, Christ is risen indeed!
Amen and amen.

The Second Sunday of Easter

Acts 4:32-35

Does the resurrection have power? If so, what type of power is it — how is it expressed?

Most church attenders (and preachers) would answer the first question in the affirmative. Yes, the resurrection has power! Didn't we just have a big hullabaloo on Easter? Didn't you see how many people showed up for worship?

Ah, yes…I love the power demonstrated by the services and splendor on Easter. We all wish that "every Sunday were like Easter." But, really now…what is the ongoing meaning of the resurrection of the Christ for our lives?

At least a portion of the answer to that second, more probative question is found here in Acts: "the whole group…were of one heart and soul…. With great power [they] gave their testimony to the resurrection…. There was not a needy person among them."

Now, THAT would be a testimony of the Lord's resurrection power if THAT happened again today! Not a needy person in America, in Europe, in Africa, Asia, or anywhere else in the world where people name the name of Christ?

Psalm 133

More power in unity. The images are of plenty…so much oil running down the beard of Aaron (at his ordination) that it trails off his head and face and into the neckline of his garment. The dew of Hermon (the highest point in northern Israel) literally runs down and feeds the rest of the country by means of the Jordan River, the Sea of Galilee, and other tributaries all the way to the Dead Sea in the desert.

Oil and water are sometimes plenteous, sometimes scarce; but the mercy of God never runs dry!

1 John 1:1-2:2

I've always loved the vivid image here of John proclaiming "what we have heard, what we have seen with our eyes…we have looked at, we have touched!"

Once something has become tangible through you by means of your physical senses, you know it in a way that can never be completely explained in words. How to describe the sound of the water rushing over Niagara Falls? What is it like to see the sun set over the expanse of the high desert with its clear skies? To feel a silken scarf as it flows through your fingers? Can you adequately describe what the first bite of a crunchy apple, freshly harvested from the orchard, is like?

In many ways, our fellowship with Christ and his people has to be experienced to be understood. But it sure is good!

John 20:19-31

Thomas thought he needed to "experience" firsthand the resurrected Christ in order to believe what he was hearing from his apostolic brethren. And, he did get a face-to-face shot with the Master.

I've always found it fascinating that he didn't really HAVE to put his fingers in the marks of the nails once he had the chance to. The simple presence of Christ brought him to his knees.

We might well say, "Well, if I could have been there when they crucified my Lord, I'll bet I would have got it right! Not like those other faithless disciples!"

Not so fast, my friend; we all have our Thomas moments. And in the end, our response can only be like his: "My Lord, and my God!"

Sermon

"Breathless"

I was driving back to the church after a hospital visit one wintry afternoon over 30 years ago.
The sun was shining bright and directly into my eyes. I turned left at a lonely country intersection and BAM! My little Datsun was slammed into by a large delivery truck doing 60 miles an hour.

He hit me right behind the back door and the car spun round and round like a top, then WHAM! I stopped, wedged into the ditch on the side of the road.

Every window in the car was broken, the steering wheel was broken, the seat was broken. My head was in the backseat, passenger side and my feet were under the steering wheel and I couldn't breathe. I literally COULD NOT BREATHE. That truck knocked the wind out of me.

The wreck was witnessed by one of my parishioners, Kitty Hightower. She ran to my car and leaned in the broken window. "Pastor, Pastor are you all right?"

Well no, I wasn't all right. I couldn't breathe. There was no air in my lungs and I didn't seem to be able to get any in there.
I couldn't speak, I couldn't even move; I just stared at her with my mouth open.

Kitty started crying, and then started screaming to the men rushing over from the country store, "He's dead, He's dead. Oh my God, the Pastor's dead!"

Which is, I assure you, a peculiar thing to have screamed in your ear when you are indeed very much alive.
After what seemed like an eternity I was able to get a bit of air into my lungs and was able to lift a hand and touch Kitty on the shoulder; which, in retrospect, was not the best thing to do, seeing as how she thought I was dead and all.

When I touched her on the shoulder, she jerked her head up and looked at me with real terror in her eyes.

Finally, I squeezed out the words, "It's alright Kitty, I'm not dead."

It was an odd thing to find myself in that position; the one who had been hurt comforting the onlooker. But that is the position in which we find Jesus in our Gospel lesson; the one who was hurt bringing solace to the witnesses.

On the Evening of that first Easter, the disciples were meeting in a room, probably the same room in which they had held their Passover.

They had the door shut, bolted, locked.
They were frightened.
They could not get their bearings.
They could not breathe.

They had given up everything to follow Jesus, and this is not how they expected things to turn out.

Just a week ago, on Palm Sunday, they had entered the city with such gigantically high hope, and now this.
This, this, disaster.
This, this, craziness.
This, this, car crash of an ending.

Indeed, they had had the wind knocked out of them.
And on that first Easter evening, Jesus the Christ came to the disciples in that locked and airless room and breathed new life into them.

At one time or another all of us are like the disciples were on that first Easter evening.

We too have had the wind knocked out of us. Some of us gathered here have lost loved ones unexpectedly, some of us are struggling with the diagnosis of a long-term illness in the family, some of us have had job losses, some of us have lost economic security, some of us have failed to get that promotion (or that call) we had hoped for, our children haven't worked out the way we hoped, our marriages are hurting.

All of us have had the wind knocked out of us, sometime; probably sometime lately.

Believe you me, in times like those, the big picture fades away and all your energy is centered on surviving, on breathing, on taking one more precious breathe, and anything other than present personal experience becomes difficult to believe in or focus on.

Writing in Christianity Today, Tim Stafford talks about an object lesson Pastor Stephen Bilynski uses with his confirmation class.

He comes to the very first class with a jar full of jelly beans and asks the class to guess how many are in the jar. He writes all their estimates on the board. Then he asks the boys and girls to name their favorite songs and he lists those on the board.

Finally the class counts the beans to see who was closest to right. Then Pastor Steve points to the list of songs and asks, "And which one of these is closest to being right?"

And of course the students protest that there is no right answer; that a person's favorite song is purely a matter of taste and circumstance; purely personal preference. (Which would, I suppose, explain my predilection for Procol Harum's "Whiter Shade of Pale.")

At this point, Pr. Steve comes to the point of the entire exercise: "When you decide what to believe about God, is that more like guessing the number of beans, or more like choosing your favorite song"

In the article, Pastor Steve says he has done this numerous times over the last 20 years, and always, always, the answer, from teen-agers and from adults, is the same:

"Choosing what to believe about God is like choosing one's favorite song."

In modern America, we have transferred faith from the realm of fact to the world of feelings. And the problem with that is, we seldom feel like believing.

Or more accurately, those personal experiences that would convince us to believe in God are few and far between, practically non-existent; and those things that would cause us to disbelieve, that knock the wind out of us, are much louder, persistent and frequent.

This is why what Jesus did in that room with those disciples is so important to us. Jesus reminded them where he came from "Just as the Father sent me," and then he reminded them where they were going, "So I send you!"

Then he filled them with the Holy Spirit the way God the Creator filled the lungs of Adam and Eve with the very air we breathe, the wind that gives us life.

Lastly, he reminded them what their calling was, what they were being sent out filled with the Holy Spirit to do "Forgive sins."

All this says to us that whether God loves us or not is not dependent on whether we're feeling the love or not.
It is dependent upon God's choice to love us; a choice God made and will never undo.
Whether God is involved in our lives is not dependent upon whether or not our grand plans and schemes for ourselves or for God are working out or not; God's involvement in our lives is again God's choice, a choice Gad has already made and will not unmake.

All the disciples, Thomas and the others, had an advantage we do not and will not have; they got to see the Risen Lord.

But we have an advantage they did not; we have seen the fact that the Church and the Gospel are still going strong 2000 years later; again, not because of us, but because of God.

Amen and amen.

The Third Sunday of Easter

Acts 3:12-19

"Dude, it's not about us!"

Peter tried really hard to deflect the attention from himself and John on the day a lame man was healed by "their" touch. Preachers are sometimes put in a similarly awkward position when we hear comments along the line of, "That was such a great sermon today, Pastor; you really did your best today!"

Of course, we want to do our best as often as we can, and it's nice to be acknowledged every once in a while. But, again, the issue here is the ways in which the power of God is made plain.

Peter makes a definite connection for his listeners: this is the God of Abraham, the God of Isaac, the God of Jacob, the God of our ancestors who has glorified Jesus, his servant. How clearly are we pointing out the presence and power of God to our listeners? How are we helping them make the connection to what they see, pray for, hope for and what God is doing in their midst?

Psalm 4

Psalm 4 speaks a word to busy worshipers (and preachers.) The word is: stop! We seem always to be in a hurry; even in our "worship" we have an order and a time frame in mind.

The old joke, at least among Baptists in the South, is that the preacher must quit in time "for us to beat the Methodists and the Presbyterians to the restaurant!"

Notice that there are two indicated pauses for silence and reflection within the eight verses of this text. (These are the "Selah" moments.) Verse 4 could be something of a theme for this psalm: "When you are disturbed, do not sin; ponder it on your beds, and be silent."

Eastertide is a good time for pondering what it is that we have seen and witnessed in recent days, as well as for considering the "holy disturbances" that God sometimes places in our lives. After all, it took the disciples some time to digest what the Easter events meant for them; why should we be any different?

1 John 3:1-7

For some odd reason, when I read John's words of exhortation and encouragement here, I am reminded of the little children's song from my long-ago Sunday School years (it's actually a "gospel song" from music evangelist Ira Stanphill):

> *I traveled alone upon this lonesome way;*
> *My burdens so heavy and dark was my day.*
> *I looked for a friend, not knowing that He*
> *Had all the time been looking for me.*
> *Now, it is Jesus and me for each tomorrow;*
> *For every heartache and every sorrow.*
> *I know that I can depend upon my new found Friend.*
> *And so, till the end, it's Jesus and me.*

(Wanna hear it? Four young ladies in a gospel quartet sing it nicely here:

https://www.youtube.com/watch?v=HjhPeTNdASQ

No, I'm not advocating the over-simplistic theological stance that you might think; but, I am trying to think seriously about what it means to live as God's child, knowing that one day, we will see Jesus "as he is"…and that, then, we will be like him.

In the meantime, how should I speak, think, act, live?

Luke 24:36b-48

See what I'm saying?

Even after a couple of post-resurrection appearances, the disciples are still pretty skittish when Jesus happens suddenly upon them. They are having quite a time trying to grasp the full meaning of the "we saw him dead but now he's alive?" thing.

I love the wit displayed by Jesus here (and by Luke in writing the story this way) — they're all happy and stuff to see him, but still scratching their heads a bit, when Jesus says, "So, I'm hungry; how about you guys? Got anything to eat?"

He doesn't chastise them or call them down for their lack of faith. He just finds a way to confront the elephant in the room and teach them yet another lesson. "I told you I'd be here, and now I am here. You can really, really, really depend on what I say to you!"
Chomp!

Sermon

"The Way Forward"

N.T. Wright says: "People often ask me, 'What after all is the point of Jesus dying and rising again? It's no doubt very nice for him to be alive again, but what does it have to do with the rest of us?'" (1)
What indeed? What is the point of the story of Jesus and why are we here at church?

Are we here because it's the tradition in which we were raised? Because church is a part of the civic fabric of our lives and we would feel a little lost without it.

Why, exactly are we in this community called a church and in this space set apart for getting together to sing strange songs while hearing short speeches and eating a meal that isn't actually a meal, more like a snack, really.

What is it all about? Why are we here? Is it because we're all from somewhere else and are a little lonely for a taste, a touch of home, and a Lutheran Church is a part of home? Is that it?

Three verses in our Gospel lesson are there specifically to tell us why we're here.

> Verse 46: and he said to them, "Thus it is written, the Messiah is to suffer and to rise from the dead on the third day,
>
> Verse 47: and that repentance and forgiveness of sins is to be proclaimed in his name to all nations, beginning from Jerusalem,
>
> Verse 48: you are witnesses of these things.

Three short verses; in English, a mere 50 words; yet they contain our reason for being and our call to action.

First of all; it is written. Luke wants the early church, and us, to know that what happened to Jesus was not a random act of ugliness; another in a long series of cruelties and indignities that powerful and corrupt people have foisted upon the weak, the innocent and the good.

Jesus life, suffering, death, and resurrection were a part of God's long term plan to deal with the very human problems of sin, evil, hatred, discord, and death.

Bishop Wright points out that the basic human condition is that the history of the world is one long litany of bad things people as individuals and as communities and as nations have done to each other.

And all our attempts to bring an end to these bad things flounder on our very human sense of self- righteousness. A few years ago the president of Iran was invited to speak to the UN and he used the occasion to accuse Israel of racism, prompting delegates of other countries to walk out and the United States to boycott the whole thing. It is a scene played out all over the world.

Wright says, "Each one claims that they have the right to the moral high ground and must be allowed redress, revenge, satisfaction." (2)

The only way forward is the way of the Christ, the way of the cross. Jesus came and lived among us and showed us that the one who had the most right, the best claim, to revenge, to redress, to satisfaction, chose to go another way. God, in Christ, turned away from revenge and embraced justice; turned away from our death, and through his own death, gave us life.

Verse 47 – repentance and forgiveness of sins is to be proclaimed in his name throughout the world.

This is the world's only hope, our only way out of the continual cycle of offense and revenge, of insult and retaliation, of wrong piled upon wrong in a deadly version of the Children's game of "King of the Hill"

The only way to bring an end to the nations' battling is through living out the Gospel call for repentance and forgiveness.

Very often, we read this is a private and individual way. If I, DELMER, repent of MY sins, then God will forgive ME, DELMER, of MY sins. That's one way to hear it, but not the only or the best way.

What about; WE must ALL repent of OUR wrongful ways, OUR destructive paths, OUR vengeful hearts.
WE are ALL called to turn from ways that lead to death, and WE are ALL called to turn to and follow ways that lead to newness of life.

And we are all encouraged; no commanded, to forgive the sins of others, to seek reconciliation instead of revenge, to look for life in the valley of the shadow of death.
What are we doing here?

That's in VERSE 48: you are witnesses of these things.
We are here, in this place, in this church,
to be reminded of the story,
to continually turn from death to life,
to receive forgiveness and to learn how to give forgiveness,
to support one another in our lives of faith,
to gather strength from the meal and the community,

and to push each other out the door to be witnesses of these things in the world.

As Luther puts it in the Small Catechism, "We are called, gathered, empowered and sent," by the Holy Spirit, into the streets, with the message of God's amazing Grace.
Christ is Risen, Christ is Risen Indeed, Alleluia.

(1) and (2) NT Wright, *Luke for Everyone*, p.301 ff.

The Fourth Sunday of Easter

Acts 4:5-12

Cheeky answer, wasn't it?

Peter is standing — along with his accomplice, John — before the very seat of power in Israel of the first century CE. This is you or I being brought before our particular judicatories (synod, conference, presbytery, deacon body, etc.) and questioned about our ministerial practice. The fact that these men were "all" members of the high-priestly family added a bit more gravitas (if any were needed.)

"By what power are you doing these things? Who, or what, gives you the right to act the way you have been acting?"
It's not a question one wants to answer lightly. They knew that they could get in real trouble.

You or I might very well find our livelihoods on the line if brought up for questioning on a similar matter. (What if your entire pension fund were riding on the words that came next out of your mouth, for instance?)

"None other than Jesus of Nazareth — the one you crucified. God raised him from the dead and his is the only name that has been given by which we may be saved."

Pretty specific; pretty well-defined. Not afraid to be gently, if firmly, confrontational. It's an all-or-nothing response, when you think about it.

Are we, who may have much less on the line, just as willing to proclaim our conviction as to the truth of the gospel today?

Psalm 23

The classic Psalm 23 provides background for the qualities of the "good shepherd." We do well to have this passage in mind when Jesus says, "I am the good shepherd."

As you re-read Psalm 23 — and do take the time to re-read it, no matter how many times you've heard it, read it, or even preached it — what quality (or qualities) of the good shepherd stand out to you? How have you experienced the presence of the Lord as your shepherd?

1 John 3:16-24

True love does a lot more than wait; it gives, it hopes, it perseveres, it trusts, it supports...and a whole lot more (refresh your memory at 1 Corinthians 13.)

Mainly, as the Elder Apostle writes here, it acts. Love is a very active thing to feel and do. Not just the words, lofty as they may be (love poems are among the highest literary achievements in human history.) It's all about what you do, baby!

Don't just tell me that you love me — show me! You don't have to live in Missouri to subscribe to that kind of wisdom! John says that we have not gone far enough when we have simply believed in Jesus...we must also love (in word and deed) one another.

John 10:11-18

If you're just in it for the paycheck, you probably aren't too interested in sacrificing yourself for anyone at the place where you work. That's just not a "normal" way to think, is it?

But Jesus says that living life his way is sort of like a shepherd in the old days — most likely, the shepherd had a literal financial interest in the welfare of the sheep. He was owner or part-owner of the flock, so it was in his best interest to deliver them to market (or to the shearer) in the best possible condition. Healthier sheep equals higher dollars.

But more than that, the shepherd shared a bond with the sheep. He knew them each by name (his own pet names for them;) he knew how they acted, which were prone to act up or skip out, which were prone to mind and follow in the way they were led.

The sheep also knew which was their shepherd; they got used to his (or her) voice. Even when penned with other flocks and other shepherds, only the voice of "their" shepherd would rouse the sheep to follow. The shepherd was sworn to protect the sheep, and — evidently — would put himself at risk in order to fulfill his duty.

So, Jesus says, I am a lot like that; I know you, you know me, we're really in this thing together. I have given my life for my sheep. All of them. Even the ones you can't see in this fold.

Trust me on this.

Sermon

"Jesus Books"

In my little backyard converted shed office, I have a couple thousand books arranged on a variety of yard sale bookcases. As I wrote this sermon, my coffee cup rested on a shelf that contains what I call my "Jesus books." In recent years there have been a huge number of books written and debate hashed out about who Jesus was, or if indeed he really was.

I own over 30 of these books, and that's just a small part of all that are out there. They have titles like: "Will the Real Jesus Please Stand up?" "The Misunderstood Jew," "Who Was Jesus?" "Lord or Legend?" "Looking for Jesus," "The Real Jesus," "What Jesus Meant," and my favorite title, not favorite book, but favorite title: "Cynic Sage or Son of God?"

(Just rolls off the tongue, doesn't it?)

For over 2000 years the world and the church have wrestled with the question of the true identity of the wandering preacher from Galilee.

The whole of Chapter 10 in John deals with this. Who does he say he is? Does his walk match his talk? Is he for real? Are the signs to be believed?

Eventually, in verse 24, the people ask Jesus – "Are you the Messiah? Are you the one sent from God?" Jesus' answer points to his actions as keys to his identity; behavior reveals character.

He asks them, "Do I act and talk like a Messiah, like a true king of Israel?" "Are the things I say and do for the benefit of the people?" "Do I honor God with the way I live my life?"

In this first part of chapter 10, Jesus talks about being the Shepherd of the sheep, about how the sheep hear the true shepherd's voice and follow, about the willingness of the shepherd to lay down his life for the sheep.

In verses 7 through 11 Jesus showed the contrast between himself and the other shepherds: "all who came before me are thieves and bandits,"
Then he says "I am the good shepherd." Later in chapter 10 Jesus again picks up the protective and caring shepherd theme.

It may be helpful to us to think not in terms of good and bad, but rather in terms of true versus false; or real versus pretend; or fake versus genuine; or perhaps faithless versus faithful.

What Jesus lays claim to here in this text is to being not a false, not a pretend, not a fake, not a faithless shepherd of Israel; but rather to being a true, a real, a genuine, a faithful shepherd of God's sheep.

The shepherd was an important symbol in Israel. For much of their history they were a nomadic people dependent upon their sheep for their livelihood. Because of this, sheep and shepherd imagery was very important.

The King was often referred to as the Shepherd of Israel, referring back to King David, the traditional author of the 23rd Psalm. David, a shepherd boy in his youth, is the king by whom all kings are measured.

The ancient kings of Israel were different from the kings of the nations around them. The other kings were held up to be gods on earth, divine beings in human form. The kings of Israel were not believed to be divine; they were known to be ordinary human beings who represented God on earth and ruled in God's name. The idea was that God had placed the responsibility for the nation in their hands.

The kingdom was not theirs to do with as they pleased. The kingdom was God's and they were to take care of it and God's people in God's name and with God's help. And even great King David failed to do it right all the time.
Between David and Jesus there were many years and many kings, and all the kings of Israel failed in one way or another. None of them lived up to the image of the good, the true, the real Shepherd of Israel, especially not the emperor in Rome or his puppet King Herod.

Now Jesus makes it plain. The sheep hear my voice, he says, they know their true Shepherd and follow and respond to him.

This is the difficult part of this lesson for me. Just hearing the voice is not enough. Many people hear, but don't appear to respond, don't seem to answer, don't look like they are following, apparently don't recognize the voice of Jesus.

Those of us gathered here in church on Sunday morning have, in one way or another heard and recognized the voice of God, the voice of our savior and friend, in the voice of the Bible, in the voice of the Church.

Some of us are more sure than others, some of us hear it more clearly and distinctly than others, but all of us have heard it. That is why we are here. But we are left to wonder about those who aren't here, those who may have heard the word but don't appear to have heard the voice.

Rather than wonder about if they have heard, or why they haven't heard in the, our calling today is to live our lives in such a way that the voice of the Christ is shared with the world in the way we live our lives and in the way we tell God's story.

Pastor John Ortberg tells this story in a recent book:
A man is being tailgated by a woman in a hurry. He comes to an intersection, and when the light turns yellow, he hits the brakes. The woman behind him goes ballistic. She honks her horn at him; she yells her frustration in no uncertain terms; she rants and gestures.

While she is in mid-rant, someone taps on her window. She looks up and sees a policeman. He invites her out of her car and takes her to the station where she is searched and fingerprinted and put in a cell. After a couple of hours, she is released, and the arresting officer gives her her personal effects, saying

"I'm very sorry for the mistake, ma'am. I pulled up behind your car while you were blowing your horn, using bad gestures and bad language. I noticed the WHAT WOULD JESUS DO bumper sticker, the CHOOSE LIFE license plate holder, the FOLLOW ME TO SUNDAY SCHOOL window sign, the FISH EMBLEM on your trunk, and I naturally assumed you had stolen the car.

(*When the Game is Over, It all Goes Back in the Box*, 2007, p. 115)

How we live our lives sends a message to the world. When Martin Luther said that the church is a "priesthood of believers," he didn't mean that we are all pastors; he meant that we all carry Christ into the world in our words and in our actions.

In the modern world, we; we, the church; we, all of us in the church; we are the shepherds; and the hurting, lonely, lost people of the world are God's scattered sheep. Our calling is to go out to them with the voice of the shepherd, calling them home to safety, calling them home to love.

We are the voice of Christ in the world.

What people know of God's law, they learn from us.

What people know of God's forgiveness, they receive from us.

What people know of God's love, they feel from us.

The voice of Christ calls each of one of us out into the world today.

How will you answer?

Will you go?

Will you go out there and love the world in the name of Christ?

Amen and amen.

The Fifth Sunday of Easter

Acts 8:26-40

We sometimes find good news in the strangest places. Philip — deacon, evangelist, obedient follower of Christ — is sent on his way with an angel's message on the road to Gaza. The text parenthetically notes that "this is a wilderness road." Having recently traveled in that area, I can affirm that this is something of an understatement.

There doesn't appear to be anybody or anything on this road; seemingly, it is the waste of a good church member to send Philip on a "mission" to such a godforsaken, barren place.

This, then, is the setup for the wonderful encounter between the Philip and the Ethiopian eunuch. Talk about outsiders! (Philip is, of course, a Greek — his partner in this episode is twice-marked as an African and "less than" a man.)

But what they find as they search the scriptures together is "good news." Both of these outsiders have been brought in to the life of God, in all its goodness, through Jesus Christ. Isn't that still the bottom line for all of us? My birth doesn't matter, my station in life doesn't matter, my sexuality doesn't matter, the color of my skin doesn't matter — what matters is the life I am offered in Christ. It is God's life, and receiving it is good news.

Psalm 22:25-31

This portion of Psalm 22 is a reminder that God's purpose for the world is just that — God's purpose for ALL the world.

Stop for a moment and think about what that means; what part of the world or its peoples seem to you to be far removed from the presence or purpose of God? How can we pray (and work) for the world to know God's dominion?

1 John 4:7-21

Okay, I admit it; I am a long-time fan of Dumb and Dumber (you know, the movie with Jim Carrey and Jeff Daniels.)

Among the scenes in that classic piece of farce is the one where Lloyd and Harry play a game of "Tag, You're It!" There are actually two occurrences of the guys playing "Tag" in the movie, and they serve to illustrate (in a wacky sort of way) the enduring bond of affection that the goofy protagonists share.

Clip -- https://www.youtube.com/watch?v=WasRS2XclpY

After surviving a crisis that threatens to sever their relationship, they are still best buds in the end.

(Stay with me here...)

When I read the passage from 1 John again, I am struck by any number of important moments:

- love comes from God
- when we love, we mimic God
- we actually "see" God when we see love in action
- God has sent Jesus as the Savior of the world — an act of love
- real love is never about fear

But the one moment that really stands out to me in my reading is what I would call the Divine "Tag, You're It" moment, in v.10 — we did not love God, but rather God first loved us. God sent Jesus as an "atoning sacrifice" for our sins.

Regardless of your theological take on atonement, it means that sin and its attendant threat of death has been taken care of — finished, kaput, removed, unplugged. God has preemptively and proactively given us life through Christ. All before we ever made any sort of move toward God. We didn't start the game — God did.

Tag, you're it!

John 15:1-8

Dr. Chilton treats the image of the vine and the vinegrower in his sermon below (and does it very well, of course!)

I am struck by the power of Christ's words here; in fact, Jesus says, "You have already been cleansed by the word that I have spoken to you." (v.3)

There is a key relationship between our "abiding in Christ" as the source of our life, and Christ's words "abiding in us." What does it mean for busy, time-starved, 21st-century disciples of Jesus to allow his words to "abide" in us?

Sermon

"Holy Heliotropism and Other Things Jesus Taught"

My subject today is Holy Heliotropism or Divine Radiation and Human Transformation or The Ministry of Plant Rotation. Let me explain.

There are two women in my life: my mother and my wife. Both are inveterate gardeners in the English mold that I call "out messing in the yard". My earliest memories are of my mother dragging her hose around the house to water her various bushes and flowers.

My sons tell me that their main memories of their pre-school days are of their mother, with sun-hat and gloves and little plastic gardening wagon, puttering around the yard.

I am not a gardener, but I have paid attention to their gardening; in particular to the methodology of plant rotation.

Some plants are tied to stakes to force them to grow in a certain way: pea vines and rose bushes and tomato plants and certain other flowers and vegetables.

Other plants are planted in pots and are rotated in the sun, and grow in the direction of the light. They are shaped by being pulled toward the light. Their growth in a certain direction is not forced, it is encouraged. This growing in the direction of the sun is called heliotropism.

Jesus is the vine, and we are the branches. (John 15:5) God is our vinegrower, the gardener of our souls. Here's a question: What method has our vinegrower chosen to use in shaping our lives into a Christlike shape? Are we forced into a particular direction or are we drawn to the light of God's love?

Conformity seems to be the world's way. Conformity to the world eventually becomes what the Prayer of Confession in the Lutheran liturgy calls "bondage to sin."

To be conformed to the world is to be staked out on the altar of popularity or acceptability, to lose your soul in the effort to go along to get along, to live a life in imitation of what others think you should be and should do.

You will live, but you will not be free; far from it, you will find yourself a slave to the will and the way of the world.
On the other hand, God's way is the way of heliotropism, of inviting us to be transformed by being bathed in the light of God's love — by daily turning our faces toward the source of life and love itself.

Martin Luther said that in sin, the human will becomes bent, turns away from God and in on itself.

In their powerful little book on the Lord's Prayer, Stanley Hauerwas and Will Willimon make reference to this when they say, "The Lord's Prayer is a lifelong act of bending our lives toward God in the way that God has offered."

In the hymn "Joyful, Joyful, We Adore Thee," we sing about this bending toward God in the lines:

 Hearts unfold like flowers before thee,
opening to the sun above.
Melt the clouds of sin and sadness;
drive the dark of doubt away.
Giver of immortal gladness,
fill us with the light of day!

-- Henry J. van Dyke

One of the great dangers of the church is that we sometimes try to make other folks conform to our ideas of what they ought to be doing if they are "true Christians."

We attempt to tie them to the stake of our preconceived ideas of how they should respond to the Gospel and we are disappointed when they resist and pull away.

We are called instead to a ministry of heliotropism. We are called to shine the light of Christ in such a way that others will be drawn to it and will begin to conform their lives to it. That is all.

Most of us, if we think about it, can figure out who those persons, those assistant vinegrowers, were for us.

We can look back over our lives and see the people who lived out the Gospel, who acted in a Christlike manner in such a way that we wanted to be like them, wanted to be the sort of person, the kind of Christian, they were.

That is who we are called to be. Assistant vinegrowers, exposing people to the bright sun of God's love in Christ. Amen and amen.

The Sixth Sunday of Easter
Acts 10:44-48

"Surely God just can't bless THEM!"

The "them" blank has been filled in with lots of suspects in Christian history. There are always people that "we Christians" are just sure reside outside the grace of God. In Acts 10, it was the uncircumcised believers; in our time, it could be Republican believers, or Democratic believers; upper 1% believers, or 99% believers; gay believers, or straight believers; "Muslim-loving" believers, or Christian-supremacist believers.

Of whom might it be said that you (or your congregation members) would be astounded to know they had received the gifts of God by the Spirit?

Psalm 98

Isn't the Bible just absurd sometimes? I mean, come on — seas "roaring" and waves "clapping their hands?" Will the earth really "break into song" and put forth a few paeans of praise? Everybody knows you can't take this stuff literally — right?

I love Bible texts like Psalm 98, precisely because they are absurd — absurdly wonderful! Let us join the cacophony of praise!

1 John 5:1-6

Well, I hope we're getting the idea the "love" is important to God! These Eastertide readings from John — nicknamed the "Beloved" disciple — have emphasized over and over again just how tightly bound God's presence in the world is to our expressions of love.

What's love got to do with it? Everything, apparently.

John 15:9-17

Key points from John 15:

• Jesus' love for us is his imitation (much more than the sincerest form of flattery!) of God's love for him; that is to say, Jesus learned love from the one he named his Heavenly Father. When he loves us, he's just passing along what he's always known!

- Keeping the commandments of Christ always issues forth in one distinguishing way: love for others. If our actions and/or words are not loving, oughtn't we pause to consider where they might be originating?
- Jesus gives loving one another the force of a commandment (it's not a suggestion, or merely an example.)
- Jesus chose us — not vice versa.

Sermon

"A Risky Gospel"

Writing in USA Today, Presbyterian Pastor Henry G. Brinton made a helpful "two kinds of Christians" argument. Or rather, he argued that each of us carries two, often contradictory, religious impulses: 1) obligation-keeping and 2) liberation-seeking. (USA Today, May 8, 2006)

I have found this a helpful tool for thinking about my faith. I have begun to ask myself: "Which of my religious notions is based in obligation-keeping and which are rooted in liberation-seeking?" Pro-life or pro-choice, peace-activist or military defender, capitalism versus socialism, science and religion; which impulse rules in what areas?

This week's lessons pose an interesting opportunity to play with this question. In both the second reading from I John and the gospel lesson from John 15, we get a lot of obligation keeping language, "I command" and "obey his commandments" and "You are my friends if you do what I command you."

On the other hand, the Acts lesson is about all kinds of liberation. Peter becomes liberated from his notions about the Gentiles and their need to follow certain rules and regulations in order to be accepted by God. And the gentile believers get liberated from a potentially very uncomfortable surgical procedure and a restrictive diet. Peter also discovers that God pours out the Spirit on whomever God chooses, strangely ignoring us and our traditional notions of other people's readiness for our level of holiness.

Peter verbalizes this shift from obligation-keeping mode to liberation-seeking mode when he says "Can anyone withhold the water for baptizing these people who have received the Holy Spirit just as we have?"

The tricky thing is balancing somewhere on the tightrope between obligation keeping and liberation seeking. Most of us know that pure obligation-keeping religion leads to an oppressive, stifling, regimented legalism that creates communities of faith with blinders on, unable and unwilling to respond either to the world or to God's new movements of the spirit.

On the other hand, pure liberation-seeking leads to "tossing to and fro on the winds of doctrine," seeking the next new thing (whatever it is) that will turn us loose from whatever restrictions we wishes to be released from.

When I was in college I was what I now jokingly call a Metho-Bap-Terian, a generic mainline Protestant with a toe in several churches and my heart and commitment in none. Feeling called to ministry, but not knowing which "company" to sign up with, I went to one of my religion professor for help. He didn't give me an answer but he did give me a tool for thinking. (Good professor, right?)

He told me that almost any decision in life is about finding a balance between two equally valuable things: freedom and security. Basically the freer you are, the less security you have and vice versa. A system whereby clergy are appointed to their churches is very secure, but there is little freedom. A pure call system is very free with an almost complete lack of security.

Many times we try to increase our feelings of security with God by trying to restrict both our and God's freedom. We try to draw inviolable lines of what's okay and what's not okay; of who's in and who's out; of what God can and can't do.

And it is very scary to embrace the freedom that comes with realizing that those lines are fuzzier than we thought, and that God, being God, is free to do as God pleases and to love whom God loves whether we like it or not.

The command to love is probably as good a balancing point as any. My Mama told me once that Jesus had to command us to love one another, because love is not easy sometimes. If it were easy, no commands, no orders would be necessary. As it is there are times when we need the command to love so that we continue to behave in loving ways, even when we don't feel like it.

Thanks, Mama.

G.K. Chesterton said somewhere, "Jesus told us to love our neighbors. In another place, he told us to love our enemies. This is because, generally speaking, they are the same people." Again, the command is very, very clear because the task is very, very hard.

So, what is it that the gospel calls to today? Some of us may need to think about establishing a few guidelines, obligations so to speak, for our lives. A little discipline never hurt anybody. Think of it as diet and exercise for the soul.

But most of us need to think through and change whatever attitudes and behaviors we are carrying around that may be protecting our own feelings of security but which are hampering the God-given freedom of others.

The story is that sometime during the early days of the reformation, someone insisted to Luther that the "obligation" to go to confession and to attend mass every week had to be retained. "If we don't require it, people won't come," they said.

Luther replied, "Well, that is just the risk we will have to take for the freedom of the gospel."

The question today is, "What risks are we called to make for the freedom of the gospel?"

Amen and amen.

The Ascension of Our Lord

Sermon
by the Rev. Dr. Delmer L. Chilton

". . . he ascended into heaven," APOSTLES' CREED and NICENE CREED

The story of the Ascension doesn't get a lot of attention in the life of the church. I think this is because it is somewhat hard to see the point of it. Laying aside all the standard, modern, empirical doubts about the resurrection appearances themselves, there is still the question of why?

If Jesus was resurrected and if Jesus could flit here and there in his new resurrection body, appearing and disappearing at will as if he had Scotty from Star Trek beaming him about, why would he pull this somewhat theatrical stunt of floating off into heaven, like the Wizard taking leave of Oz in his balloon? Why didn't he just say good-bye and go?

Well, for one thing it was important that when he went to "sit at the right hand of the father," people knew that he was really gone this time. Gone and not coming back until he came back for good, came back to "judge the living and the dead." If he had just disappeared again, well there would have been more Jesuses seen in Jerusalem than Elvises in Las Vegas.

It's difficult to get busy with the important business of loving the Christ in your neighbor if you are constantly on the lookout for another resurrection appearance.

The Ascension of Our Lord is the completion of his resurrection. Christ came from God to take on our flesh, our life, our troubles, our sin and yes, our death.

In the mystery of the Three Days, sin was removed and death was defeated. For forty days Jesus walked and talked among the believers, making sure they knew that this new life was real and not imagined. And then he went back to God, in the spirit and in the flesh, fully human and fully divine forever and ever, amen.

And he left us here. We were all, in one sense, left behind. We were left but we were not abandoned. The Ascension marks the end of the earthly ministry of Jesus and prepares the way for the birth of the church with the gift of the Spirit at Pentecost. Up until this moment the Gospel has been about what God in Christ has done for us; from this day forth the Gospel is about what God is Christ is doing through us in the world.

This need to get on with ministry is reflected in Acts, "While he was going and they were gazing up toward heaven, suddenly two men in white robes stood by them. They said, "Men of Galilee, why do you stand looking up toward heaven?"(Acts 1:10-11, NRSV)

Every time I read that I remember being twelve years old and doing, or rather, not doing, my chores. I can hear my father come around the corner of the barn or see him suddenly appear beside me in the field. He would scowl and look disappointed and said, "What are you doing just standing there? Get busy; we've got a farm to run."

In the same way, we are reminded to stop looking up and to start looking around at the work we are called to do, at the world full of hurting people who need to hear and feel the love of Jesus in their lives.

The Seventh Sunday of Easter
Acts 1:15-17, 21-26

You gotta love Matthias; he is the poster child of unsung heroes of the church everywhere.

It is "The Twelve" that get most of the attention during Jesus' ministry — and, of course, it is the Big Three (Peter, James, and John) who get the most ink on top of that. After the shocking betrayal of Judas and the hurry-scurry days that followed Jesus' resurrection, it takes a while for the leadership core to get around to filling out their numbers with another apostle.

An aside — I've sometimes wondered why Jesus himself didn't ask them to pick a replacement for Judas. Was it just not on his radar during his post-resurrection appearances? He certainly had business with Peter ("feed my sheep") and Thomas ("don't doubt any longer") and others who needed him. Or was Jesus just not that concerned with the numbers? I know that we have a nearly legendary concern for numbers, and reports, balancing the books, filling up committees — sort of ecclesiastically rearranging the deck chairs on the Titanic, if you know what I mean. Not that there's anything wrong with that! Or is there? Are we consuming a good bit of our time and energy with the functional details of ministry, when we could be spending it on things that are more relational?

At any rate, Matthias is chosen to round out the Twelve. Check his record of consistency and persistence: he had been with Jesus and the other disciples "during all the time that the Lord Jesus went in and out among us, beginning from the baptism of John until the day when he was taken up from us."

Never held a position, never had a title, never noticed until the moment of need, not even a consensus candidate during the first round of balloting. But, in the end, he was present, available, willing and able. I like the guy…may his tribe increase!

Psalm 1

Psalm 1 is perhaps the clearest presentation of the Hebrew concept of the "two ways" in all of the Bible. Exercising the distinct human gift of free will (choice,) we may follow the way of the LORD — the righteous path — or the way of the wicked.

Both ways have attendant rewards and consequences; both paths require effort. It is the latter point that impresses me as I read Psalm 1 again. We often hear words along the line of, "It's just too hard to follow God; God expects too much of me; I just can't keep all those commandments."

But we fail to realize that it takes a good deal of effort to walk the opposite path — to follow the advice of the wicked, one must first take time to listen; taking the path that sinners tread requires actually walking along that way; sitting in the seat of scoffers doesn't "just happen." You have to decide to stop and sit a spell, so to speak.

1 John 5:9-13

John writes very much in line with the concept of the "two ways."

The church's testimony has always been, as summarized in v. 11, "God gave us eternal life, and this life is in his Son." That's it. Jesus is the Savior of the world.

In our fractious dissent (borne of that same pesky free will we just mentioned?), we have often debated just exactly HOW Jesus is the Savior of the world — but never IF.
Whatever the HOW, John holds that the inevitable conclusion is: "Whoever has the Son has life; whoever does not have the Son of God does not have life."

Thus, has the church been given a "great commission" to teach, tell, instruct, show, demonstrate and by any and all means get the message out to the world — "believe in the name of the Son of God, that you may know that you have eternal life."

John 17:6-19

Jesus' prayer of protection for his followers — also known as a prayer for the unity of his followers — is rooted in this same mission of making God known in the world. "I have made your name known to those whom you gave me from the world."

Part of the church's life (at least) is to live in imitation of Jesus; what he does, we seek to do. Making God's name known — through the life of Jesus — seems to me to be a basic part of the church's job description.

Who are the ones that God has given us from the world? Who are we to pray for, protect, love, minister to? In whom — and in what ways — is God making our joy full as we share the life of Jesus?

Sermon

"At-one-ment"

Jesus prays in John's Gospel, "Holy Father, protect them in your name that you have given me, so that they may be one, as we are one.

We are called to be united as the community of faith; yet we look around us and see much disunity and division in the churches.

One of the churches I served in North Carolina had had a church split in the 1890's. It involved hurt feelings and loud meetings and even a Synod President (now called a bishop) threatened with arrest. After the dust settled there were three churches where for the previous 150 years there had been one.

Most of us agree that we want unity, we desire oneness. We lament the divisions and debates that drive us apart, we do not want to be divided, yet all too often -- we are.

Why? In the face of our Lord's command and our desire, why do we so frequently find ourselves at odds with each other?

The witness of Scripture is pretty clear on two points here:

    1) Our disunity springs from seeking to do things our own way, and
    2) The path to unity and oneness lies in seeking to do things God's way.

Many hundreds of years before Christ, King Solomon built a temple, a place for the people of God to gather in worship.

II Chronicles 7:14 tells us of God's response to King Solomon's prayer of dedication:

> *If my people, who are called by my name, will humble themselves and pray and seek my face, and turn from their wicked ways; then will I hear from heaven, forgive their sins, and heal their land.*

Time and time again when the people of God lose their focus on God, trouble ensues. This trouble is not punishment from God; it is the natural result of what are essentially spiritual beings failing to attend to necessary spiritual things.

It is in unity with the holy, the divine, the spiritual, that we find wholeness within ourselves and unity with each other.

The words atone and atonement have an interesting history in English. We generally speak of atoning for our sins as somehow doing something to earn forgiveness, or performing some act of penance or restitution to make up for the bad that we have done.

In theology, atonement has become the name for the doctrine of what God in Christ accomplished by his death upon the cross.

What's interesting is that the English root word doesn't exactly mean making up for or paying for one's sins or mistakes or crimes. The root word means "reconciliation."

It comes from the Middle English atonen "to become reconciled" and from the French at on "in harmony" at +on = one (Webster's Seventh New Collegiate Dictionary, p.56). How do we achieve unity, oneness, harmony? With God and with each other? Well, it seems obvious it begins with Christ and the cross.

Jesus stood amongst his disciples at the Last Supper and prayed that they might be one.

Then he went out and did something about it. He reconciled, he harmonized, he "at-oned" us.

Christ made us one with God and one with each other.

My favorite professor at the Lutheran Seminary in Columbia, SC, Dr. J. Benjamin Bedenbaugh defined God's act of reconciliation as "God hugging the world to himself in an embrace of love."(*Classroom lecture*, Spring 1983)

God has made peace with us and, by extension, between us. If we are one with God, then we are also one with each other.

Dr. Paul Tournier, author of THE MEANING OF PERSONS has been quoted as saying: There are two things we cannot do alone. One is to be married, and the other is to be a Christian."

We need to be one with one another within the body of Christ, the church, if for no other reason than without it we cannot learn to love and to be loved alone.

It is within the daily bump and grind of life together, of living and working and playing and praying together as the people of God that we find out what it means to be genuinely forgiven for our failures, praised for our efforts, appreciated for our virtues, prayed for in our sorrows, helped in the midst of our troubles, and loved in spite of ourselves.

It is only within the community of faith that we learn to be genuinely loving and praising and forgiving and helping toward others. We need each other in order to learn and to practice what it means to be Christian, to each other and to the world.

Our calling today is to do all that we can to be agents of at-one-ness. It begins here and goes spilling out those doors into the world, walking out of here with arms wide open, seeking to embrace the world with love of God.

Amen and amen.

Day of Pentecost

A few years ago, USA Today ran a story about the Connie T. Maxwell Home in Greenwood SC in its Life section.

The article told about how the Baptists of the state had started the home as an orphanage and as times changed had adapted to serving children in any sort of need.

They had an interview with the director, a cheerful but harried woman, who told heart-breaking stories of the children's lives before they were brought to Connie T. Maxwell.

The reporter asked how she, and the other staff, cope with such constant stress and pain in others.

The director smiled and said that you had to keep a sense of humor and perspective. She showed the writer a file in her desk where she kept an anonymous collection of cute, poignant or funny things the children had said.

The director said, "Whenever I get over-whelmed, I just open this drawer and read a few of these and I feel better." USA Today printed several of the things the kids said.

My favorite is this, from a 9 year old boy:

"Germs, germs, germs! Jesus, Jesus, Jesus! That's all I ever hear about around here and I ain't never seen either one of them."

That young boy sums up a problem that Jesus addresses in John 15: 26-27.

It is Maundy Thursday and Jesus is in the midst of trying to explain everything to his disciples before he leaves. I'm not so sure they're getting it, and neither is Jesus.

He realizes that when he's gone they'll be like that little boy; hearing and talking about Jesus without ever seeing him. So Jesus promises an answer, a solution to this "Never Seeing Jesus" problem – the Holy Spirit.

In our text Jesus talks about a "Counselor" and the "spirit of truth," but it's the Holy Spirit he's talking about.

It is likely that the disciples heard that and looked at each other quizzically and nodded like they understood; but they really didn't and after he quit talking, they promptly forgot what he said.

We are all familiar with this; it's what we all do when our husband or wife or boss or teacher or other significant other tells us things we don't understand and don't care enough about to ask for clarification.

So, they kind of forgot about it, and then the crucifixion and the resurrection and the hiding out and then the resurrection appearances of Jesus' popping in and out of their lives for a few weeks happened and then the ascension, with Jesus' floating off into heaven happened, and in midst of all that, who could remember a little un-comprehended promise about a counselor; I mean, really?

So, here they were minding their own insignificant little messianic Christian storefront cult business, singing hymns and praying and still hiding out from the authorities when whoosh, Jesus' promise comes gloriously true.

Noise, wind, fire, voices shouting, movement, out of control religious excitement; of one thing we can be absolutely certain; the first church was definitely NOT Lutheran!

The church was born in answer to the problem of talking about Jesus without being able to see him.

Germs, germs, germs. Jesus, Jesus, Jesus. That's all I hear about around here and I ain't never seen either one of them. Though I understand what that young boy was talking about, I would beg to differ.

He saw Jesus every day in the very existence of that home, built and supported by the church. He saw Jesus every day in the people who bathed, fed, disciplined, taught and loved him.

The church is the place and the people where and among whom Jesus is not just talked about but is shown to the world. It is not by accident that the New Testament constantly refers to the church as the body of Christ.

Too often we think of the church in personal terms, in terms of what I'm getting out of it, of "am I being fed," "are my needs being met," etc.

To think that way is to misunderstand the nature of the church.

The church is mentioned in the third article of the Creed, the part devoted to the Holy Spirit because the church is a work of the Holy Spirit in the world.

Luther's explanation of this part of the creed says the church is:"called, gathered, enlightened, made holy and sent"

The Holy Spirit is active in the church calling the world to God. Each of us has been called here by the spirit. we have been gathered together not for convenience; not because talking to a lot of people at once is more efficient than talking one on one or because we need more voices to make the hymns sound better, or the more people we have the better we can pay the pastor.

No, we are gathered because it is the nature of human beings to need each other, to need to learn with and from each other, to learn to support and care for each other.

It is in the midst of the gathered community that we become truly holy, not perfect, not ideal, not without problem or moral struggles and flaws, but holy, devoted to God and aware of God's presence in us and in others and in the world.

And it is as we have been gathered and enlightened and made holy that we realize that we have not been made those things for ourselves and for our own benefit and for our own personal growth, but for the world. We realize that we have been gathered so that we might be sent, sent into a world that needs love, that needs care, that needs compassion, that needs to see Jesus in the midst of the toxic germs of modern life.

In his book *Red Letter Christians*, Tony Campolo tells of sitting down to dinner in a restaurant in Port-au-Prince, Haiti. Seated next to the front window, he looked up from his plate to discover three little boys with their faces pressed against the window, staring at his plate full of food.

The waiter came by and pulled down the shade and said, "Don't let them bother you, enjoy your meal." (P. 24)

There is a world just outside these walls that is starving both for food and for what God has to offer them. And the question is: are we going to pull the shade? Or are we going to get up and go deal with them?

Amen and amen.

Trinity Sunday

Isaiah 6:1-8

I don't know that any of us will ever be able to capture or imagine the awe and terror of Isaiah's vision of a visit to the throne of the Lord. The hem of God's robe fills the temple; now that's a big robe!

Seraphim are there, hovering and shouting (though we often think of angels "singing," the text never really says that they sing.)

The house is shaking and there's smoke everywhere — much more dramatic than our sanctuaries on most Sundays, I'd say.

The cumulative effect is that Isaiah comes quite undone. "Woe is me," is the best hymn of praise that he can squawk out. Something about truly seeing God as holy reminds us deeply and painfully that we are not.

And, yet — the call of God comes: "Who will go for us?" Since there's nobody else present, Isaiah steps us with one of his most famous lines: "Here am I (gulp); send me."

The old evangelist used to say, "When it comes to the call of God, it's not your ability God is interested in. It's your availability!" I kind of like that, even if it makes me nervous!

Psalm 29

The psalm text offers accompaniment and counterpoint to Isaiah's grand vision of God. The emphasis is on the commanding, calling "voice of the LORD."

This voice is not for the faint of heart, yet it is a source of both strength and peace.

Romans 8:12-17

Our readings in Romans 8 continue, opening doors to yet more aspects of the limitless, ever-present Spirit of God.

- The Spirit leads and guides
- The Spirit "puts to death" our fleshly inclinations
- The Spirit does not lead us to fear
- The Spirit allows us to cry out to God, as a young child to a loving, trustworthy father

- The Spirit assures us that we are, indeed, children of God

John 3:1-17

We have encountered portions of this reading already through the church year; there is much of note in this third chapter of John's gospel. On Trinity Sunday, however, perhaps the center of the text is found in v. 8:

"The wind blows where it chooses, and you hear the sound of it, but you do not know where it comes from or where it goes. So it is with everyone who is born of the Spirit."

One of the most difficult illusions for we human beings to give up is that of control over our lives. Experience teaches us that there are really very few things that are within our capacity to control.

Certainly, we do not control the Spirit of God — anymore than we can control the wind. (As I write these words, we are entering the "hurricane season" in Florida with a tropical storm just off the coast. If you've ever survived a hurricane or similar natural disaster, you realize just how little control you have!)

That image helps me connect to Isaiah's experience in our first reading. His experience of God was somewhat out of control, to the point of being terrifying. Much like the roaring of hurricane-force winds and the sound of trees splitting or being ripped up by their roots.

May we not forget the power we are dealing with when we blithely mention the presence of the Spirit, pronouncing the Spirit's blessings on the lives of those to whom we preach and with whom we minister.

Sermon

"Golf and the Holy Trinity"

Today is Holy Trinity Sunday. Brief attempts to explain the Trinity remind me of my Daddy's sister, Aunt Mildred. She talked on the phone with her friends a lot; a whole lot. The family joke was that she ended every conversation with the line, "I would tell you more, but I already told you more than I heard myself."

Our Scripture lessons all make some sort of reference to a trinitarian understanding of the nature of God. Isaiah contains the line, "holy, holy, holy," which can be stretched into a reference to the trinity if one is so inclined.

Romans says things about crying "Abba, Father," and being a "joint heir with Christ," and the "Spirit of God" letting us know that we are children of God.

John's Gospel contains Jesus' famous conversation with Nicodemus about being "born from above" and "born of water and the Spirit," and most memorable of all, "For God so loved the world that he gave his only Son."

Nowhere do we find the word trinity or an explanation of how God is both three and one at the same time. Like I said, we have to be careful not to say more than we heard ourselves.

Me, I'm lazy. I use golf theology. Used to play golf with a minister friend of mine and we came up with the term.
We got to thinking about all the people we knew who spent a lot of time on the golf course complaining about their lie, or trying to improve their lie, legally or, most often, illegally

and sneakily, moving the ball out of sand traps and from behind tress when they thought no one was looking.

Or they were obsessing about their score, or they were trying to improve their score, or they were lying about their score, etc.

And we realized that neither of us worried too much about all that. We were just glad to be out of the office and out on the golf course, whacking away at the ball in the general direction of the hole.

Then, being preachers, we started thinking of all those pastor friends we knew who were always trying to improve their theological lie, trying to make things make better sense, etc. And we decided that we were golf theologians; we preferred to take things as they came, to play it as it lay, to whack away in the general direction of heaven.

So, rather than spend a lot of time on the philosophical understanding of the Trinity, I prefer to think a lot about the Trinity's implications for the Christian life.

I like to meditate on the fact that God exists in community, in a family, a family of equals who share one calling and goal and life, but exist within that community and family as unique individuals who are stronger together than they could ever be apart.

That helps me understand the notion of the church better, because if we're made in the image of God and God needs community, then it makes sense that we need community too; a community that is called together to move in the same general direction, loving each other and serving the world.

And sometimes when I think about the Trinity, I think about how each of us have different spiritual personalities and how some of us respond to Abba, the Father, the Creator, and how others of us really relate to God in Christ, the Son. There are many others who are touched deeply by the Spirit.

It just fascinates me how the idea of the Trinity manages to touch all those spiritual bases and keep them all in balance. Our calling on Holy Trinity Sunday, is neither figuring out the Trinity nor explaining it.

Our calling is to live the Holy Trinity in our lives and in the holy and loving community we call the church.

Amen and amen.

Proper 3 – Season after Pentecost Sunday Closest to May 25

Hosea 2:14-20

God has chosen the "life situation" of the prophet to illustrate God's own relationship to Israel. Hosea's wife, Gomer, has been unfaithful to him. Though she has borne three children (only one of which is confirmed as his,) she decides to up and leave Hosea holding the (diaper) bag.

As the rest of the book reveals, Hosea still loves her, and would do pretty much anything to win her back. In today's poignant passage, God makes clear that this is how God feels about the people.

"I am now going to allure her…I will betroth you in righteousness and justice, in love and compassion."

God never, ever gives up.

Psalm 103:1-13, 22

Classic lines from this great worship psalm:
- "all that is within me" – give it all you've got!
- "forget not his benefits" – remember the good stuff
- "forgives your iniquity" – doesn't hold it over your head
- "heals all your diseases" – healed, sealed, the real deal!
- "redeems you life from the Pit" – life IS the pits sometimes, but God lifts us up!

- "as high as the heavens are above the earth…as far as the east is from the west" – that's a very long way, indeed; you can't really measure God's love!

2 Corinthians 3:1-6

"Do I need to get that in writing?"

In our society, in just about any business or personal deal that is made, you are pretty much always better off to get it in writing. It's not safe to assume, anymore, that a person is a "man (or woman) of his (her) word."

Paul uses one of scripture's most beautiful images when he tells the Corinthians, "you are our letter, written on our hearts."

No, you don't have to get the evidence of Christ's working in you and our labor among you written down – just look into your own lives and hearts.

Mark 2:13-22

We've already talked about it – Mark's gospel moves fast! Sometimes, I almost feel like Jesus is just too quick for the people around him.

Levi certainly seems to pick up on Jesus' urgency. He responds with alacrity, and even hosts an immediate dinner party for his new rabbi. Of course, the "old gang" that he has always known come along for the ride, and that doesn't exactly make for the crowd that you would expect in the church fellowship hall for a potluck supper!

Jesus gives his nemeses, the "scribes of the Pharisees," three quick reasons why he's doing what he's doing. I can't help but think that all three whizzed right over their heads (and probably a bit over ours.)

Whatever else wedding guests, unshrunk cloth, and new wine may mean – they are certainly signals that what God is doing through Jesus is not like what has come before. I wonder if God's work among us is every really what we were expecting?

More to the point, I wonder if what we are expecting is every truly God's work among us?

Sermon

"Those Who Are Sick"

I am told by my mother (frequently I might add) that when I was about three years old, she took me and my sister and brother, who were 6 and 5 respectively, to the doctor for some childhood illness that required us to get a shot. Dr. Jarrel was a country doctor, long on common sense and short on wither formality or a good pediatric bedside manner.

He took the three of us into the examining room together and, with his back to us, prepared a needle while chatting with my Mama about the weather and farming and her relatives who were also his patients. Suddenly he turned around with the needle in his hands and I started climbing the walls, trying to scramble over the radiator and out the window, all the while screaming over my shoulder, "Only them two's sick! Only them two's sick!"

I thought of that story when I read our Gospel Lesson for today. The "scribes of the Pharisees saw that he was eating with tax collectors and sinners." And they said to the disciples, in effect; "Only them two's sick! Only them two's sick!" All too often all too many of us are like that aren't we? We know what's wrong, and we're pretty sure it's not us. We know who's wrong, and again, we're pretty sure it's not us.

One of my childhood mountain preachers put it this way, "According to most of us, it must have been for those other people that Jesus came and died, cause we haven't ever done anything bad enough to lose sleep over, much less go to Hell for."

In our text, Jesus responds to the scribes of the Pharisees with a hint of both sarcasm and resignation, "Those who are well have no need of a physician, but those who are sick; I have come to call not the righteous but sinners." The sarcasm lies in the fact that Jesus knows full well that these folks are neither spiritually well nor completely righteous. The resignation comes from the fact that he also knows that only those who know they need help will both ask for it and benefit from it. As long as "only them two's sick," there is nothing anyone, not even Jesus, can do for them.

When I was in my early twenties, while still in divinity school, I was assigned to a small parish as a student pastor. After a few months I went to the District Superintendent and poured out all my frustrations with my church, which mostly had to do with their unresponsiveness to my suggestions.

He listened patiently and then said, "Delmer, if you are going to last as a clergyperson you will have to learn that you cannot minister to people who do not want to be ministered to. As long as they think they are fine the way they are, they will politely 'yes, but . . .' you to death. It's only when they know that they need to change, that they need help, that you can make an impact. In the meantime, work with those who want your help and continue to preach the good news to those who don't."

Amen and amen.

Proper 4 – Season after Pentecost Sunday Closest to June 1

1 Samuel 3:1-10, (11-20)

We get a glimpse into the call of Israel's true "minor" prophet – Samuel. So many images to play around with here for preaching:

- Eli, the "priest in charge" in Israel, is getting old and has lost touch, in many ways, with his own call from God. Yet, though his eyesight had "begun to grow dim," he is not yet blind or spiritually bereft. He maintains enough sensitivity to guide young Samuel.
- The "lamp of God" has not yet gone out – a symbol of the presence of God with God's people. Sometimes, God presence feels a little dim in our own lives, yet the lamp has not gone out!
- The old saying goes, "Third time's a charm;" well, it actually took God four tries to get Samuel tuned in, but God is patient and eventually accomplished God's call on Samuel's life.
- Pity poor old Eli (sort of.) He knows that he is most likely deserving of whatever fate God hands down to him, but he "takes it like a man." Again, even a fading servant of the Lord can still find a chance to be faithful (and faith –full.)

Psalm 139:1-6, 13:18

Quick thoughts from the psalm: There is very little (nothing, actually) that God does not already know about us, before we ever approach God's presence in prayer or worship.

There is nowhere we ever are, or will go, that God is not already there.

Before we ever were – God was.

To be made by God is an awesome and wonderful thing.

God's thoughts are "weighty" – a term that indicates great worth (worth your weight in gold, at least!)

Deuteronomy 5:12-15

There is a time and place reserved only for God, and for our communion with God. It is "Sabbath."

Psalm 81:1-10

One might say that Psalm 81 describes the original "praise band" in the worship of God. Put that in your organ pipe and smoke it!

2 Corinthians 4:5-12

From this passage, we know Jesus as both "Light" and "Life." By comparison, our bodies are but "jars of clay" that dampen the light, and we are infected by and afflicted with death. The good news is that Jesus' light and life are ours, the gift(s) of God.

Mark 2:23-3:6

A rabbi and twelve disciples walk into a grain field…stop me if you've heard this one!

Seriously, an excellent treatment below by Dr. Chilton.

Sermon

"Quality Time"

Our Gospel lesson today has to do with Sabbath observance. The main focus of this lesson is to encourage us to pay attention to our relationship with God. All relationships thrive on people taking the time to pay attention to one another. It's not so much what happens during the time – the time itself is what's important.

When my sons were school-age I read an article about the myth of "quality time." Parenting. The idea was that very busy, two job parents can do adequate parenting by carefully planning the time they have with their children. The point of the article was simple; there is no such thing as "quality time," to a kid. Quality time is a very adult, productivity centered concept. "How much "good work," can I get done in the limited time I have available? To a child, the important thing is not what is done in the time with the parent, the important thing is the time itself. Attention being paid to the relationship is the key.

A study of counseling techniques used by the Marriage and Family therapists showed that the particular style of counseling was not as important to the healing process as the frequency with which the couples made visits to the therapist. The researcher concluded that the most important factor in improving relationships was that the couple took time at least once a week to pay attention to each other and nothing else. Again, what was done during the time was nowhere near as important as the time itself.

What is true of these basic human relationships is also true of our relationship with God. Sabbath observance is about taking time out of our ever increasingly busy schedules to "pay attention" to our relationship with God.

In Mark's Gospel, Jesus confronts the Pharisees about their misuse of the Sabbath. They turned a gift of rest into a burden; filling it with unreasonable rules. We don't have that problem today, do we? There is practically nothing we do on any other day that we would not do on Sunday. If the Pharisees were guilty of abolishing the Sabbath by making it a chore; we are guilty of the opposite sin – that of abusing the Sabbath by taking it too lightly.

When Jesus said, "The Sabbath was made for humankind," he meant it literally. He meant that the Sabbath was created as a gift to us, a gift that flows out of our kind and benevolent God's love and concern for us. In Deuteronomy we learn that everyone, including the farm animals, was to receive the day off. Everyone, from the highest to the lowest, was equally important in the eyes of God and was to be given time to nurture their relationship with the holy.

Sabbath observance is not about what you do or don't do on the day the calendar says in Sunday. That's not the point. Sabbath observance is about recognizing our total dependence upon God. Sabbath observance is about making significant room for God in our lives. What we do and when we do it is nowhere near as important as taking the time to pay attention to your relationship with God in Christ.

I heard a story about an American academic philosopher who went to Japan on a lecture tour. While there he consulted with a famous Zen master about some of the finer points of Buddhism. He built an hour into his "very busy" schedule to visit the master in the monastery. As the master attempted to answer the professor's questions, he kept interrupting the master with a string of "questions," which were really just a statement of his own opinion. Finally, the master poured the professor some tea. When the cup was full the master kept pouring. Indeed, he kept pouring until he emptied the teapot and the tea ran over the cup, over the saucer and onto the philosopher's pants. When he protested, the master observed, "You are like the cup, you are so full of yourself, you have no room for God."

From the foundations of the earth, God knew we would be like that, knew that these beloved children would be so full of themselves that, without help, they would seldom take time for their souls, take time to nurture their relationship with the holy and with each other. And so, God gave us a day, a day every week to do nothing else but pay attention; to ourselves, to each other and to God.

Amen and amen.

Proper 5 – Season after Pentecost Sunday Closest to June 8

1 Samuel 8:4-11, (12-15), 16-20, (11:14-15)

Mel Brooks made the catch-line famous, in his 1981 film, History of the World, Part I: "It's good to be the king!" (Get an idea with this 4-minute excerpt from the film, set to Mel's own "hip hop" song lyric:

https://www.youtube.com/watch?v=XO99nL_at0o)

For Brooks fans, the line becomes something of a leitmotif in his other films, including Robin Hood: Men in Tights, Spaceballs, and The Producers — not that that has anything to do with anything — except that I am reminded of it when God, through Samuel, tries to tell the Israelites that gaining a king to rule over them might not be all they think it is cracked up to be!

"It's going to cost you!" is something of a biblical leitmotif where sin is concerned, yet over and over again, we humans are willing to enter the bargain anyway. The Israelites (who play our part in this drama) use the argument familiar to every teenager who has ever been confronted by a parent over dubious behavioral choices: "Well, everybody's doing it!"

What's a prophet — or a God — to say?

Psalm 138

This God — the LORD of Israel — is greater than all gods; this God is the true King above all kings.

Noticeably, the LORD, as the high King, is very close to those who recognize their own lowliness; but remains "far away" from those whose self-attitude is haughty. Those who seek the help of the LORD when they are in trouble will find it; those who maintain an "I got this" state-of-mind are not so likely to find themselves aided by God's strong "right hand."

Genesis 3:8-15

Ah, speaking of the "fruit" of our own choices!
I have long been intrigued by the fact that God never said a word to these first humans before they exhibited their first sign of guilt; they "heard" God walking in the garden and they "hid" themselves in the trees.
Apparently, not only does the guilty dog bark first, he/she also tucks tail and hides at the first sound of accountability coming!

Psalm 130

Does God keep score?

The psalmist asks a question (v.3) that still resonates. How in the world could I ever answer for every single time I "sinned?" (i.e., broke a rule, crossed a boundary, told a lie, hurt another person, etc.)

There is something powerful to consider here about just how forgiveness works. If I can never even the score of my wrongdoing, then sooner or later I would just give up trying

— and sin would progress to its inevitable conclusion: hurt, destruction, and death.

But, if there is a way to "wipe the slate clean" and get a fresh start — starting over seems like a genuine option. After a time, I know the deep need of my life for cleansing and renewal; I feel it "in my bones."

Honest confrontation of my shortcomings and confession of my sin are the prerequisites of right living and right relationship — with God and others. Like waiting through a long, dark night for a glimmer of hope and sunshine, passing through the anguish of repentance brings redemption to my soul.

2 Corinthians 4:13-5:1

How thankful have I been for grace lately?

V. 15 says that "grace, as it extends to more and more people, may increase thanksgiving...." Just makes me wonder how thankful I have been for the incredible grace given to me. Have I stopped the flow of God's grace through my life in any way by ingratitude?

Mark 3:20-35

"That boy done lost his mind!"

There was a certain young man in my hometown of whom that statement was made regularly when I was growing up. Theories varied as to exactly why Ray Skinner (not his real name, by the way) was crazy — or if he even was really mentally unbalanced — but none of us "kids" were ever brave enough to actually talk to him and find out. He was sort of our local Boo Radley, I suppose.

The setting for today's gospel reading is a very Boo Radley-like experience Jesus has with his own family — those who should have been best-positioned to know him. Jesus is, of course, talking about his "kingdom," which was his favorite subject. He really believed that God had sent him to establish a kingdom that was sort of, kind of on this earth — but wasn't really, exactly like the other kingdoms of the earth.

Yeah, that was some crazy-sounding stuff right there! No wonder his momma and them came to try to talk him into coming home with them.

Just how crazy are the demands of the kingdom of God for those who would claim to follow Christ today? Are we "brothers and sisters" of our Lord Jesus?

Sermon

"Who Are You?"
I left home — the farm in the foothills of North Carolina — when I was 18, to go to college. Though I still speak with a decided southern accent, I do not sound like the folks in and around Mt. Airy, NC anymore. Years of higher education in the Research Triangle area of NC and serving transplanted mid-westerners in Lutheran congregations in Atlanta and Nashville have taken the edge off enough that when I go home to Mt. Airy I get, not the "you ain't from around here" look, but the "you went off and got different" look — which is almost as bad.

When Jesus goes home in today's Gospel lesson, he gets the "you went off and got different" look from his community and his family. They knew who he was, he was Mary's boy, he was James' brother. But then again, he wasn't; something was different, something was wrong, he had changed.

A woman slips into the living quarters back of the carpenter shop, "Mary, I saw your boy. Yeah, Jesus the one that went off to be a preacher. Boy, he sure talks funny, like them city folks he's been hanging around with. And, well, it ain't just the way he talks, it's what he says. That boy of your'n' has sure got some funny ideas. People are talking like he's nuts or something. You better do something about it."

So Mary gathers up the family and sets out to find her boy. There are two motivations working in their effort to stop Jesus. One is the fact that Mary and James and the rest still live in Nazareth and what Jesus does reflects on them. Family honor and business are on the line. The second, and I suspect more powerful, motivation is love. They love Jesus. They didn't understand him, but they loved him.

They were wrong to try to stop him, but they were wrong for the right reason. They loved Jesus as a son and brother and they wanted him to be happy, they wanted him to be successful, they wanted him to fit in, they wanted him to be safe, they wanted him to come home; if not home to Nazareth at least home to traditional values.

When they found Jesus they discovered that things were worse than they thought. Not only was Jesus talking funny and doing weird things; he was also openly defying the public officials, engaging in public argument with the temple scribes. This was serious business indeed.

The scribes were accusing Jesus of being a Satanist, of being in league with the devil. Can you imagine the fear that struck at Mary's heart when she heard it said that her sweet, precious, first-born son was not only odd but that he was also evil? And Jesus only made it worse by arguing with the scribes, by making them look like fools.

Mary had to act and act quickly. She sends in one of the boys with a message for Jesus to come out and go home. And Jesus, unbelievably, rejects his mother and his mother's pleas.

Jesus turns his back on his family. He looks around the crowd and says, "Who are my mother and my brothers? Here are my mothers and my sisters and my brothers; those who do the will of God!"

In that moment, Jesus redefined for all time the meaning of family. It was shocking then and it is shocking to many of us now.

For the people of Jesus time and place, family was not an important thing; it was everything. Who you were, what you did, who you married, your entire relationship to society and to God were defined by your family.

Jesus was not just Jesus who used to be a carpenter in Nazareth and was now a Rabbi. No, Jesus as Jesus, Son of Joseph, of the house and lineage of David, a descendant of Abraham. Without those family connections, Jesus was nobody, at least not anybody who had to be recognized or dealt with; he was permanently "not from around here." He had done "gone off and got different."

You have heard it said that "Blood is thicker than water," but in that moment Jesus declared that "the waters of baptism are thicker than the blood of family."

Now, this did not mean that Jesus no longer loved "his Mama and them," as we say back in Mt. Airy. It did mean that Jesus declared a rearrangement in the order of his relationships; and by so doing, rearranged the order of our relationships too.

I am still son and brother and husband and father and pastor and neighbor and friend to many and probably am considered a jerk by more people than I would like to know about.

But all those relational definitions are secondary to one overarching and defining relationship; I am a child of God and younger brother of Jesus Christ, who is my Lord and Savior. That relationship takes priority over all others and makes sense of all others. As long as I remember that Christ is first in my life, everything else falls in line.

For more than 600 years the Hapsburgs ruled much of Europe. In 1916 Emperor Franz-Josef I of Austria died. A procession of dignitaries and elegantly dressed royal mourners escorted the coffin which was draped in black and gold silk. A military band played somber funeral music as the torch-lit procession made its way down winding narrow stairs into the catacombs beneath the Capuchin Monastery in Vienna.

At the bottom of the stairs were great iron doors leading to the Hapsburg family crypt. Behind the door was the Cardinal-Archbishop of Vienna.

The Commanding officer rapped on the door and cried out. "Open!"

The Archbishop replied, "Who goes there?"

"We bear the remains of his Imperial and Apostolic Majesty, Franz-Josef I, by the grace of God Emperor of Austria, King of Hungary, Defender of the Faith, Prince of Bohemia-Moravia, Grand-Duke of Lombardy . . . ." And so it went, through the entire list of his 37 titles.

"We know him not, "the Cardinal said, "Who goes there?"

The officer spoke again, using the informal title, "We bear the remains of Emperor Franz-Josef I of the Hapsburg line." "We know him not," the cardinal said again. "Who goes there?"

This time the officer replied, "We bear the body of Franz-Josef, our brother, a sinner like all of us." At that the doors swung open and Franz-Josef was welcomed home.

Whoever else you may be, whatever other relationships you may have, there is one title and one relationship that can never be taken away from you; you are always a child of God, born out of the waters of baptism and sealed with the Holy Spirit forever.

Though that means that wherever you go on earth, you will be considered and bit odd and "not from around here" because you have "done gone off and got different;" it also means that you are always welcome and at home in the family and kingdom of God.

Amen and amen.

Proper 6 – Season after Pentecost Sunday Closest to June 15

1 Samuel 15:34 – 16:13

"Well, there's my youngest boy — but I doubt you're looking for him. He's just a shepherd."

You can almost hear the overtones in Jesse's voice as he dialogues with the great prophet, Samuel, can't you? Saul — the tall, handsome, strike-fear-in-the-hearts-of-our-enemies king of Israel is on his way out. The search is on for his replacement.

Like any good call committee, Samuel and the people he represents are pretty sure THEY know what they want. What God wants may be something else entirely.

We most likely want to be very careful in our discerning of "God's will" in our lives — the Eliabs in our lives do look awfully good sometimes. If we can, though, it's always best to hold out until God says to us, "Now there you go; that's what I really had in mind."

Psalm 20

Verse 6 seems to center this selection in its relationship to the first reading. God always helps God's "anointed." When God is in the midst of our choices and the direction of our lives, there is help (regardless of the number of chariots and horses we may have — or not have — at our disposal!)
Ezekiel 17:22-24

What a great image: God is the one who is tall enough to break off a sprig from the topmost branch of a "lofty cedar." Having recently returned from some vacation time among the redwoods of California, I imagine just how impossibly high the top of one of those great trees looks to be from my location down on the ground.
God's reach is impressive, indeed!

Psalm 92:1-4, 12-15

Whenever I read this text, I hear the strains of Eugene Butler's excellent choral setting, "It Is a Good Thing to Give Thanks Unto the Lord."

God's presence with us is not on the clock; steadfast love in the morning, faithfulness by night — all set to the music of the lute, the harp, and the lyre. What a deal!

2 Corinthians 5:6-10, (11-13), 14-17

Several great theological "one-liners" in this passage:

- "we walk by faith, not by sight" — very apropos when considered with the first reading
- "away from the body, at home with the Lord" — a concept that brings much comfort, eh?
- "if anyone is in Christ, there is a new creation" — says it all, really

Mark 4:26-34

The kingdom of God — its spread, its flourishing, its end results — is so far beyond our control or even our imaginings that it's hard to describe. But, as usual, Jesus' parables do a pretty good job.

Our work matters; what we do as laborers in God's field is important. But, ultimately, if you want to see just exactly how much it all depends on you or me, consider that God works whether we are awake or asleep. Our efforts are mustard-seed-sized in the totality of the kingdom; they could be blown away by the slightest puff of wind.

And, yet, God chooses to bless them and grow them — at times — beyond our wildest expectations.

Sermon

"Do the Work"

Today's Gospel lesson is the sort of text you might expect an old farm boy like me to really get into. Plowing ground, planting seeds, watching them grow. Good stuff, right?
Well, truth is, I wasn't much of a farmer; just never really had any interest in it. I mean, I could do the work and I did it well. It just didn't excite me.

Frankly, I found the whole business, well, boring. It took too long, it was too unpredictable, too uncontrollable, too frustrating. Plow the ground, put in the fertilizer, plant the seed, chop out the weeds, and wait and wait and wait; and pray and pray and pray.

Pray for rain; pray it doesn't hail; pray for the rain to stop; pray for it to warm up; pray for it to cool off. While you're praying, you need to be spraying; spray for bugs, spray for weeds; praying and spraying for weeks on end.

And after all that, it's out of the farmer's hands anyway. No matter how hard you try, sometimes it doesn't work. Most of the time; it's too hot or too cold or too wet or too dry or prices are too high or too low.

If it's a good year, everybody has a good year and there's an oversupply of the crop and prices are too low. If it's a bad year; everybody has a bad year and supply is down and prices are high, but you don't have anything to sell.

In the end, there was too much luck involved for me to be a farmer. I wasn't a very good farmer because I didn't have the right disposition. I'm not patient enough. I'm not comfortable with the fact that success ultimately is in the hands of fate, or the weather, or God; depending on how you look at it.

So, you can see, this text from Mark about farming really bothers and challenges me. If the Kingdom of God really is like farming, like sowing seed and being patient; or like the text from Ezekiel about planting sprigs and waiting for trees to grow; well, I'm probably in trouble.

Reading this text reminds me that the same things that made me a lousy farmer also work against me as a pastor and a Christian. I worry too much and I want to be in control and I don't trust God enough. There, I said it and I feel better for it.

There is a difficult lesson her for those of us who have a hard time letting go and letting things take their natural, God-given course. Jesus says to us that we are to plant the seed and let God worry about the growth.

Jesus says we are not responsible for making the church grow. We are not responsible for making sure everybody "gets saved." We are not responsible for making the Kingdom of God a smashing success.

Our job, our responsibility is planting the seed and reaping the harvest. God is responsible for the growth.

Faith is often defined as trust, and in this case, faith is trusting that the things we do for God will turn out right, in God's way, in God's time. Faith is keeping on with the work of the Gospel and trusting that in God's own time the crop will grow, even if we never live to see it. Faith is, in part, letting go of our control over the results.

We live in a world in which people are afraid of losing control, or more correctly, of letting someone or something else control their fate. We have been taught that in order to succeed one must have a goal – after all, as Yogi Berra said, "If you don't know where you're going, you might end up somewhere else."

Jesus teaches us that the Kingdom of God, the work of grace and mercy and compassion and in the world, works from a totally different theory.

These parables remind us that we are called to do the work, indeed we are called to do the work to the best of our ability; but they also remind us that the ultimate purpose and outcome of this work is not in our hands but in God's; which is, I assure you, a reality that is both frustrating and reassuring.

It is frustrating to those of us who don't like to wait, who like to be in charge and in control of our own fate and destiny, who like to see progress being made, who like to be able to measure and calibrate and control.

But it is also reassuring and liberating to know that in God's eyes success is not judged by the size of the harvest but by our faithfulness in sowing seeds.

Amen and amen.

Proper 7 – Season after Pentecost Sunday Closest to June 22
1 Samuel 17:(1a, 4-11, 19-23), 32-49

Who doesn't love a good "David and Goliath" story?

Here we have David, the prototypical underdog – a skinny, knock-kneed, snot-nosed teenager filled with ambition and foolish enough not to know any better – against the prohibitive favorite in the fight, Goliath – the mighty, battle-hardened, swaggering bully who never met an Israelite body he didn't want to separate from its head.

If we want to help our parishioners feel some of the tension that was present on this day, we need only understand that the word "Philistine" with which we are so familiar from childhood Bible stories is the same word that passed through the Latin language via the Roman Empire and became transferred as "Palestinian." This battle account could be today's headlines in a "holy land" war story.

Of course, one of the prerogatives of coming out as the winner in a war is the chance to write the history books – so this one turns out A-OK for Israel and their God.

How did the ancient people of Yahweh hear this story? With much favor, as well as fervor, no doubt! The young boy-who-would-become-king rejects not only the curses of the enemy, but the artificial aid of his own ruler and countrymen. In this account, David needs absolutely nothing other than his faith in God and his trusty sling. (A curious question — why did he select five stones, if God was going to aid him with the first shot?)

In short order, the score is Yahweh 1, Pagan Gods 0. What else can you say?

Psalm 9:9-20

Given the background of David's victory against Goliath, I have often wondered if v.20 might not be translated: "Put the fear in them, O Lord; let the nations know that they are only human."

1 Samuel 17:57-18:5, 18:10-16

We get a glimpse of the paranoid Saul — a sad departure from the days when he was the champion of Israel. After the departure of the Spirit from his life, he is left only with jealousy and rage. The figure of Jonathan, his son, is the most redemptive aspect of Saul's life that remains. Through Jonathan's friendship with David, the "soul" of Saul's reign is joined with the "soul" of all that David would come to represent in Israel.

Psalm 133

Verse 1 is in stark contrast to the tone of rivalry, bitter jealousy, and rage in the earlier readings. In comparison, unity is indeed refreshing and renewing. (Mt. Hermon is the highest point in Israel — the water that runs down from its "dews" and snows feeds the Jordan River, which in turn feeds the Sea of Galilee and most of the rest of the land.)

Job 38:1-11

The Creator God revealed in Job, who is powerful enough to lay a foundation for our earth and to cause the oceans to cease their crashing at our shorelines, is certainly powerful enough to sustain and protect us, eh?

Psalm 107:1-3, 23-32

After the storm-tossed passages of our lives, it truly is a blessing sometimes to enjoy the quiet of a desired haven. God is good when the storms are raging, but seems even better when they have passed.

2 Corinthians 6:1-13

Paul understands a thing or two about storms and being tossed (not to mention the occasional beating and prison term.) So, when he urges us to take care of today's business today, it's a pretty important idea. You never know where the storm will blow you tomorrow!

Mark 4:35-41

Speaking of storms…

It is so easy to berate the disciples in this story for panicking over the waves. I've seen the type of boats that were used on the Sea of Galilee during Jesus' time (not that different from the boats that are still used today) and, let me tell you, I would be a little nervous, too! The sides aren't more than 12-18 inches above the waterline. They were getting swamped!
I am also amazed that Jesus manages to sleep through the storm; I think we're supposed to take our cue from that and learn something about the essence of faith. Relax, God's gonna take care of you…or something along those lines.

That is certainly true, whether we hit the panic button or not. God is going to take care of us. Notice that Jesus' "rebuke" to the disciples is much more gentle than that he gives to the wind and the waves. In hindsight (which, they say, is always 20/20,) I'm sure the disciples could see it all playing out much more clearly. God's provision and care depend, not on our faith nor on our confidence, but on God's faithfulness.

So, if you get a little scared next time your boat starts filling up — it's okay. Try to have at least a little faith.

Sermon

"Do We Trust God…Really?"

In a move that some might find whimsical or even bizarre — which is precisely why it fits here on the Lectionary Lab — we honor the confluence of the Nativity of Saint John the Baptist with the Fourth Sunday after Pentecost in this homiletical offering by Bubba #1.

THE NATIVITY OF SAINT JOHN THE BAPTIST

Texts: Malachi 3:1-4, Acts 13:13-26, Luke 1:57-67 (68-80)

Well, did you get all your "Nativity of St. John the Baptist" shopping done on time? Did you get your Nativity cards out? Did your Nativity office party go well?
Boy, wasn't it a pain doing all that decorating and putting lights on the house, particularly this time of year when it's so hot and all? What? You didn't do any of those things for "the Nativity of Saint John the Baptist?" You didn't even know we were celebrating the Nativity of St. John the Baptist? Well, to tell you the truth, until recently, I didn't know much about it either.

At a recent pastor's meeting, our Bible study leader shared research on the celebration of the Nativity of John the Baptist and I learned a lot.

For example, I learned that it was placed on this date for biblical reasons. John said of Jesus, "I must decrease that he may increase."

Well according to the calendar in use when the date was set, June 24 was when the days started getting shorter, decreasing; just as the Nativity of Our Lord, Dec. 25, was when the days began getting longer, increasing.

I also learned that John the Baptist (the "Forerunner") is extensively celebrated in the Eastern Orthodox Church. Besides June 24, they also celebrate:

- January 7: The Commemoration of St. John the Forerunner
- February 24: First and Second Finding of the Head of St. John the Forerunner.
- May 25: Third Finding of the Head St. John the Forerunner.
- August 29: The Beheading of St. John the Forerunner
- September 23: Conception of St. John the Forerunner.

(Here's an interesting question: Why can't they keep up with his head? I mean John only lost it once, and they had to find it three times. I tried to find out more about that but came up empty. I'll keep looking, maybe something will turn up.)

One thing is for certain – all this celebrating points to the importance of John the Baptist, or John the Baptizer, or John the Forerunner as the Orthodox call him, or John the cousin of Jesus as he was probably know around Nazareth; for the

Bible tells us that his mother Elizabeth was a cousin of Mary, the Mother of our Lord.

And the question for us today is a simple one. So what? Why should we care? Why should we think about and celebrate the people involved in the Nativity of St. John the Baptist? And what about their journey can help us as we move through our own journey of faith?

In order to understand today's Gospel lesson, we have to remember what happened nine months before.

Zechariah and Elizabeth were, like Abraham and Sarah, quite old and childless. He was one of the priests who served in the temple in Jerusalem. He was serving on the altar one day. He was in the Holy of Holies, in the Sanctuary of the Lord, where no one but the appointed priest went.

He was standing at the altar of incense when suddenly an angel appeared beside him, and scared the daylights out of him. The angel told him that he and Elizabeth would have a child, but frankly, Zechariah didn't believe him, and said so. "We're too old. It's not going to happen." So the angel Gabriel said to him, "But now, because you did not believe my words . . . you will become mute, unable to speak, until the days these things occur."

Zechariah wanted a relationship with God, but he wanted it on his own terms. He wanted to tell God what was and was not possible. God said to Zechariah, "I'm not arguing with you over what I can and can't do. I'll just show you while you have to stand silently by and watch."

And so it was. Zechariah was unable to speak for nine months. And Elizabeth indeed got pregnant, and Zechariah could say nothing.

Finally the day came, and the baby was born, and they went through the naming argument, at the end of which Zechariah made a statement of faith, writing down the name the angel had told him. At that moment his tongue was loosed and he was able to give voice and words to the miracle of God that had happened in his life.

Unless we believe, deep in our souls, deep in our hearts, that God can and will love and redeem all humanity; unless we trust to the very core of our being in the steadfast and endless grace and mercy of God, we have nothing to say to the world that cannot be better said by any number of secular, non-profit, benevolent organizations.

Without that gut level willingness to throw ourselves into the arms of the divine, we are just playing church, dancing around the edges of the holy. To really believe is to make it personal, to move from ideas about God to a relationship with God, to move from discussing God with others to talking things over with God.

Zechariah knew a lot about God, but he didn't know God, not until that day at the altar. And until he put aside the terms by which he would be able to relate to God, he had nothing to say. But when he laid aside all his defenses and trusted God completely, his long unused voice burst forth in song.

So it is with us. We as individuals and as a community are called upon to trust the promise of God. God has promised to love us, to forgive us, to support and sustain us through all life's difficulties and troubles.

Do we trust God? Do we trust God's love? Do we trust God's care? Do we trust God's compassion? Do we trust God's mercy? Do we?

We invited today to join in the Song of Zechariah. We are invited to feel deep within ourselves the joy of knowing that we are a beloved children of God, and as that oy wells up within us, our tongues will be loosed and our voices heard.

Amen and Amen.

Proper 8 – Season after Pentecost Sunday Closest to June 29

2 Samuel 1:1, 17-27

One might assume that David had plenty of reasons to exult over the death of Saul. The mad king had taunted him, hunted him, and perhaps would gladly have spilled David's blood had he had the chance. Yet, David's grief at Saul's passing is evident in this song of lament.

Saul's tormented reign brought with it much to be sad about, no doubt; yet, there is no life that is completely devoid of goodness or accomplishment. David reminds Israel of the days when Saul "clothed [them] with crimson, in luxury, who put ornaments of gold on [their] apparel."

The depth of David's grief is reserved for his friend and Saul's son, Jonathan. War is costly, and its price is illustrated far too vividly here. No wonder David would later write the poignant line, "Pray for the peace of Jerusalem…." (Psalm 122:6)

Psalm 130

If God were determined to "keep score" of our iniquities forever, there would, indeed, be none of us who could stand before God's righteous presence. But, the good news of the psalm text is that God does forgive — and in the great power of forgiveness there is redemption. This is a message that is badly needed still in our world today.

Wisdom of Solomon 1:13-15, 2:23-24

God's good intent in creation was — and is — for good.

Lamentations 3:22-33

No wonder the oft-used saying has such power: everything looks better by the light of a new day. Jeremiah tells us why — "The steadfast love of the Lord never ceases, his mercies never end; they are new every morning."

Take a minute to stop, look, listen, and feel all around you the ways that God's mercies are reborn with the new day.

Psalm 30

There is hardly a more soul-healing verse in all of scripture than v.5: "God's anger is but for a moment, but God's favor is for a lifetime. Weeping may linger for the night, but joy comes in the morning." Yet another reason to hope for the next new day.

2 Corinthians 8:7-15

A great passage on the balance that comes in our giving out of our resources to meet the needs of another's lack. This is far more than a text for the annual stewardship emphasis; it is a look into one of the core competencies of Christian discipleship. We give because Christ gave; we share out of what we have, not out of what we don't have.

In God's miraculous plan of economy, nobody has too much and nobody has too little. (I have to wonder, would this really be too difficult for our elected officials to understand?)

Mark 5:21-43

Oh, the power of touch!

This wrapped-about twin healing has always fascinated me — Mark mentions (parenthetically) that Jairus' daughter was twelve, and the woman in the crowd had been bleeding for twelve years.

I have wondered if they both began their journey toward Jesus on the same day twelve years earlier? (Sorry if that's a bit of a theologycal red herring, but I can't help thinking of stuff like that!)

At any rate, the request for Jesus to come and "lay hands" on the little girl is interrupted by a woman who wants to "just touch" — not Jesus — but the edge of his clothes. Just a brush, an "I-hope-he-won't-notice-but-I'm-going-to-give-it-a-go-anyway" act of faith.

One might argue that Jairus is bold and that the woman is a bit cowardly, or at the very least embarrassed. Maybe there is no great risk on the part of either of them since they have nothing to lose.

What's really cool, to my way of thinking, is that it doesn't matter to Jesus: he takes whatever faith we are able to place in him and makes it work.

The power of a touch.

Sermon

"Of Faith and Fear"

Early one fall morning when I was nine years old, I awoke to a cold and silent house.

I got up and looked around. My brothers were not in their beds in our communal bedroom; the lamp would not turn on. I stumbled downstairs to the kitchen; no one was there. I ran through the entire house; it was empty. I tried every light switch, and the TV and radio. Nothing worked.

I ran out to the barn; still no one. And still, nothing worked. Then I did what every reasonable nine-year-old fundamentalist child would do; I fell on my knees and cried for Jesus "to come back and get me," for I assumed that the rapture had come and I had been "left behind."

There was, in biblical terms, much "crying and gnashing of teeth," as collapsed onto the cold, dewy grass in my underwear.

At that moment, I heard a tractor coming over the hill from behind the house. I had indeed been "left behind;" by my forgetful Daddy when he gathered up the family to help him get a wagon load of cured tobacco from the storehouse to take to market. That and a power outage explained my personal "rapture," moment.

In our Gospel lesson, I was struck by the words fear and faith.

After the woman with the flow of blood touched Jesus and he stopped and asked who touched him, it says she "came in fear and trembling, fell down before him and told him the whole truth. He (Jesus) said to her, "Daughter, your faith has made you well."

In the wrap-around story of Jairus' daughter, at this point, the text says, "some people came from the leader's house to say, "Your daughter is dead. Why trouble the teacher any further?"

But Jesus says to the man, "Do not fear, only believe (have faith)."

When I was a child I had a lot of faith; I also had a lot of fear. My faith was faith in the reality of God, not any sort of trust in the goodness or compassion of God.

And my fear was rooted in a fear of the power of that real but vengeful God I had conjured up from Sunday School and fundamentalist preaching and comic books and horror movies and God knows what else.

As I have grown older, faith and fear have remained in dynamic tension in my life. Just as my faith has matured and become more sophisticated, my fears have grown less generalized and more realistic.

But they are still there as they are for all of us. All of us fear things: terrorism, avian flu, economic collapse, earthquake, fire and flood, to name a few.

And the last few years have shown us that our fears are realistic and founded in reality, not fantasy as were mine. And the question is, as we face these realistic fears, where do we place our faith, our assurance, our hope for the future? In money and its accumulation and clout? In armies and governments and secret agents? Where? In whom?

The scriptures call us to trust in God, a thing much easier said than done. Lamentations reminds us "that the steadfast love of the LORD never ceases, (God's) mercies never come to an end." and then goes on to talk about those times when one feels abandoned by God. This is a realistic look at faith in the face of fear.

The Psalm repeats this theme, as in "then you hid your face, and I was filled with fear" but also cries out, "O Lord, My God, I will give you thanks forever." And our lesson from 2 Corinthians reminds us not to hoard our money in time of other's need, but to share our resources with the needy, trusting in God to provide for us in our time of need. Generosity is shown to be an act of faith overcoming fear.
In the last several years the church has been in the midst of uncertain times. The question is: are we going to face the future with fear or faith?

Are we going to reach out to one another the way the woman in the story reached out to Jesus for comfort and healing? Remember; the church is, we are, the body of Christ, and we have God's spirit and healing power flowing through us. Are we facing the future with fear or faith?

Amen and amen.

Proper 9 – Season after Pentecost Sunday Closest to July 6

2 Samuel 5:1-5, 9-1

There's something to be said for biding your time. Well, for biding God's time, I suppose.

David has waited patiently while the drama that was Saul's life played out. He has known for some time that he was the "anointed" of the Lord — chosen by God and sealed by the prophet/judge/priest Samuel. It would have been easy for him to have "got the big head," as my grandma used to say.

But, he did what was set before him — no more, no less. In God's time, it came to pass. And, it was good (well, for the most part.) Forty years of rule were built out of patient days, weeks, and months of quiet service.

One never knows just exactly what one is being prepared for when God's call to service comes.

Psalm 48

The psalm provides fitting accompaniment to the first lesson's closing line: "David became greater…for the LORD, the God of hosts, was with him."

It is God's greatness that is to be praised.

Ezekiel 2:1-5

'Zekiel got the call of the Lord…the same one that many of us as preachers get.

"You go tell them what I tell you to tell them," says God, "no matter whether they listen or not."

That's not always an easy commission to fulfill. But they cannot say that there was no one to give them the words of the Lord!

Psalm 123

Servants and handmaids never had much hope for grace, unless it came from the master or mistress of the house that they served. God's mercy is much keener than that of an earthly master; it is the perfect antidote for contempt.

2 Corinthians 12:2-10

"Thank you, Lord; could you heap a few more weaknesses, insults, hardships, persecutions, and calamities onto my life?"

I doubt that any of us are lining up to pray that prayer. I also doubt that Paul wrote this portion of the letter to glorify his suffering. The incomparable goodness of Christ that strengthens us in the midst of difficulty is one of the more quizzical components of discipleship — something that is awfully hard to explain to those who have never experienced it.

In what ways have you experienced the grace of God in times of weakness? Has it been sufficient for you? How?

Mark 6:1-13

Sometimes, we are just bound and determined NOT to believe our eyes.

It strikes me that the residents of Jesus' hometown were perfectly willing to admit that when he spoke, his words reflected wisdom.

They had no doubt that he was able to perform deeds of power with his own hands (and evidently sans smoke and mirrors.)

Yet, they still decided to "take offense" at him — because, after all, he was JUST the carpenter's son. He really had "got too big for his britches" (which is somewhat akin to gettin' the big head — see above.)

I have never quite figured out how one cuts off one's nose to spite one's face — sounds like a painful proposition — but the folks in Nazareth evidently had it perfected to an art. Sadly, even Jesus Christ himself couldn't be a successful pastor in his own hometown. Some folks are just too hard-headed to help!

Sermon

"Did We Win?"

I learned my most important lesson as a "sports Dad" when my younger son was playing coach pitch baseball. They weren't a very good team, losing a lot more often than they won.

They were seven years old, and most of them had the attention span of a gnat. They spent more time jostling and picking on each other than paying attention to what was happening on the field.

After the game was over, as they lined up to shake hands with the other team, I would hear the boys ask the coach, "Did we win? Did we win?"

If the coach said "yes," they would cheer, if the coach said "no," they would kick the ground. And after that they would ask, "What's for snack?"

Adult winning and losing is often much more complicated than that. But it is important for all of us to learn to deal with losing, with failure, with disappointment, because long experience shows that most of us, most of the time, lose more than we win.

And when we lose, it takes more than a snack to cheer us up and make us better.

Each of the lessons we read from the Bible deals with someone in the midst of a losing situation. We encounter these people at a time of very real and painful failure in their lives.

And their losses, their failures, go beyond competition and games and what's for snack.

Their failures are failures at life, failures at vocation, failures in health, and failures in faith.

Ezekiel: the prophet to whom no one would listen.
Paul the Apostle: the healer who could not heal himself.
Jesus: Downhome Miracle Man who could work no miracles for the crowd.

Each of them learned a valuable lesson from their failure.

Each of them learned how to know when a loss is a win.

Ezekiel's story begins like all good prophet stories; the people are acting like total pagans. They have turned their backs on God and Godly ways. God decides to send a prophet to straighten them out.

In Chapter 1 Ezekiel has a vision. In Chapter 2 God begins to speak to Ezekiel. In verses 1 and 2 God says, "Listen up, I want to talk to you," and in verses 3 and 4, God complains, "My people are rebellious, I want you to tell them."

So far, so good and so normal. This is how it works with God and prophets and the people of Israel in the Bible.

Then, in verse 5, God says a strange thing: "Whether you succeed or not, win or lose, is not the issue. The important thing is that they hear the truth; that they know that "there has been a prophet among them."

As it happens, the people didn't listen, and God sent them into exile, and the people rewarded Ezekiel for this preaching by treating him very shabbily.

By all external measures, Ezekiel failed and failed miserably. But Ezekiel's loss was a win; because he a faithful to the truth. When Ezekiel was finished, the people knew there had been a prophet among them.

Nobody knows what Paul's "thorn in the flesh," but that is not important. What really matters is that Paul prayed very hard and very long and very faithfully for this thorn to be removed and it wasn't.

Paul lost the struggle for victory over a physical problem, and this loss created for him a spiritual problem, a crisis of faith.

This failure to pray himself out of this physical problem led him to question his faith. It was an experience that could have shattered his trust in God, but instead it humbled him and strengthened his faith in God. Paul's thorn in the flesh was a loss that turned into a win.

The story of Jesus returning home to preach occurs early in his ministry. Up until now, Jesus' version of Brother Love's Traveling Salvation Show and Tent Revival had been a roaring success.

The first five chapters of Mark are filled with healing stories and reports of huge crowds of people coming to hear Jesus preach. Immediately before this he had raised Jairus' daughter from the dead and healed the woman with the flow of blood.

So, he takes it on home to Nazareth; and falls flat on his face. In verse 3 we read that they "took offense at him." And in verse 5 we learn that, somehow, their resentment resulted in his inability to perform miracles and other healings.

Verse 6 contains one of the most human portraits of Jesus in the gospels; "He was amazed at their unbelief." Jesus just couldn't believe their lack of belief. He was stunned, left with his mouth hanging open. Jesus learned a hard lesson; that there was a limit to his power; it was limited by the people's willingness to receive it.

That day in Nazareth, Jesus had a loss that was a win. From it he learned the limits to his power.

He learned you can control what you say, you cannot control what people hear. He learned you can control what you do, you cannot control how people respond. He learned you can control how you show your love, you cannot control how people receive it.

I think when we get to "heaven," most of us will be like the seven year old baseball players. "Did we win?" we will cry out, because we really won't know. And the coach will smile and say, "Who wants snack?"

Proper 10 – Season after Pentecost Sunday Closest to July 13

2 Samuel 6:1-5, 12b-19

The reading, as assigned, feels a little disorienting, in that there is a three-month break in the action between verse 5 and verse 12. The quizzical and tragic incident involving Uzzah — who was probably just doing what he thought was best — is omitted, as is the aforementioned 90-day hiatus of the ark in the house of Obed-edom, as David was "afraid of the Lord."

But, once it became clear that the ark was a source of blessing and not of curse (as long as you kept your hands off of it,) David proceeds with the processional. And, I mean, proceed he does!

The former shepherd boy does the Holy City Hoedown, as it were, and his wife — Michal, Saul's daughter — is ashamed of him. (Maybe she was still ticked off that David had won her in the Goliath contest…who knows?)

Whatever the source of her bitterness, it didn't serve her well; she remains barren for the rest of her life, a symbol in Israel of the withdrawal of God's blessing. (But you don't get that part of the story in today's reading, either — look to v. 23)

Worth noting: the blessing by David of God's people took a very tangible form. He distributed food to every household. Might be a good reminder for us of just how the blessing of God is intended for every one of God's people, everywhere.

Psalm 24

A fitting psalm for the processional. Lift the gates, open the doors; the celebration is for the LORD, who is strong and mighty. As we learned from David's earlier encounter with Goliath, "the battle is the Lord's."

Amos 7:7-15

To whom are we ultimately accountable for our lives? Against whom are we measured? Ever and always, it is God's measurement (judgment) that counts. God's will is the rule of life.

Psalm 85:8-13

When we are quiet long enough to hear God speak, what we will often hear is God's message of peace. Love, faithfulness, righteousness, and peace — these are "the good" that God desires to give.

Ephesians 1:3-14

We are, indeed, blessed with a number of "spiritual blessings" in Christ:

- we are chosen before the foundation of the world (God works way ahead of the curve!)
- we were destined to be adopted into God's family
- grace is freely bestowed on us, as are redemption and forgiveness
- we have an inheritance (who wouldn't like to get one of those?)
- we have heard the word of truth, the gospel of salvation, and we live for Christ's glory

- we have been sealed by the Holy Spirit — a "down payment" of sorts on the life we will live forever with God

Mark 6:14-29

Some days, it just doesn't pay to be a preacher!

John has famously and steadfastly proclaimed the message from God: "Repent, for the kingdom of God is at hand!" For Herod, that repentance involved not marrying his brother's wife — but, he just couldn't help himself!

While Herod is uncomfortable with John, he also respects him and is intrigued by him. But, with his blood all riled up after watching his niece/daughter dancing after dinner, Herod pretty much traps himself into killing a man he really wanted to protect.

Rather than let his pride suffer (not to mention the hell he would have to pay for refusing his wife,) Herod lops off John's head and serves it up on a platter.

Oh, be careful little mouth what you say!

Sermon

"Hiding in the Basement"

Figuring out what led up to the events in today's gospel lesson is like trying to follow the story line of a soap opera. It can get a little confusing.

King Herod here is not the same King Herod who was around when Jesus was born. That was his Daddy, Herod the Great. This is Herod Antipas.

He was, by all accounts, not much of a man or a ruler. And this royal family's bedding and marrying habits were unconventional and messy to say the least. It really was a soap opera.

Herod Antipas had married his brother's wife. This wouldn't have been so bad, except that his brother was still living and Herod forced him to divorce Herodias so he could marry her.

And the daughter who does the dancing? Jewish historian Josephus tells us her name was Salome. She was the Herod's niece and his wife's daughter and she ended up marrying his brother, her uncle. Sounds like a bad redneck joke, doesn't it?

Into the midst of this came John the Baptist. He surveyed the whole mess and called Herod out on issues of morality and leadership. He pointed out to Herod where he had failed to be a good leader to the people, both politically and in his personal life.

Herod's reaction is interesting. On the one hand, he has John arrested and put in jail; but on the other he protects John from his wife's revenge. She is really angry and wants John dead, but, for now, Herod is a more afraid of John then he is his wife.

As the text says," . . . for Herod feared John, knowing that he was a righteous and holy man, and he protected him. When he heard him, he was greatly perplexed; and yet he liked to listen to him." (verse 20)

What if he is Elijah? What if Herod does need to repent? What if God is displeased with the way Herod is leading his life?

Herod is a perplexed seeker, a dabbler in the mysteries of God. He believes just enough to keep him awake at night but not enough to change his way of living.

All too often, we too are like Herod. We keep holy things hidden away in the basement of our lives. We're not willing to throw them out, but we're not really sure what to do with them. We live our lives without paying much attention to the holy, to the call of God on our lives, because we are perplexed as to how taking that stuff seriously might challenge us to be different.

And truth be told, most of us are happy with the way we are and don't want to change; if we really wanted to, we would. Look at Amos and King Jeroboam in our first lesson. Amos spoke the truth and nobody wanted to hear it. So the priest told Amos to go way, and then, in verse 13 said this, "never again prophecy at Bethel, for it is the king's sanctuary, and it is the temple of the kingdom."

We all have to be careful on this point; it is God's house, it is God's sanctuary, it is God's temple, it is God's church. It's not our church, it's not the pastor's church, it's not the bishop's church, it's not the ELCA's church; it is God's Church.

When pastors are ordained and then later when they are installed in various ministries, they are asked to promise to preach and teach according to the scriptures and the theological tradition of the church. And the congregation is asked to hold them to that promise and to question them when it's not clear they're doing that.

But we are also to remember it is not the preacher's calling to "tickle our ears" with pleasant things we want to hear; it is her calling to rightly divide the word of truth and challenge us to grow in our faith and godly actions.

Ellenita Zimmerman was a missionary in China, Hong Kong, and Taiwan; and then the long time organist, choir director, and church worker at Holy Trinity Lutheran in Nashville, Tennessee. Her son Ted is professor of New Testament at the Lutheran Seminary in Hong Kong. Ellenita and I worked together for several years and she told me often that her definition of the Gospel was this: "God loves you just the way you are. And God loves you too much to let you stay that way."

Both the Bible and the preacher have been sent to us from God to constantly remind us of those two basic truths. And like Herod and Jeroboam, we often doubt God's love and resist being changed.

And the Good News is God will not give up on us. God will continue to send messengers of love into our midst to perplex us and challenge us and ultimately transform us into the image of Christ.

Amen and amen.

Proper 11 – Season after Pentecost Sunday Closest to July 20

2 Samuel 7:1-14a

Not every idea that we have for ministry or for "God's glory" is necessarily a good idea — at least for the moment. There is something significant about waiting and working on God's timetable.

David's motivation for the temple project was most likely very sincere. But, God urged David to wait on that project. God just wanted David to do what God had set before him: be the king, lead the people.

Unfortunately, David — like so many of us — had a very short attention span when it came to listening deeply and waiting patiently for the will of God. We tire of the plain old day-to-day tasks of ministry and long for something more exciting, something grander.

Soon, David will "find" an object for his attention and energy — in the form of Bathsheba, another man's wife. We stray from the path God sets for us at great peril, my friends.

Psalm 89:20-37

What an incredible word of God's faithfulness to us, in spite of our actual and potential unfaithfulness!

God plans in advance to remain faithful to God's own covenant promises. We may (and certainly do) stray from God's commandments, and that always has a cost (vv. 31-32.) But, God does not give up on us (vv. 33-34) — God determines to continue the work of building our lives and making God's righteousness known throughout the earth.

Jeremiah 23:1-6

Not every leader among the people of God is a good and faithful leader. This fact is sad, but true. There are "flocks" that have been hurt by unfaithful shepherds — just as there are faithful shepherds that have been injured by their flocks — but that's another story.

Wherever there has been hurt in the lives of God's people, God is present to bring healing and restoration. (v. 3) God is the God who makes it right. (v.6)

Psalm 23

God is the restorer of our souls — when we are physically depleted, God guides us to the place of rest (green pastures.) When we are spiritually and emotionally drained, God allows us to drink deeply from the still waters of God's own compassion.

Ephesians 2:11-22

This passage forms part of Paul's clear vision for God's work in building all the people of the earth into a "new humanity." Begun in the covenant promises given to Israel, that work is now moving toward completion through the life of Jesus Christ.

There is one Spirit, Paul says, that grants us all access to the Father. As the Spirit completes the work of fashioning our lives into a temple, we look forward to the time when God will dwell with God's people — all of them, without division or hostility. (v. 14)

Mark 6:30-34, 53-56

Compassion costs.

The apostles return from their mission work excited, but a bit exhausted, as well. They have seen and felt the power of God made manifest through their lives. Many, many others have been "blessed" by God as a result of their faithful ministry. Jesus tells them that they have earned a respite — a little rest.

But, alas, there is very little rest for the weary in ministry, it seems. There is almost nowhere that Jesus and the guys can go that there are not needy people waiting on them, hoping for a touch of the Christ.

Where will the crowds gather in our lives — hoping to be touched by Christ through us? Careful, it's costly!

Sermon

"He Had Compassion"

I used to love watching the TV Show Evening Shade. It starred Burt Reynolds as a small town football coach in Arkansas. One night the coach's two small children were leaning out the upstairs window, looking at the stars.

> Boy: I'm glad I've got you guys. It sure would be lonely without you.
> Girl: Remember Sunday School.
> Boy: Remember Sunday School? What do you mean by that? Oh, yeah. You mean how God is always here so we're never alone.
> Girl: Yeah, that's what I mean.
> Boy: Well, I know that's right, but sometimes I just need somebody with some skin on 'em.

I think most of us know how he feels. The world can be a difficult and dangerous and lonely place. And as comforting as it is to believe in a God in Heaven who loves us and cares about us and has a plan for our lives; sometimes you just need somebody to talk to who will talk back.

That's why people flocked to Jesus. Sure there were those who had heard about his miracles and just wanted to see a good show. And there were those who were there just because everybody else was there.

It's like the Friday night high school football in the small-town south. When my son was in the band I used to sit in the stands and listen to women talk about church and teenagers talk about who's dating whom. One night the Methodist preacher told me where to sit. He said, "This is the section for the football fans. The other people are just here because everybody else in town is here."

So there were the thrill seekers and the crowd seekers, but there were also the God seekers, those who had heard about Jesus; had heard about his words and his actions and had come to catch a glimpse of the Holy.

Jesus and the apostles had been really busy and really needed a break. So Jesus said, "Come away to a deserted place all by yourselves and rest a while."

They were going on retreat, on vacation, on holiday.

But it was not to be. By the time they got where they were going, a crowd had gathered.

Jesus looked at them and weighed his own and his companions' weariness against something he saw in the faces turned up at him, something in the crowd's eyes.

What was it that swayed Jesus to give up the plan to rest? I think he looked at them and saw their hunger. Not a hunger for food, but a hunger for companionship, a hunger for community, a hunger for love, a hunger for God.

Verse 34 says, "he had compassion for them, because they were like sheep without a shepherd." Compassion literally means "to feel with." Jesus felt compassion for them because he had felt what they were feeling.

After Jesus' Baptism, the Spirit drove him into the Wilderness to be tempted by the Devil. There he learned what it feels like to be abandoned, deserted, alone in the universe. He also learned what one does and does not need in a time like that.

One of his temptations was to feed the world by turning stone into bread. There in the wilderness, Jesus realized that fixing every human hurt was not to be his mission. People didn't need a Superman jumping to their rescue. People needed to know that God was in the world with them, not off in heaven above and beyond them. People needed to know that God cared, and that God wanted them to care, and to act with caring as well.

So, there in the desert, Jesus came to a momentous decision; he would purposely withhold his power, restrain himself. Throughout his ministry opportunities for healings came to Jesus, but he didn't go looking for them. Every time he worked a miracle it happened because of those three little words; he had compassion.

It's interesting to me how many people don't believe that; don't believe that God is love, that God is forgiving and kind and merciful. Too many people in the world believe that God is anxious to send us all to Hell, that God has plans to send holy warriors to earth in to wipe out the evil doers in a grand final battle. And if you don't think a lot of people believe that, check out the popularity of the Left Behind series of novels.

That he had compassion is the most important thing we can say about Jesus, and about God. In the midst of a world in which everyone is afraid of their own shadows, and, if they believe in God at all they believe God to be either remote and uncaring, or cruel and vindictive; we in the church have been called to witness to the fact that he had compassion.

Sisters and brothers, we live today in a world full of fear and war. We are afraid of rising gas prices, we are afraid of failing health care systems, we are afraid of immigration and disease and forest fires and drought and drugs, and, and, and . . .

It has been a long time since I have seen this country, and indeed the world, so depressed and sad and frightened and on edge about the future. And into this bog of sadness and sorrow, we the church are called to imitate our Lord and find ways to break into the cycle of fear and violence with words and acts of hope and assurance, words and acts of compassion and healing.

Now, that is a mighty tall order isn't it? What can one little church do? What can one little Christian do? In the face of all this hurt and pain, who am I?

Those must have been the sorts of questions a little Albanian nun asked herself over 50 years ago when she found herself in Calcutta, one of the worst and most hopeless places in the world. And what she decided to do was to do what Jesus did in our story, she had compassion on the ones right in front of her. She dealt with the need she was given and did what she could.
She began to pick up the dying beggars off the streets of Calcutta and to give them a decent place to die. That was it. She washed their wounds and their bottoms, she cleaned their sheets and their latrines. She fed them, and bathed them and turned them on their pallets when no one else

would touch them. She had compassion, one dying person at a time.

We are called to have compassion, to preach compassion, to teach compassion, to live compassion. We are called to break whatever rules and taboos and cultural barriers necessary to let the world know God is not harsh, God is not out to get them, God is not punishing them for their sins, God is love, God is steadfast, everlasting, never-ending love.
God is reaching out into the midst of our fear of death with an offer of life, of life eternal.

He had compassion. Jesus had compassion then, and God has compassion now. Open up your hearts and let God love you. Open up your arms and show God's love to the world.

Amen and amen.

Proper 12 – Season after Pentecost Sunday Closest to July 27

2 Samuel 11:1-15

Boy, oh, boy! What can we say about King David and his wandering eyes?

There are any number of approaches possible for preaching this text; certainly, "be sure your sins will find you out" is a tried and true message. The futility of trying to "hide from God" (a la the story of the Fall in the garden of Eden) might be another. Seeing if you can find somebody else to take the fall for you ("go on down to your house, Uriah, and 'wash your feet' –[wink, wink]") is another fool's errand.

I am struck by the depth of the desperation that ensued as David sought any remedy other than honest confession for his sin. Those in the recovery community learn — at a price, to be sure — that every offense is only made right by an act of atonement. Responsibility must be accepted and amends must be made.

You can't send Joab to do your dirty work for you.

Psalm 14

I recently re-watched Peter Jackson's movie adaptation of The Lord of the Rings, by JRR Tolkien (all three movies — it was a holiday!) When I read this psalm, I get a visual image of the "all-seeing eye" of Sauron flashing in my mind.

Of course, you can Google it and find an image — or you can just go to:

http://img3.wikia.nocookie.net/__cb20100425151333/lotr/images/1/1e/Eye.jpg

I'm not certain that this is what the psalmist had in mind with his line, "The Lord looks down from heaven…" — but there is something to be said for the pervasiveness and thoroughness of God's vision when it comes to considering the thoughts and intentions of our hearts.

2 Kings 4:42-44

The Hebrew Bible version of loaves and fishes: loaves of barley and fresh ears of corn (well, at least of grain — what else other than corn comes in ears?)

At any rate, Elisha's miracle — based on a word from the Lord — foreshadows the trust that Christ would call forth from his disciples on the hillside. Little is enough — and more than enough! — when God is in the mix.

Psalm 145:10-18

This is one of the most encouraging psalm texts in scripture — and that's saying a lot! Both God's words and actions are intended for good (v.13.) God is near to "all who call" on God. Truly.

Ephesians 3:14-21

Love, strength, grace, glory, riches — Ephesians is filled with these "power" phrases, available as Christ dwells in the hearts of believers. Indeed, in the fullness of God's good intention — its height, depth, and breadth — there is very little that God cannot accomplish. Certainly, more than we can imagine (if not always exactly what we have imagined!)

John 6:1-21

No rest for the weary — and, on this occasion, no food, either.

John's telling has Jesus slyly testing the disciples. They are excellent foils for his plans to illustrate what faith in God looks and acts like. Jesus works with very little (compare the relative bounty in Elisha's story, above) but leads the disciples to see that God provides not just enough — but much more than they ever could have imagined (see Ephesians, above.)

For the disciples, it's personal. When the lesson has ended, they each have their own basket to carry away — a reminder of God's sufficiency in the time of need.

The second episode, with Jesus walking on water in the midst of a storm (and transporting not only the disciples, but their boat, to safety with Mr. Scott-like efficiency) illustrates even further how little we need fear when God is the strength of our lives.

It's tough in the midst of our own storms — admittedly. But let the words of Christ dwell richly in us: "It is I; do not be afraid."

Sermon

"Gathered at the Table"

I was recently invited to preach for a "Homecoming" at a former parish, Friedens Lutheran Church in Gibsonville, NC. I have to confess that I said yes partly out of ego and partly out of a desire for some good North Carolina home cooking at the after service "covered dish dinner," (what Midwest Lutherans call a "hot dish.") When it comes to congregational dinners, rural and small town Lutherans in North and South Carolina are much more southern than they are Lutheran.

We're talking about fried chicken and country ham biscuits and pork barbecue and fresh boiled corn and creamed potatoes and field peas and cornbread and greens and squash and thick tomatoes the color of blood and sliced as thick as a hockey puck. And cakes and pies and fruit cobblers and . . . oh my; my cholesterol just went up a few points writing that Faulknerian sentence. (Oh yeah, the iced tea; thick and brown and cold and sweet enough to rot your teeth,)

There is something about a good church dinner that reminds us of what the Kingdom of God is supposed to be like.

Everybody's there, even the ones who aren't there very often, or who don't like the pastor, or who are at odds with others in the church about this, that or the other thing that is of vital importance right at this moment, but which will be forgotten in a year or two.

In the face of the "Fellowship Meal" in the "Fellowship Hall"; all of that seems to fade away and there we are together, sampling each other's food and admiring each other's children and asking after each other's health and listening to each other's stories and enjoying each other's company.

In the southern evangelical churches of my youth, we didn't really have Feasts or Festivals in the liturgical calendar sense, just Christmas and Easter really. But we had "Feast Days" anyway. We found many opportunities to celebrate with a feast. Homecoming with "dinner on the grounds;" numerous family reunions, held at the church after service and everyone invited (and would have come anyway, since we were all related by marriage or something); the first Sunday night of a revival, the last night of Vacation Bible School, etc. etc.

We knew instinctively that eating together in that way was something the church was supposed to do. And we knew that it was about more than food, it was about more than good fellowship and camaraderie and community spirit. Deep in an unarticulated part of our souls, we knew it was about God, and about growing in God's grace and about growing as the Body of Christ, and about remembering that we were more than just some folk who liked to get together to sing hymns and listen to sermons; we were God's children gathered around God's table. We are a people of the feast.

This connection between God and community and feasting is reflected in several of our scripture lessons for today. In Second Kings we read a story about Elisha and the feeding of a hundred men with a limited amount of food. It is a parallel story to the feeding of the 5000, even down to there being a collection of leftovers.

Psalm 145:15-16 reminds us that, "The eyes of all look to thee, and thou givest them their food in due season. Thou openest thy hand, thou satisfiest the desire of every living thing."(RSV)

There are many things going on in the Gospel lesson, but one of the important ones is a reminder that God is a god of abundance and blessing, a god who calls upon God's people to be a community of abundance and blessing as well.

For a few years I travelled the country as a church consultant, working with churches from Seattle to Savannah, from Northern New England to Southern California. They were also across the board denominationally; from high church Episcopalians to low church Quakers. There was one thing all those congregations had in common; they liked to eat together.

The real differences between them were not matters of geography or liturgy or theology. Their differences had to do with who was invited to eat with them. The churches who vigorously pursued opening the feast to everyone, especially those who took the feast outside the walls into the community, were healthy churches.

The congregations who were mostly interested in eating with each other, and who only grudgingly allowed others a seat at the table, were dying a slow death.

Our calling today is to open our hearts, open our doors, open our tables. Invite one and all to join the feast of God's goodness. And when we are afraid that what we have is too little, we must remember the little boy and offer up what we have, trusting God's abundance and blessing to make it enough.

Amen and amen.

Proper 13 – Season after Advent Sunday Closest to August 3

2 Samuel 11:26 – 12:13a

Two phrases from this poignant story resonate with me: "You are the man" and "I have sinned." Boil it all down, and you have all one really needs to know about the gravity of sin and its resolution.

David is outraged and moved by the story of the defenseless lamb. Alas, it is always much easier for us to see sin in the lives of someone else; our own shortfalls are arguably "not so bad." But, Nathan's accusation is straight up and to the point. "You know you did it, David."

When confronted with our sin, we can aver, justify, minimize, shift the blame or use any number of other strategies to avoid owning up. In the end, not a one of them will avail our need for cleansing and righteousness. There is only one way through to forgiveness — confession. "I did it; I was wrong."

The cost for sin is great; confession does not take that away. But it does make restoration possible — it opens the door for hope from despair.

Psalm 51:1-12

The textual notes tell us that this is written by David after he has been confronted by Nathan about his sin with Bathsheba. The language speaks for itself; the depth of agony, sorrow, and penitence are as palpable here as any place in the scripture.

Exodus 16:2-4, 9-15

"Huh?"

Can you imagine that response to a miracle? The Israelites have been dreaming of bread and "fleshpots" back in Egypt, and Moses tells them God will send them food the next morning. "Just look for it when you open your tentflap and step out."

So, they do — and they may have been a little underwhelmed at first. "What's that?" Kind of like children confronted with a plate of spinach or stewed carrots, perhaps.

We aren't always immediately thrilled with God's answers to our prayers, are we? Sometimes, it takes some time to get acclimated and to catch up with the wisdom of what God is doing. Manna may not have been a four-course meal, but it sure did get them through some tough times in the wilderness!

God tends to come through in the clutch, even if it's not the way we would have done it ourselves.

Psalm 78:23-29

The psalm text calls God's manna from heaven, "the bread of angels." Probably a little poetic license here — we don't literally know if this is what angels eat for breakfast every morning.

But it is the symbol of abundance and provision. Good enough for angels, good enough for you and me!

Ephesians 4:1-16

The Apostle reminds us that we are definitely all very different parts of the same body. No two of us perform exactly the same functions (or see "eye to eye" on all things, necessarily!) But, we all definitely need each other in order to perform most effectively.

Besides, there is a powerful argument presented here for finding unity in the midst of our considerable diversity: we all share one hope, one calling, one one Lord, one faith, one baptism (even if I use more water than you do!) — there is one God who looks parentally upon each of us.

We are a family, after all, and though we may fuss and fight like one — in the end, we are here to stick up for one another, as well.

John 6:24-35

People are always hungry.

Things were no different for Jesus; after a couple of "feeding the five thousand" episodes, there are those who find themselves standing in line, coming back for more. He is hard-pressed to keep up with the demand, as he evidently did not come into the world "to save the people from their hunger."

He tries really hard to point them to the bread of heaven — not exactly the same thing as the manna they had all heard about (see above) — and promises that their spiritual hunger and thirst will definitely be satisfied if they believe in him.

"Fine, but we're still hungry here, Jesus. What are you going to do about that?"

As we will see in next week's lesson, Jesus will tell them that eating his flesh is the answer- but he doesn't get many takers.

Ministry sure is hard.

Sermon

"Who's on First?"

Have you ever seen the old Abbot and Costello comedy routine, "Who's on first?" (Catch the YouTube version https://www.youtube.com/watch?v=kTcRRaXV-fg)

It's a conversation about a baseball team whose players have names like WHO, WHAT and I DON'T KNOW. The dialog goes like this:

> Lou: "Who's on first?'
> Bud: "Yes, WHO's on first."
> Lou: "That's what I want to know, who's on first?"
> Bud: "Exactly, WHO's on first."
> Lou (exasperated): "That's what I want to know. What's the fella's name on first?"
> Bud: "No, no. WHAT's on second, WHO's on first."

Lou: (pulling hair and glaring): "Let's try something different. Who's on third?"
Bud: "No, no, no. WHO's on first. I DON'T KNOW's on third."
Lou (yelling): If you don't know, who does?"
Bud: "Yes WHO knows, he's the captain."

And so it goes for several minutes.

I think of "Who's on first?" frequently when I read the Gospel of John because it is full of stories about Jesus talking at cross purposes with people.

The woman at the well and water, Nicodemus and being born again, Pontius Pilate and what it means to be a king, etc.

And now, today's dialogue about signs and bread and Moses and God and what must we do and it's all a gift.

This recurring theme talking at cross-purposes high-lights John's basic theme; we are separated from God and Jesus has come into the world to heal that separation.

In his book, The Deeper Life, Yale professor of Philosophy Louis Dupre meditates upon Michelangelo's painting of the creation on the ceiling of the Sistine Chapel.

Adam is stretched out on the ground, dazed and confused, one arm, one finger reaching out toward an old and slightly wild looking God, who stretches out his arm, one finger almost touching Adam's finger.

Dupre says that our entire life is lived in that tiny space between God's finger and Adam's hand.

It reminds us that we are separated from our source and that religion is a quest to reconnect to God.

The problem is, we don't know how. We try to be good enough, or smart enough, or spiritual enough, and none of it really works. None of it works because it is based on us; on our talent, or our ability, or our intelligence, or our persistence. And none of it works. The only thing that will work is the grace of God.

Jesus says, "Do not work for the food which perishes, but for the food that endures to eternal life, which the son of man will GIVE you" And the people respond, "Uh, what must we DO?"

What part of gift don't we understand? Jesus said, "I'll give it to you." And they said, "What do we have to do?" "Who's on first?" "That's right, WHO's on first."

Jesus tries again. "This is the work OF GOD. (God's work; not our work) that you believe in him that God sent. Again, it's a gift. God does the doing, the sending.

People: "Uh, that's nice. Give us a sign. Something concrete. Something we can sink our teeth into. Like Moses. He gave us Manna. Something like that."

Jesus almost laughs at them, "Moses didn't give you bread. God gave you that bread, that manna. And God is doing it again. God has sent the rue, the living bread from heaven."

The people, "Now you're talking. Give us that bread." Still, they're thinking food for the belly, not food for the soul.

Then Jesus makes it as plain as he can. "I am that manna. I am the living bread from heaven."

Jesus is the one who fills up that tiny space between God's finger and Adam's hand.

And what sign does Jesus give? He has already given signs of a compassionate presence with us in the midst of the difficulty and pain of our lives: the feeding of the 5000 and the healing of the sick and suffering.

In 1967, Doug Nichols went to India as a social justice missionary. He worked to dig wells and improve agriculture. While there, Doug got malaria and entered a sanitarium. Though he was not then a missionary, Doug was a Christian and he had brought along some pamphlets and some copies of the Gospel of John in the local language, which he did not speak. During his recovery, Doug tried to give away his literature. Everyone politely refused to take it. For several nights, Doug woke up at 2:00 AM with a hacking cough. One morning he noticed an old man across the aisle trying to get out of the bed. He tried and tried and then would give up in defeat and fall back into the bed weeping.
The next morning Doug realized why the man was trying to get out of bed. He had messed himself and the stench was awful. The other patients yelled at and insulted the old man. Angry nurses complained bitterly as they cleaned up the mess. The old man curled up into a ball and wept.

That night Doug again woke up coughing. He saw the old man sit up on the side of the bed and try to stand. And again he failed and fell back into the bed. In what he did next, Doug admits no purity of motives. He just didn't think he could stand the smell again.

He got up, and went over to the old man, picked him up out of the bed and carried him to the toilet. There he held him under the arms while the man took care of himself. Then he took him back to bed and went to bed himself.

The next day Doug was awakened by another patient giving him a cup of tea and picking up one of his pamphlets. Throughout the day other people came by his bed and asked for a piece of literature.

Doug was mystified by all this until a pastor friend who knew the local language came to visit and had a conversation with some of Doug's fellow patients in nearby beds. They told the pastor that they took the material because they wanted to learn what vision of God would motivate someone to do something like that for another person. (Many sources: one in particular Harold J. Sala, in the *Christianity Today* blog MEN OF INTEGRITY – Oct. 26, 2000)

Jesus Christ has come to us in the hospital ward of our souls, come to us midst of our confusion and doubt, some to take care of us in the midst of our inability to tend to ourselves.
Jesus Christ has come to us with one sign, the sign of love and compassion, the sign of tender mercy and gentle healing.

Jesus Christ has come to us in the sign of the cross, where with one hand stretched out to God and the other stretched out to us, he fills up that tiny space that separates us from God and from each other.

"Who's on first?" We are. First on God's mind, first in God's heart, first in line to take up our own cross and follow Christ into the world as a sign of God's never-ending love and compassion.

Amen and amen.

Proper 14 – Season after Pentecost Sunday Closest to August 10

2 Samuel 18:5-9, 15, 31-33

Our children, no matter how rebellious or "unloving" toward us, are always still our children.

There are very few words in scripture more pathetic (as in, filled with pathos) than David's declaration of his grief over the death of Absalom. David would gladly have traded his life for his son's, wayward child that he was.

The fulfillment of Nathan's prophecy aside, what parent among us cannot identify with the pain in David's heart? After sitting with the inconsolable grief for a few moments, which of us cannot be moved by imagining the same pain within the heart of God toward each of God's wayward children across the earth?

Psalm 130

A plaintive and elegant song for the times we, too, must "cry from the depths" of life's dark places.

1 Kings 19:4-8

Dr. Chilton deals extensively (and, quite well, one might add) with this text in the sermon below. I can't add a whole lot, except to say that there are those places that we, both as preachers and people of God, are sometimes called to go that just feel far too wearying to endure on our own. Laying down and waiting to die sounds like a pretty preferable alternative on some days.

But, on those days, God is still there. May the "bread of heaven" that sometimes appears in the strangest ways and places fill us and strengthen us for the journey.

Psalm 34:1-8

At all times.

That's the key phrase in this psalm text — at least, it's a key phrase. Blessing God is fairly easy when the good times are rolling by like a parade (though, admittedly, we often forget to bless God as our first instinct.)

When the bad times roll in like a fog, our first instinct may be to offer a prayer more along the lines of "help me, God!"

I'm with Anne Lamott, who quoted a wise friend (in *Traveling Mercies*, still one of my favorites of her work) as saying, "The two best prayers I know are 'Help me, help me' and 'Thank you, thank you, thank you.'"

Ephesians 4:25-5:2

More practical applications of the grace of God for everyday living from Ephesians. This is good stuff. I like that all of it comes out of the phrase, "be imitators of God… live in love, as Christ loved" in 5:1-2. A pretty good set of companion ideas when paired with Psalm 34:1 (see above.)

John 6:35, 41-51

More than one wag has commented on this series of gospel readings, "When will Jesus ever stop talking about bread?"

We all love images of freshly-baked loaves, still warm from the oven, served up delightfully for us on platters with plenty of butter or cream cheese. Now that's some "bread of heaven" we can get into!

As Jesus' images turn toward eating his flesh, we find that the number of takers begins to dwindle pretty sharply. More than one Christian, when faced with the complexity and difficulty of living out the Christ lifestyle, has bemoaned, "This is not what I signed up for!"

Well....

Sermon

"Too Tired to Run"

In her novel At Home in Mitford, Jan Karon tells the story of Father Tim, rector of a tiny Episcopal church in a tiny North Carolina mountain village. One day Father Tim is having lunch with his friend and mentor, Brother Absalom Greer, a retired Baptist minister in his late eighties.

Father Tim is complaining about his spiritual dryness, his feelings of being far from God while at the same time running himself ragged being about the Lord's business.
Brother Absalom nods and smiles and says, "I know what you mean, brother, I know what you mean. You're too tired to run and too sacred to rest."

That's Elijah in our first lesson, sitting under a broom tree, "too tired to run and too scared to rest," too exhausted to think, and too disgusted with himself to want to go on living. How did Elijah get here? What brought Elijah to this moment of despair?

Strangely enough, this moment of great tragedy had its beginnings in a moment of great triumph. In a story with echoes in the story of John Baptist and Herod, King Ahab had married a foreign woman named Jezebel and Jezebel had brought with her into the kingdom the worship of the fertility god Baal. Elijah spoke his mind about Jezebel and her religion and a few other matters and Jezebel was not amused.

The conflict culminated in a dramatic confrontation between Elijah and four hundred and fifty priest of Baal on Mount Carmel. It's pretty exciting and you can read all about it in chapter 18 of I Kings.

There was a huge altar and two young bulls for sacrifice and the contest was to see who could call down fire from heaven. Elijah put on a show, trash-talking the priests of Baal when they failed, soaking the altar with water when it was his turn. And when he prayed for fire he got fire. It burned up everything. Then Elijah had the priests of Baal killed. What a performance, what a triumph!

Then, in the first few verses of chapter 19, King Ahab tells Jezebel what has happened and she sends a message to Elijah that he will be dead by tomorrow night. And Elijah runs. He flees. He gets out of town as fast as his puny little prophet legs can carry him. He didn't take time to pack or to leave a forwarding address; he just left and went deep into the wilderness.

This is where we find him in today's reading, sitting under a broom tree, "too tired to run and too scared to rest," beating his chest and asking God to let him die. "It is enough," he says, "take away my life. I am no better than my ancestors." Elijah has come to the crisis point in his life, the point where his faith will be most severely tested.

His words, "I am no better than my ancestors," are a confession of sin and failure, of helplessness and despair. Elijah is acutely aware that his running away from Jezebel has undone all that had been accomplished in facing down the priests of Baal. He is ashamed and sits alone and exhausted, "too tired to run and too scared to rest," and mush too aware of his own failures and much too unsure of God's grace and love.

And so, Elijah falls asleep in his sins. He has made his confession, he is ready to die. As far as he knows, when he falls asleep he is falling into the eternal sleep of death.

But God has a different plan, a different ending in store for Elijah. Elijah is awakened to the gift of new life. Elijah is awakened by the touch of a holy hand and the sound of a divine voice inviting him to "arise and eat." Get up and get on with your life. Get up God is not finished with you yet. Get up and get on with it. Get up and quit taking yourself so seriously. Arise and eat God has more future in store for you.

God's response to Elijah's confession of helplessness and hopelessness was not judgment and death. God's response was forgiveness and life. The cake of bread and jar of water are more than just necessary provisions to keep Elijah's body alive for another day. No, they are a gift from God to keep his soul from wasting away. They are a message, a sign to Elijah that the past is over and forgiven and the future is alive and in God's hands.

When we come to our moments of sitting alone under the broom tree, "too tired to run and too scared to rest," when we look back on our lives and see only our faults and failures, our disappointments and unfulfilled ambitions looming up and chasing us like Jezebel's pursuing minions, when we feel like we have done all we can and despite our best intentions, we find we are no better than our ancestors, we must remember how God responded to Elijah and how God will respond to us.

We must listen carefully and hear God say to us, "Arise and eat. I know who you are and what you've done and filed to do and I love you anyway. Here, have some bread. I made it myself; I call it the bread of life."

Amen and amen.

Proper 15 – Season after Pentecost Sunday Closest to August 17

1 Kings 2:10-12; 3:3-14

All good things must come to an end.

So with the life of the great king of Israel, David. Honestly, we have seen David at both his best and his worst over these past few weeks of readings. A great reminder that the people of the Bible's stories are just like us — imperfect, unholy, obedient, faithful, willing and willful. God loves us and uses us for God's own good purposes, just the same.

Young Solomon now ascends the throne, and begins his reign well, according to the text: "Solomon loved the LORD, walking in the statutes of his father David…." So far, so good. But, we do get a little hint of trouble to come with the rest of that verse: "…only, he sacrificed and offered incense at the high places."

Solomon will follow God, and be blessed greatly by God — as the rest of today's passage clearly indicates. But, he will always have a bit of a weak spot for other ways, other women (lots of them,) and other gods.

As we have learned repeatedly: nobody's perfect.

Psalm 111

A nice text for worship, we are immediately assured of the virtue of seeking God with our "whole hearts." Not half-hearted, mind you — God wants and deserves it all!
In an additional nod to the accession of Solomon to the throne, we have v. 10 which echoes the famous words of Proverbs 9:10 — "The fear of the Lord is the beginning of wisdom."

Whole heart, healthy respect. These are two of the prerequisites for entering the worship of the God of heaven and earth.

Proverbs 9:1-6

Wisdom is personified in Proverbs, a wise woman who provides counterpoint to the fleeting pleasures of youthful desire embodied in the "adulterous woman." While it may be a difficult choice to make in the throes of ardent, hormone-induced passion — the mature choice is life and insight, not momentary satisfaction.

Psalm 34:9-14

One of the most poignant questions ever asked of me was by a young college student who had just returned from a short-term mission experience in Africa. Regarding this psalm, she queried me: "Pastor, I don't understand. I met some of the most passionate believers in Christ I have ever encountered, but they are starving to death! Why does this psalm say, 'Those who seek the Lord lack no good thing?'"

I'm still puzzling that one out.

She went on to say that the people she had left behind were not the ones who were complaining; it was those who had come from cultures of plenty and more. We decided that maybe a part of her experience was a call to wake up to the wealth with which she was blessed, and to turn that toward sharing with those whose lack was a daily part of their lives. Could it be that the "good" that is needed in the life of another faithful brother or sister in the Lord, is currently residing in my own pocket or bank account or other reservoir of the overflowing blessings of God?

Or, as a member of my current congregation said to me recently, "When my cup's overflowing, I believe I need to let it run into somebody else's saucer."

Ephesians 5:15-20

"Be careful how you live."

That's not a statement of fear or restriction, but a call to careful examination. Keep a lookout on your life; walk around it, kick the tires, be sure things are in balance.

Getting drunk? Not your best move for a real purpose in life. Walking around singing psalms, hymns, and spiritual songs 24/7? Well, maybe that's not exactly what the apostle is talking about, either!

Give thanks to God at all times…have an attitude of gratitude, as the old saying goes. Not everything that happens to me is going to elicit a "hip, hip, hooray" kind of reaction — but I can be aware and open and observant to what is happening around me. And, I can remember to thank God in my abundance and to ask for God's help when I encounter need.

John 6:51-58

See Dr. Chilton's explication below.

(I can't really add anything to it…and if you can't say nothing nice, don't say nothing at all!)

Sermon

"There's Power in the Blood"

Most of us are so accustomed to hearing liturgical language about the bread and wine being the body and blood of Christ, that we no longer really hear the crude, primal, visceral nature of such language.

At least not the way Jesus' audience heard it when he said to them: "Very truly, I tell you, unless you eat the flesh of the Son of Man and drink his blood, you have no life in you." When the text says they "disputed among themselves" about this that is putting it mildly. The better translation would be "argued violently/angrily."

As we shall see in next week's Gospel, many got so upset that they left off following after and listening to Jesus altogether.

This business of eating flesh and drinking blood was indeed a most offensive thing to say to Jewish people. Many of the laws about keeping kosher have to do with the avoidance of drinking blood, or of eating flesh with blood still in it, etc.

How are we to understand this? What are we to make of such language? What is John trying to tell us with all these "bread" stories we find in chapter six?

There's the feeding of the 5000, the many references to the exodus from Egypt and God's provision of manna from heaven, Jesus' claims to be the true bread from Heaven, and now this cannibalistic reference to eating and drinking Jesus himself.

It's all a bit much for our modern, antiseptic sensibilities. We prefer our religion neat and clean and appropriately done and appropriately metaphorical if you please. And, so did many of the people to whom John was writing when he composed his Gospel several years after the death and resurrection.

They were not only offended at this language about eating and drinking Jesus; they were also offended by the very idea that Jesus was really human. They preferred to think that he was a sort of ghost who only appeared in human form, but was really all spirit.

There was an idea about that the body was bad and the spirit was good and that true religion consisted of being really spiritual and escaping the body. Therefore, many who became Christian with this idea decided that Jesus, the ultimate "Spiritual Person," wasn't really human; wasn't "really real" I suppose.

John's emphasis on Jesus' fleshiness is meant to counteract this notion. The Greek word used here is sarx. It denotes meat, flesh. The alternate word John could have used is soma, which means body. By choosing sarx John is making it clear that Jesus was a real live human being who ate and slept and went to the bathroom.

This was important then, and it's important now. If Jesus just appeared or seemed to be human, then his death was not a real death, his suffering was not real suffering and his resurrection was just a show, a trick, an illusion.

For the economy of salvation to really work, it is necessary that Jesus be a real human being who lived and taught and was tried and suffered and died and went to hell and was brought back to life by the power of God.

Otherwise, it's just a nice story and it really doesn't change anything. In the end it doesn't communicate anything to us about God's love and our life.

Jesus say, "Whoever eats of this bread will live forever; and the bread that I will give for the life of the world is my flesh (*sarx*)"

In his book *Written in Blood*, Robert Coleman tells the story of a little boy whose sister needed a blood transfusion. For various reasons, the boy was the only donor whose blood could save his sister. The doctor asked, "Would you give your blood to Mary?" The little boy's lower lip began to tremble, then he took a deep breath and said, "Yes, for my sister."

After the nurse inserted the needle into his arm, the little boy began to look very worried, then he crossed himself, finally he looked at the doctor and said, "When do I die?"

Suddenly, the doctor realized that the little boy had thought that to give his blood to his sister meant he had to die, and miracle of miracles, he was willing to do that for his sister.

Jesus did that for us. That's what John wants us to contemplate. It's not a metaphor, not a parable, not a mythological construct about dying and rising gods. John is clear about that and wants his readers to be clear also.

This is why we have the language about eating Jesus' flesh and drinking his blood. John uses a word for eating which is probably better translated "gnaw" or "chew". Again, he wants to drive home the point of the grounded reality of Jesus' life and death and resurrection.

As we come to the table, we are called to be mindful of Jesus' presence in our midst. It was a real presence then and it is a real presence now.

The Gospel is that Jesus really, truly came down from heaven to live among us as the fleshly love of God.

The Gospel is that Jesus really, truly died upon the cross, giving up his flesh and spilling his blood, to save us from our sins.

The Gospel is that God almighty really, truly raised him from the dead, brought him out of the grave to a new and eternal life.

The Gospel is that God almighty really, truly has just such a future in store for each and every one of us.

Amen and amen.

Proper 16 – Season after Pentecost Sunday Closest to August 24

1 Kings 8:(1,6,10-11), 22-30, 41-43

It is a magnificent occasion when Solomon and the team bring the ark of the covenant to its "resting place" in the new temple. Lots of flash, music, fire and smoke — kind of like the opening/closing ceremonies of the Olympics, I guess, only without British pop legends.

Lots of striking impressions here — the temple was one impressive structure for its day, and the ark is one of the most famous religious relics in history. (Just look at all the people who chased Indiana Jones around the world to get it!)

But the verse that "strikes" me most in my consideration for this week is v. 27: "But will God indeed dwell on the earth? Even heaven and the highest heaven cannot contain you, much less this house that I have built!"

Solomon prays one of the most important theological concepts in all of scripture — no matter how grand our efforts to construct a "home" for God, God can never and will never be contained by our imaginings.

Psalm 84

Where are "the courts of the Lord," exactly? If one day there is better than a thousand anywhere else, I'd kind of like to try it out!

The dwelling place of God, ultimately, is with God's people. (Cross reference the great twenty-first chapter of Revelation.)

Wherever God decides to take up residence, that is the place of royalty — the rule and reign of God that the New Testament names *basileia*.

God's presence is not dependent on any place, though dedicated worship spaces are among the most inspiring locations throughout the world. Ultimately, it is trust in God that builds a sanctuary in our lives.

Joshua 24:1-2a, 14-18

"Pants on fire!"

The children of Israel meant well on this day, when Joshua encouraged them to choose which gods they were going to serve. "Far be it from us that we should forsake the LORD…!"

But they did. And so do we. We turn our backs on God fairly regularly, I imagine.

Why God is so patient and long-suffering with our paltry efforts to be faithful, I'll never know. But God is faithful. Lord, give me a heart and a commitment like Joshua's!

Psalm 34:15-22

We make prayer awfully hard sometimes, don't we?

As if God can't hear us, or is not watching us. This psalm makes it abundantly clear that God is neither deaf nor blind.

In fact, God is quite eagerly awaiting the opportunity to reach out and "rescue" us.

What kind of mess are you currently in that could use a little redemption and rescue? God is waiting, watching, AND listening for your prayer!

Ephesians 6:10-20

It's all there for us: the whole armor of God. God never offers us half of what we need in order to stand in God's strength. It is up to us to put it on, however. God is not a squire, expected to dress us for battle. Make a little effort, will you?

John 6:56-69

Well, you knew this day was coming. Rubber will meet road. Pedal will be applied to metal. Few will fish, while many will cut bait.

Jesus puts it all out there for his disciples: "Those who eat my flesh and drink my blood truly abide in me."

It was not a popular thing to say.

After the brilliant success with the feeding of the 5,000…we are now left with the abandonment of the masses. Jesus turns to see that the crowds are gone. Nobody, but nobody is following him now.

> To his closest disciples: "Do you want to leave, too?"
> Peter's classic response: "We've got nowhere else to go."

(Well, I kind of merged his statement with Zack Mayo's in *An Officer and a Gentleman*, but you get the idea!

(See the clip) http://movieclips.com/LTqFV-an-officer-and-a-gentleman-movie-i-got-nowhere-else-to-go/)

In the age of "I'm Spiritual But I'm Not Religious" — what does it mean to choose to follow Christ in the extreme? Where do we find our "words of life" today?

Sermon

"You Gotta Serve Somebody"

As best I remember we received two weekly and two monthly periodicals in my childhood home. Weekly we got *Life* magazine and the *Grit* newspaper; monthly, The *Progressive Farmer* and *Decision*.

Decision was the newsletter of the Billy Graham Evangelistic Association; the title referred to the need for everyone to "make a decision for Christ." We attended an evangelical church where every service, even funerals, included an "altar call;" an invitation to "accept Jesus as your personal savior."

Many of us are pretty uncomfortable with this sort of "decision theology." I suspect that's partly out of theological conviction and partly out of a bit of class consciousness. One of my friends in North Carolina says that "Lutherans would rather be sinful than tacky. God will forgive your sins; your neighbors will never forgive your tackiness." What is true of Lutherans is, I suspect, equally true of other mainline Christians.

But in both Joshua and John's gospel we are confronted with issues of decision, of choice, of invitations to accept or reject God's call on your life.

In Joshua we find the Hebrew people in the promised land, but many are beginning to have second thoughts, they have discovered that although God has given them this land there is still much work to be done, there are obstacles to be overcome, there are already people living here.

What are we to do?

Joshua lays out for the people a history of God's saving acts beginning with the calling of Abram and Sarai and moving through their liberation from Egypt, their wandering in the wilderness, etc. Joshua reminds the people of their sacred history, of how God has seen them through, God has provided, God has made a way. Then he says, "Now if you are unwilling to serve the LORD, choose this day whom you will serve, whether the gods your ancestors served in the region beyond the River or the gods of the Amorites in whose land you are living; but as for me and my household, we will serve the LORD."

Choose this day. Decide. As Bob Dylan said in the song, "You gotta serve somebody." Who's it going to be?

In our Gospel lesson Jesus' ministry has come to a turning point. For the last month we have been reading and preaching about the 6th chapter of John. In this chapter we have seen Jesus preaching to large crowds, feeding the five thousand, being followed about by crowds of people from here to there. His moment has arrived. The people are at his beck and call, he has them in the palm of his hand, and then . . .

Jesus would have flunked Church Growth, Mega-church Ministries 101. Instead of soft-pedaling and making it easy and telling them that if they follow him their spouses will love them, their children will become docile and obedient and all their business plans will work out; Jesus does a stupid thing – he tells them the truth.

He tells them "I am not just another Rabbi, a faith healing miracle man. I am the Son of God. I am the Bread of Life, I am the Christ."

And the people say, "Whoa, this is heavy. This is; this is weird. This is hard. This is leading somewhere I'm not sure I want to go."

It has become clear to the people who have been following Jesus around, listening to him talk, watching him heal people, and eating at his overflowing table; that to follow Jesus from here on out would be to go against their own culture. It would make them religious and social outcasts. They are being asked to "choose this day," and they do. They choose to go away, in droves. This is too hard, too difficult for them.

Jesus turns to his closest companions, the chosen ones and gives them the choice as well, "Do you also wish to go away?" And Peter, as usual, speaks the words of faith, "Lord to whom can we go, you have the words of eternal life."

In both Joshua and John, we have situations in which people are asked to choose, but they are not invited to choose blindly, like picking a door on The Price is Right. They are invited to put their personal future into the hands of the one who has been there for them in the past.

"Choose this day whom you will serve. As for me and my house we will serve the LORD."

"LORD, to whom shall we go? You have the words of eternal life."

"O God, you have called your servants to ventures of which we cannot see the ending, by paths as yet untrodden, through perils unknown. Give us faith to go out with good courage, not knowing where we go, but only that your hand is leading us and your love supporting us; through Jesus Christ our Lord. Amen. (*Evangelical Lutheran Worship*, p. 317)

Proper 17 – Season after Pentecost Sunday Closest to August 31

Song of Solomon 2:8-13

Plato is said to have remarked: "At the touch of love everyone becomes a poet."

The Song of Songs is known as the erotic thriller of the Hebrew Bible, and is a great place to look when it comes to understanding the ways of the heart.

In today's gospel lesson, Jesus quotes Isaiah (who is, of course, quoting God) by referring to the phrase: "…their hearts are far from me." Perhaps a little brush-up with the song can awaken, in all of us, the kind of love for God and others that leaps upon mountains and bounds over hills!

Psalm 45:1-2, 6-9

This is a very "scentual" psalm — fragrances everywhere!

As with the king, so for all of us; our ultimate source of success is God. It is God's throne that endures forever, God' scepter that is equitable. A good psalm for election season!

Deuteronomy 4:1-2, 6-9

Slippery minds is a condition that we are all prone to. "I forgot," becomes something of a mantra for us, especially when there are literally thousands of images, sounds, and bits of data blowing through our heads each day.

- "Did you pick up the cleaning on the way home, dear?" I forgot.
- "Did you send my mother the flowers for her birthday?" I forgot.
- "Did you help Molly with her algebra before she fell asleep last night?" I forgot.

Moses wants to encourage the Hebrews NOT to forget the mighty acts of God that they have witnessed, nor to let slip from their minds the commandments God has set before them.

Great check-in possibility for us, as we try to encourage one another from week to week: "Hey, did you do your best to love God and your neighbor this week?" I remembered!

Psalm 15

Speaking of God's commandments, Psalm 15 makes a nifty sort of "pocket version" of the law — *God's Will for Dummies*, maybe?

Pull out this list for a quick review before heading out each day; it's bound to help!

James 1:17-27

We've been playing a sort of game in the Young Adult Bible study class that I teach on Sundays; we try not to let each other get away with using "churchy words" when talking about our faith.

The game is called, "Ah! Ah! Ah!" — and is accompanied by a dramatic finger-wag, as in, "Ah, ah, ah! You can't just say 'I was blessed....' Tell us what you really mean!"

Reading the letter from James is always a bit bracing; James does not allow much "phoney-baloney" language about faith. For James, every good gift that we receive in our lives is seen as a gift from God. He calls us to live responsibly with those gifts.

Mark 7:1-8, 14-15, 21-23

So, so easy to see the crap going on in another person's life, right? And hard to detect the malodorous stench of our own foibles.

The gospel for today calls us to think a little less about what's on the outside, and a bit more about what happens on the inside of our lives. What kind of thoughts, purposes, motives do we harbor? Where is it that we are empty on the inside, searching for things that will fill us from the outside? And, most importantly, what WILL fill us up — make us whole?

> (If you don't know the contemporary hymn, "In Christ Alone," you can check it on YouTube. https://www.youtube.com/watch?v=8welVgKX8Qo)

I like it for the answer to this question.

Sermon

This is a true story – you can't make stuff like this up. It happened in Charlotte, NC. A man bought a box of very expensive cigars. He protected his investment by taking out an insurance policy on the cigars. He insured them against; "decay, spoilage, theft and fire."

In the next few weeks he proceeded to smoke all of the cigars in the box. then he filed a claim with his insurance company, stating that the cigars were lost in a series of small . . . .fires. Of course, the insurance company rejected the claim, which ended up in civil court.

Even though the man admitted smoking the cigars, he won the case because . . ."the company declared the cigars insurable property, and did insure them against fire, and the Company failed to specify what sort of fire was excluded, therefore the claim is legitimate."

The man collected $15,000. As he was leaving the courthouse, the man was arrested and charged with 24 counts of arson. After all, he had confessed to setting "the series of small fires" which had caused his loss of property. He was convicted and sentenced to 24 months in jail and was fined $24,000. (*News of the Weird*)

Ever since God handed Moses the Ten Commandments on top of the mountain, there has been a debate concerning the letter and the spirit of the law. Both our text and my little cigar story point out the danger of following the letter of the law while violating its intent.

In our Gospel lesson it is important for us to remember that Jesus was a Jew, an observant Jew, a Jew who treasured the

Law of God. Jesus took the Pharisees to task for following the letter of the law while ignoring its spirit.

We Christians tend to forget that the Law was given to the children of Israel as a gift, not a burden. Thomas Cahill, in his wonderful book The Gifts of the Jews, reminds us of that fact.

"... in the prescriptions of Jewish Law we cannot but note a presumption that all people, even slaves, are human and that all human lives are sacred. The constant bias is in favor not of the powerful and their possessions, but of the powerless and their poverty."

This was something new, something unheard of in the ancient world, something that had not been seen in other religions or other codes of law. Jewish Law was a gift to the Jews and to the world; a gift to remind us that our lives are sacred and so are the lives of everyone else.

The problem that Jesus confronts in this text is that the Pharisees chose to obey the rules without remembering the relationships that lie beneath the rules. If we are honest, we will admit that this is sometimes true of us as well. We make religious rules that are intended to help us live together as Godly people. Then, over time, we forget that the rules are there to help us, not to hurt us, in our relationships with each other in the community of Christ.

It's been a while since I was over at the Car Collectors Museum in Nashville, TN. There used to be a 1918 Dodge Touring Car on display there. Its little placard told an interesting story.

In 1918, the father of Albert Hillyard bought this car for $785. In 1921, Albert and his brother got into an argument over who got to drive the car into town on Saturday night. Their father drove the car into the garage and shut the door. There the car remained until found 38 years later, covered with dirt and chicken manure, with only 1800 miles on the Odometer.

I've thought about Mr. Hillyard and his Dodge Touring Car many times over the years. He attempted to heal the breach between his children by making a rule when what was needed was reconciliation. He said, "Okay, neither one of you gets to drive it!" But I'm willing to bet that the boys just went on to argue about something else, and then about something else, and then about something else. The car wasn't the problem. The problem was the jealousy and strife that lived in that family and in those brother's hearts.

So it is with all of us. Since our problem lies within our hearts the healing must also start there.

Jesus calls us to understand that it's not about the rules; it's about the relationships; the relationship between us and God; and the relationships between us and each other.
That's why Jesus says that the things that come out are what defile. And later for it is from within, from the human heart, that evil intentions come.

Along these lines, St. Augustine said that there is a hole in our hearts that only God can fill, that our hearts are restless until they rest in God. No amount of rules and regulations and guidelines can change our hearts. Only God can do that.

Only God's Spirit can move us that way. Only the Cross of Christ; only the broken body and spilt blood of Jesus can break our hearts enough that we will let the love of God flow in to change and reshape us.

Believe it or not, my first real job besides working on the farm with my family was as a daycare worker. Besides supervising the playground and changing diapers and serving lunch I had the great pleasure of watching Sesame Street every afternoon from four to five o'clock. Seriously, it was a great pleasure; I really liked it.

One night recently I saw a documentary on the making of Sesame Street. Someone asked the producer about the reaction of the child actors to working with the Muppets, who are, after all, puppets with a human being crouched on the floor holding them up with one arm.

The producer said the kids don't pay any attention to the humans; they just talk to the Muppets.

In fact, he said, there was one child who saw BIG BIRD take off his top half and an actor step out.

The child stared and then yelled to his mother, "Mom, Mom. Do you think Big Bird knows he has a man inside?"

The goal of the law is to remind us that we have a human being inside, in our hearts, in our souls, in our center of being; in that part of us that makes us something other than a thinking animal.

The law also reminds us that other people have that hidden humanity, that heart, soul, mind; that center that belongs to God, as well. Our calling is to remember that broken center in our dealings with each other.

It is our calling to remember that we are called to transcend the rules in the name of love. It is our calling to remember that not only did Jesus die for us, but Jesus died for everybody so that we could all be reconciled to God and to one another. It is our calling to spread this gracious Good News throughout the world, beginning with our own hearts.

Amen and amen.

Proper 18 – Season after Pentecost Sunday Closest to September 7

Proverbs 22:1-2, 8-9, 22-23

What we do, matters.

There is an apparent "law" of sowing and reaping, explicated in other places in scripture but very explicit here. Acts of injustice and anger have predictable results. So do expressions of generosity — simple acts, like sharing some bread with a hungry person.

Like so many other choices we face in life, the question becomes: "What kind of 'crop' do I wish to yield from the 'garden' of my life?"

Psalm 125

Mountains seem awfully solid, at least from our perspective with feet planted firmly on the ground.

Of course, we know (in our heads) that even great mountains can be moved — humbled by the incredible forces at work in the natural world. But, still, the image the psalmist draws reaches our hearts and our senses, and we are led to agree, "That's right! God's strength is like that mountain — unshakable, immovable!"

Similes like this one make me smile!

Isaiah 35:4-7a

Opening blind eyes and unstopping deaf ears sounds pretty cool; so does the lame leaping like deer (that's really a pretty impressive feat, if you stop and visualize it!) and those who previously couldn't carry a tune in a bucket breaking forth into virtuoso arias!

God swooping down with vengeance and "terrible recompense" — maybe not so much! Some of us tend to shy away from such war-like images in the scripture.

I'm having to sit for a bit as my mind tries to imagine the setting that has Isaiah crying out. Were I in captivity, or under assault from a deadly enemy or life-threatening plague — I might well welcome a little "terrible recompense."

What do you know...?

Psalm 146

God is certainly on the side of the oppressed and the hungry. The Lord is with those who are incarcerated (in prisons of their own, or others' making.) Those blind, bowed, surrounded by strange circumstances — all on God's list. Orphans and widows — check.

So, if these are the people who merit God's attention, shouldn't we pay attention to where (and if) they register in our awareness?

James 2:1-10, (11-13), 14-17

James has as good a grip on the answer to the question just posed (see above comment on Psalm 146) as any writer in scripture.

"Go in peace; keep warm and eat all you want," never did much to fill the stomach of a hungry person. Righteousness, or "faith" as James describes it, is empty –DEAD — without some action to back it up.

Mark 7:24-37

To paraphrase Ulysses Everett McGill: "Well, ain't this parable a theological oddity!" (Fans of O Brother, Where Art Thou? should get the reference.)

We are uncomfortable and uncertain in the face of Jesus' apparent callousness to the need of the Syrophoenician woman. Perhaps that is part of the function of Mark's story (our discomfort,) but the point is that a woman who came to Christ exercised faith — and received the blessing of God.

We are perhaps not quite as vexed by the appearance of the deaf man with a speech impediment — though I could imagine a bit of foot-shifting going on in the crowd as some thought, "Oh, no — this is going to be embarrassing!"

Notice that Jesus takes the man aside privately — away from the crowd. I'm trying to imagine Benny Hinn or Ernest Angley taking a similar step out of the limelight. (If you don't know Benny or Ernest, there's always Google!)

Sometimes, the work of God appears to be "strange doings." But it is always, ultimately, on the side of those oppressed and in need.

Sermon

"Things We Don't Understand"

About twenty years ago at a conference at St. Olaf College, I heard a story about the famous theologian Karl Barth. During World War I he served a village congregation in rural Switzerland. His grandmother lived with him in the parsonage. One afternoon he returned home to find that his grandmother had organized a Bible study group that was meeting in his living room.

Young Pastor Barth stepped into the room, greeted everyone and then excused himself and slipped upstairs to his study. Throughout the afternoon he heard much loud and animated conversation from the Bible study.

At dinner that evening he asked his grandmother what book they were studying. "Ezekiel," she replied. "Ezekiel!" Pastor Barth sputtered, "Why Ezekiel is a very difficult book. It is full of problematic and hard to understand passages." "That's alright," Grandmother said, "the things we don't understand we explain to each other."

Okay, anybody ready to explain to me how my Lord and Savior, my Sweet Jesus, my king of kings and my lord of lords, the Son of God incarnate on earth; could stoop so low as to call a polite woman in trouble and asking for help – a dog? Anybody got a ready explanation for that?

There are a lot of theories that float around: he didn't really say it, he didn't really mean it, we don't really understand it because of cultural differences between the first century and now, etc. etc. The collective Bible study of the New Testament Scholars has had a lively and occasionally loud discussion trying to explain it to each other.

Barth's story sent my thoughts down a different track; what if the Syrophoenician woman was the one doing the explaining in this passage? What if Jesus was the one who did not fully understand and needed some help interpreting God's will and way in this case? Maybe Jesus needed to have his vision cleared and his worldview adjusted do that he could see just exactly how large God's love is.

All three of our scripture lessons remind us that the coming of the kingdom of God has intense, this world, practical results. When Isaiah talks about healing, he is not speaking metaphorically. The blind see, the deaf hear, the lame not only walk; they run and leap and cavort; the mute not only speak, they sing for joy.

James takes his readers to task for failing to live out the faith that is within them. In particular, he rebukes them for showing favor to the rich and pushing aside the poor. While Martin Luther did in one place call James "an epistle of straw," because he thought it favored works over faith, he also said, "I think highly of the epistle of James . . . he wished to guard against those who depended on faith without going on to works."

(Luther's *Works*, Vol. 35 – The Preface to James and Jude)

In our Gospel lesson we see Jesus living out the coming of the kingdom by healing a young girl with a demon and a deaf man with a speech impediment.

But, but . . . there's this difficult part about exactly who it is the kingdom has come for. Is it only for the "children" of Israel, or is it also for the "dogs;" the Gentiles? Taking the text as it is, it appears that Jesus is saying that his mission is only to the Jewish people. If that is what he means, then he has failed to remember that the promise is that the kingdom will come from God through the Jewish people in order to bless all people everywhere.

In this story, Jesus stands corrected. Just like Barth's Grandma's Bible study, the woman has helped Jesus to understand a difficult part of the scripture and a difficult part of his call. The further Jesus goes in his ministry the deeper his understanding of his mission becomes. And this deeper understanding is a result of his encounters with people who aren't afraid to confront him with hard and difficult truths.

A young adult youth leader I know was chaperoning his youth group at the ELCA's National Youth Gathering in New Orleans this summer. While out and about in the city one afternoon they ran across a couple of homeless men on a park bench.

The youth leader lives in a major city neighborhood with a lot of street people, so he assessed the time, the space, and the group's safety; and while one of the men approached him and started talking, he reached in his back pack and pulled out an apple while signaling the kids to keep moving. The man was insulted, "I asked you if you believe in God and you try to give me an apple!"

The youth leader was struck dumb and somewhat appalled at himself. "Here I had spent all week talking to these kids about carrying Christ into the world, to the most needy among us, and the first chance I got to live that out in front of them I blew it."

But the moment was redeemed. The young man apologized and started talking with the man. Their time together ended with the man asking the group for prayer and so they prayed for several minutes together. It was, the group said, a very holy moment.

The Good News of God's grace and love changes people. It heals them, changes their relationships, changes the way they see right and wrong, rich and poor, us and them. It even changed Jesus and the way he saw the world and the way he saw himself in it.

May God's grace come to each of us and change us. May it loose our tongues so that we may speak explanations of difficult truths to one another. May it open our ears so that we may hear the truth when it spoken to us in love.

May it free our arms to embrace those in any need. May it strengthen our legs so that we can go where God is calling us. Most of all, may it heal our hearts so that we can invite all God's children to the table of God's love.

Amen.

Proper 19 – Season after Pentecost Sunday Closest to September 14

Proverbs 1:20-33

So, just how long are you willing to stay the way you are? When we are hurting, we often must choose to move toward healing; when we are angry, we must choose to move toward peace. Here, Wisdom asks, "How long will the simple love being simple?" There's knowledge for those who would rather be well-informed.

In John's gospel, Jesus once asked a man, "Do you want to be made whole?" (John 5:5-7) The man was initially too busy complaining and citing his list of infirmities to receive the healing offered by the Christ.

Sometimes, it's simply a matter of being willing to receive what God freely offers.

Psalm 19

My friend and colleague, Dr. Bubba #1, prays the concluding verse of this psalm each week after finishing the reading of the gospel and before commencing on to the sermon. I like it; it's a good prayer.

I wish sometime that I could employ the "speech" of the heavens as they tell the glory of God. No words, no voice — just mute-yet-powerful testimony.

"Let the words of my mouth be shut up long enough to allow your glory to shine forth, O Lord, my rock and my redeemer."

Wisdom of Solomon 7:26 – 8:1

A great piece of bumper sticker theology: "God loves nothing so much as the person who lives with wisdom."

Isaiah 50:4-9a

Filling the pulpit week after week is both immensely satisfying and incredibly burdensome. None of us "preachers" is really up to the task without the word that God places on our tongues.

I am convinced that it is often we who are "weary" as we come each week; and it is God who sustains us with merely a word.

Psalm 116:1-9

"If loving the Lord is wrong, I don't wanna' be right!"
So says the good Reverend Brown — played by Arsenio Hall — in Coming to America.

(https://www.youtube.com/watch?v=9k260wEclC8)

Cheesy as the good reverend's character may be, that's pretty good advice. The psalmist urges us to remember why we love the Lord. Not the least of the reasons: God bends down and listens; the ear of God is close when we need to pray.

James 3:1-12

"Nobody's perfect."

Well, duh. Like many modern admonitions, this one actually has a long history and a strong biblical basis. James was keen to remind us that "all of us make many mistakes."

We live and die, bless and curse, by the words we use. They should be administered very carefully!

Mark 8:27-38

I don't think Jesus was being paranoid here, nor was he looking for an ego boost.

Getting the disciples out and away from their normal stomping grounds around Capernaum gave all of them —

Jesus included — a chance for a fresh perspective on just exactly what was going on.

It is, after all, an important question for each of us to answer. Not so much, "what does everybody else think about Jesus?", but rather, "what do you think about Jesus?"

Sermon

"If Jesus is the Christ"

Cary Grant was walking down the street in New York one afternoon. He was spotted by someone who excitedly did the whole stop, stare, double-take, stare, stammer thing.

"You're, you're, you're . . . Rock Hudson. No, that's not right. You're, you're, you're uh, uh, Gary Cooper. No, that's not it, you're, you're Burt Lancaster, no, uh . . . '

Seeking to help, Grant helpfully suggested, "Cary Grant?" Man shook his head and muttered, "No, that's not it."

Today's Gospel lesson turns on a question of identity - exactly who is Jesus? Well, it's pretty clear that the author of Mark wants us to know that Jesus is the Messiah, the anointed on of God, the Savior, the Christ.

And he wants us to know that Jesus' identity as the Christ, the Messiah, has implications for Jesus that the disciples did not want to hear. "Suffer?! Die?! No! That can't be right." Peter took Jesus aside to tell him, "Now, listen here Jesus, that's not who you are.

It's like the movie fan and Cary Grant. Peter presumes to know better than Jesus who Jesus is. And Jesus' response to Peter carries us deeper into the mysteries of identity, of suffering and death, denial and the cross. This question of identity isn't just about Jesus; it's also about us.

If Jesus is the Christ, what does that mean for us? What does it mean for us to say week after week in the creed that Jesus is the Christ?

Well, for some this text is an invitation to believe the right things about Jesus. "Who do you say that I am?" is seen by many as the essential question of the faith, as if our eternal salvation will be determined by what we "thought" about Jesus, that our relationship with God depends upon our thinking and believing the right things.

And the next part of the text, the part about Jesus predicting his own suffering and Peter's unwillingness to accept it, and Jesus crying out, "Get behind me Satan," are reminders of Jesus' own suffering for us on the cross.

In the midst of all this, many still see this text as being about what Jesus did for us and almost never about what we are called to do with Jesus for the world.

Often times "deny self" is interpreted as something like: "Quit your meanness and get back to church."

"To take up one's cross," is "Put up with whatever less than ideal conditions you find yourself in, it may be bad but it's not as bad as what Jesus went through to save your sorry self from Hell, so quit complaining."

And "following Jesus" apparently consists of being in church a lot and giving enough so that the church can meet its bills.

When I was in college I went to a weeklong missionary conference of evangelical college students. (I went with the purest of motives, there was this girl . . .)

There was this big rally and the Rev. Dr. Somebody Famous preached on this text and said that the focus of this story needed to be moved from salvation to service. This text was a challenge to us to consider what God was calling us to do with our lives.

And, apparently, the answer to "deny self, take up a cross and follow Jesus" was to give ourselves to something called "full time Christian service," and, while I pondered as to how there could be anything else but "full-time" Christian service, (I mean being a part-time Christian just doesn't seem to make much logical sense; either you are or you aren't) it was further explained that the preferred full-time Christian service was outside the United States among people who would never hear the Gospel if we assembled here in this hall don't carry it to them.

And again, is that really what "deny self, take up a cross, follow Jesus" means?

I recently read something by Fred Craddock that makes the most sense to me. (Craddock taught preaching at Vanderbilt and Emory Universities.)

Craddock said that most of us think that this call to denial will come in a startling moment of moral and existential clarity, that we will have a Damascus Road experience that causes us to shed our old life in order to totally and completely embrace another life for the sake of the Gospel.

And the truth is, for most of us, most of the time, it doesn't happen that way. Craddock's analogy is that we think we have a million dollars and we have to spend it all at once on something big.

The reality is that we give away the million dollars a quarter at a time, all day long, every day of our lives. We give it away in little acts of sacrifice and kindness to others and devotion to God.

We listen to the neighbor kid's problems, we go to a boring but necessary committee meeting, we spend a night at the homeless shelter, we provide a meal at the battered women's shelter, we give a cup of water to a shaky old man in a nursing home, we call the pastor and tell her that her sermon helped us this week, we; treat the teen-ager at the drive through with respect whether they deserve it or not, the list goes on.

Usually, giving our lives to Christ is neither glorious nor spectacular. It's done in little acts of love, twenty-five cents at a time; living the Christian life little by little, day after day, over the long haul. (Fred Craddock – *Cherry Log Sermons*.)

I think of it this way, we go through life shedding little pieces of our old self, tiny bits at a time. And we pick up little splinters and pieces of our cross along the way as we attempt to follow a Christ who is just out of sight over the horizon, until, near the end of our journey, we look back and realize we are no longer who we once were and the change in us is all because we followed him.

Amen and amen.

Proper 20 -- Season after Pentecost Sunday Closest to September 21

Proverbs 31:10-31

This text, so often proclaimed as "The Worth of a Noble Woman," may sound a little patronizing to some ears. Should a woman's value only be found in her ability to raise the reputation of her husband? Is her joy dependent merely on rearing a happy, healthy brood?

No, though the "utterance of King Lemuel" goes to the deep value of relationships and reflects on just what it is that has lasting value in a lifetime. Men, women, children, youth — we could all do with a healthy dose of this way to happiness and blessing. (v. 28)

Psalm 1

Ah, more of the "way of happiness!"

Psalm 1 presents the Hebrew Bible's classic "two choices" — the way of the sinner, and the way of the righteous. Straightforward and no-nonsense, the choice is up to each of us.

The answer, my friends, is blowing in the wind. (v. 4)

Wisdom of Solomon 1:16-2:1, 12-22

One might wish to take a moment and consider one's course when "lying in wait for a righteous" person. There are many plans that roll around in our heads that sound awfully good when we first conceive them. Later — well, not so much!

The human capacity to outthink ourselves is legendary; thanks to sin, we are, indeed, sometimes blinded by wickedness. Better to trust the "secret purposes of God."

Jeremiah 11:18-20

Does God still reveal God's will to individuals and congregations? Jeremiah claims that, "the Lord made it known to me, and I knew."

There you have it. Perhaps easier said than done, to be sure; but, somehow God must direct those who have committed their cause to the Lord.

Psalm 54

The psalmist does not proclaim, "For the Lord has delivered me from some of my troubles." Nope, it's every trouble!
As Brother Jerry Clower was wont to say, "Ain't God good!"
James 3:13 – 4:3, 7-8a

For James, wisdom and understanding are not a matter of "book learning" or cerebral intelligence. These traits issue forth in good deeds that are done with gentleness.

In other words, if you say you believe it — then do it!

Mark 9:30-37

Busted!

I don't know that this gospel story requires a Jesus that can hear every word we utter in secret or not; most likely, the disciples weren't that stealthy as they walked along the road back to Capernaum, jostling over who was going to get the choicest assignments in God's kingdom come.

At any rate, Jesus brings the party to a screeching halt with his question — "What were you arguing about?"

"Umm, not much Jesus. Why do you ask?"

"Last is first, service is greatness. Are you guys ever going to get this into your heads?"

Sermon

"Here's Your Sign"

I am a big fan of church signs. Traveling as much as I have over the past ten years, I see a lot of them. Across from Tennessee State University in Nashville there is a congregation that has the longest name I've ever seen on a church sign:

> *The House of the Lord, Which is the Church of the Living God, The Pillar and Ground of the Truth, Without Controversy, Incorporated.*

Without controversy! Whoever heard of a church without controversy?

A church sign I saw in Decatur Georgia seems more accurate to me. This church said it was "Free For All Baptist Church" When I saw that sign I imagined elderly deacons in their Sunday suits engaged in an ecclesiastical version of a bar fight; throwing down their Bibles and wrestling each other to the floor in front of the altar.

The truth of the matter is, the people of God have always been and probably always will be a contentious lot, given to fussing with each other about all sorts of things, some of which matter and most of which don't.

In today's Gospel lesson, Jesus finds his disciples arguing about one of those things that do not matter, not in the family of God, anyway. They have been fussing and fighting over which one is the greatest.

It is particularly ironic and disappointing that they are arguing about this right after Jesus has told them that as the messiah he will have to suffer and die for the world, and that as his followers they will need to "deny self and take up a cross" as well.

He presents them with a model of complete helplessness and weakness and they respond by contending for positions of power and influence. In other words, they don't get it.

In his commentary on Mark, N.T. Wright points out that not all Jews of the time believed that God would send a messiah and among those who did believe a messiah was coming; no one believed that the messiah would have to suffer, much less to die. Most believed that "the one" would come in power and might and strength. They believed the messiah would come as a military leader, smiting the Romans and their evil, pagan allies, conquering the world in the name of Truth, Justice and YHWH.

So Jesus disciples just didn't get it when Jesus said in verse 31, "The son of Man is to be betrayed into human hands, and they will kill him, and three days after being killed, he will rise again." If they heard his words, they certainly didn't hear his meaning. They had figured out he was the messiah so they were trying to sort out their positions of importance in the new regime.

Jesus overheard their arguing and called them on it, asking them "what were you talking about?" And the text says they were silent. They couldn't answer him. Could it be that in trying to formulate an answer to that question, it began to dawn on them just how wrong they were; just how far they had strayed from the path Jesus had called them to follow?
I imagine Jesus taking a deep breath, sighing and with a somewhat forced smile, saying, "Come here y'all, sit down, let's talk. Let me see if I can find a better way to explain this to you."

He proceeded to talk about how whoever wants to be first must be last and a servant of everyone. This "great reversal" is consistent with things Jesus says over and over throughout the Gospels about how in the Kingdom of God things are almost the mirror opposite of how they are in the world.

Then, Jesus did a monumentally important thing in the history of the church. There, on the spot, he invented the children's sermon, complete with an actual child as the object in the object lesson.

Jesus and the disciples were in the ground floor room of a house, it had open windows and doorways, and a crowd had gathered to listen to him teach his disciples. Jesus reached into the crowd and pulled a child, probably a toddler, into the room. Then he said, "Whoever welcomes one such child in my name welcomes me, and whoever welcomes me welcomes not me, but the one who sent me."

With these words, Jesus proclaims his ultimate great reversal. In the ancient world, children were symbols of powerlessness. Outside of normal parental affection, children were, almost literally, nothing. Lutheran pastor Peter Marty, in the Lectionary Commentary, says that "in the Greco-Roman world a father could punish, sell, pawn off or even kill his own child."

It is interesting to note that the Greek words for child and servant have the same root and that Jesus used both of these images; child and servant, as symbols of who the messiah is and who we, the followers of Jesus, are called to be in the world. Children and servants, powerless and defenseless ones, that's us.

Our modern world, gives highest honor and respect to those with power and authority and importance. People in our world seek positions of strength from which they can control and manage others.

And the call of the Gospel to us today is the same as it was to those to whom Jesus spoke personally. It may be that way in the world, but it must not be that way among you my followers.

It may not be possible for the church to be the church and also be, as the sign said, "without controversy." On the other hand, just because we have controversy, it is not necessary that we be a "free for all" either.

Through his teaching about the great reversal, the call to child-like-ness, to servant-hood, to powerlessness and humility, most of all though his own humiliation and death on the cross, Jesus has shown us the way forward though our disagreements and controversies.

Rather than aspiring to power and influence and control within the world and within the community of the faithful;

our calling is seek to be servants of one another, actively loving each other in the name of the one who first loved us.

Amen and amen.

Proper 21 – Season after Pentecost Sunday Closest to September 28
Esther 7:1-6, 9-10; 9:20-22

I have always been partial to the phrase, "Hoist with his own petard." (Shakespeare, Hamlet, Act III, Scene iv)

I never knew until recently that a petard was actually an explosive device used in medieval warfare for blowing up tunnels and gates and such. If an explosives engineer didn't construct said petard correctly – and it went off unexpectedly while still in his possession – well, you get the idea. The poor gentleman was "hoist" (the older English past participle form of the verb for "to lift") with his own device.

Certainly, Haman qualifies here in the story of Esther. His best-laid plans for the destruction of the Jews came back to haunt him in a bad, bad way. Famously, without ever mentioning the name of God directly, Esther's story points us to the truth expounded by Joseph hundreds of years earlier: "You meant [your actions] for harm, but God intended it for good to accomplish what is coming to pass – the saving of many lives." (Genesis 50:20)

Psalm 124

"If it had not been the Lord who was on our side...."

How many times can we as people of faith look back and feel the truth of the psalmist played out in our experience? If God hadn't been present through some of the darkest days of our lives, how would we have made it?

Life grinds us down, chews us up, spits us out. But, God is with us and we are saved. This is the proclamation that we are privileged to share. We remember it every time we speak in worship: "Our help is in the name of the Lord, who made heaven and earth."

Numbers 11:4-6, 10-16, 24-29

"Manna? We don't need no stinking manna!"

Okay, so it's a bit of stretch to place the words from *Treasure of the Sierra Madre** in the mouths of the Hebrew children. But, they do appear to have been pretty tired of the miraculous "bread from heaven" that had become their nutritional mainstay in the wilderness.

Are we, as children who often exhibit a "restless discontent" with the provision of God, guilty of wanting meat when what we have is manna? Do we ever implicitly carry the attitude with us before the Lord, "Is this really the best that you can do, God?"

Perhaps the intended function of this passage is to support the idea that, when God places the Spirit on the lives of others who may "preach" or "proclaim" differently than we do — we may need to back off a bit and trust God's working. There are, after all, different gifts but the same Spirit. (1 Corinthians 12:4)

Jesus will have a word for his disciples on this matter in the gospel reading (below.)

* *The "famous" line from the 1927 novel and its film adaptation in 1948 passed into the popular consciousness by means of comedic master Mel Brooks in Blazing Saddles (1974.) It has been widely misquoted and maladapted ever since, so we feel that we are on solid ground here at the Lab!*

Psalm 19:7-14

Sometimes, you just have to sit back and realize about some passages in scripture: "It don't get no better than this!"

Psalm 19's description of the power of the law of the Lord is intended simply to wash over us, cleanse us, renew us. As I read vv. 7-10, I find myself responding over and over again, "Yes, Lord; make it so in me."

James 5:13-20

Prayer is a mighty powerful thing!

How do we handle this in our own lives? How are we challenging our congregations to grasp the power of prayer? Are we ever afraid of "letting go" to the point that we might have to actually believe that "prayer changes things?"

Mark 9:38-50

What we do for Christ matters. And so, evidently, do the deeds of others — even if they aren't "like us!"

We can be a tad prone to territorialism in our churches and denominations. Those "other" Christians don't do things like we do them. Are we sure we can trust them?

Heck, we even get suspicious of folks who DO do things the way we do them! There are few fights more bitter than those that pit Baptists against Baptists, Lutherans against Lutherans, Episcopalians against Episcopalians, etc. Even nuns are fighting the pope (or vice versa, I suppose, depending on your perspective) these days!

Verse 40 is what I would call a "chillax" verse; Jesus assures us that he is keeping an eye on things and that those other folk — the ones who don't do things the same we do — they're not really against us, after all.

And, if they are…well, God's going to take care of them. Worms not dying, fire going unquenched and all that. God is the Righteous Judge who will dole out any consequences that are needed. That's not our job; we are to "be at peace with one another.
"
'Nuff said, don't you reckon?

Sermon

"It's Practical, This Theology"

When I went to seminary, back when students used electric typewriters and libraries instead of laptops and the internet, we had courses in Practical Theology. Now I think they call it Contextual Education or something like that.

I always liked the term "practical theology." It reminded me that our theology, our talk about God, really comes alive when we put it into practice. Our three scripture readings for today contain lessons in doing what we say we believe about God and Jesus and the Holy Spirit; about loving God and loving each other. In particular, these readings teach us about inviting divine healing into our bodies, souls and communities.

In the first lesson in Numbers we read about a time when, in the midst of community dysfunction, the Israelites turned on their leader, Moses, who then proceeded to blame everything on God.

God responded with a plan that moved the community from an authoritarian, charismatic leader model to a "spirit dispersed on the people" style of decision making by bestowing the Spirit upon the seventy who had been selected by the people. The community was able to bring a halt to the "blame the leader" syndrome and move into a healthier "share the responsibility" model of life together.

One of the interesting sidelights of this story is the bestowal of the Spirit on Eldad and Medad, who were not in the seventy picked by the people. This seems to be a reminder that the wind of the Spirit still blows where it wills and, though structures are good for us, God's activity in the world is not limited by them.

While the reading from James is about physical and spiritual healing, it is less about the charismatic gift of healing (which I have witnessed and do not deny) than it is about our call to take care of each other.

This passage is about community and compassion, especially as it moves into language about the reconciliation of sinners. James is reminding us that healing is both physical and emotional; it's not only about our bodies, it's also about our souls and our relationships.

The first part of the reading from Mark brings to mind the Numbers episode about Eldad and Medad, and the bestowal of the Spirit on those outside the camp. Then it moves quickly into really scary language about drowning one's self and cutting off body parts and tearing eyes out of their sockets.

Of course, this is all hyperbole, exaggeration for the sake of emphasis, designed to bring us up short and get us to pay attention to the fact that this cross-bearing, following Jesus, stuff is serious business.

The question we need to ask ourselves is, "What do I need to cut out of my life? What am I doing that is keeping me from being the complete and whole person God made me to be and means for me to be?"

My late mother-in-law was always on a diet. And she was always cheating on it, eating things she knew she shouldn't. When daughter or her husband would find a wrapper from a drive-thru breakfast hidden in her purse, she would sigh and say, in her soft, sweet, eastern North Carolina accent, "Ah, biscuits, them's my downfall."

An empty package of cookies in the trash? "Ah Oreos, them's my downfall!"

A takeout plate from Wilber's Barbecue under the car seat? "Ah ribs, them's my downfall!"

Sisters and brothers in Christ, what's your downfall?

We all have good intentions of living a life close to God. We all want to be better people than we are. We all want our churches to be communities that are full of love and compassion, capable of healing and transforming one another and the world.

What's stopping us? What is our downfall?

Again, all three of these lessons turn on questions of practice: "What does it take to heal us, to make us whole, to turn us into the people God made us to be, wants us to be, calls us to be?"

And the answers all have to do with doing things God's way in the holy community instead of stubbornly clinging to our own individual way.

In community we are called to let go of power and embrace the spirit of God speaking in the community; even sometimes speaking to us through voices outside the community. (Numbers)

In community, we are called to heal and be healed by reaching out to one another in humility and compassion, loving the community and trusting the community to love us back. (James)

In community we are called to take the welfare of others, their faith and their life, so seriously that we are willing to sacrifice things that are good for us rather than injure or harm them. (Mark)

In the Christian faith, the way forward is always through the cross, putting aside our yearnings for power and control to follow Jesus along the way of sacrifice, death to self and rebirth in the image of Christ.

Amen and amen.

Proper 22 – Season after Pentecost Sunday Closest to October 5

Job 1:1, 2:1-10
A little liturgical limerick:

> *"There once was a man down in Uz,*
> *who lived a good life, just because.*
> *He never cursed God, though his wife sure did prod;*
> *A just man, he, if ever there was!"*

Psalm 26

On most days, I don't think I'm quite brave enough to pray v.2 from this psalm.

Asking for God to test me, try me, and prove me (isn't there an old gospel song that goes something like that?) sounds like a dangerous thing to do. Look where it got Job! (see above)

Haughty spirit aside, v.3 is a wonderful prayer thought to keep in front of us: "Your steadfast love is before my eyes, and I walk in faithfulness to you."

I believe that's the key: it is God's faithfulness that we watch — and that we just keep heading toward.

Genesis 2:18-24

"No, I don't think that's gonna do it for me!"

Can you imagine the seemingly endless refrain, as God paraded one creature after another before the man in the garden, searching for a "helper as his partner." (v.18)

Bird — no. Goat — no. Elephant — no. Baboon — definitely not!

But when God decided to whip up a woman — well, then God got the man's attention! Now, I don't want to get too patriarchal or sexist here, but there is something about this whole "bone of my bone, flesh of my flesh" thing that clearly brings a little snap, crackle, and pop to the man's morning! What a wonderful creation human love — in all its forms — truly is. Gift of God, grace upon grace. And behold, it was very good!

Psalm 8

Babies and bulwarks are among the images that I don't get right away when I read the NRSV of v.2.

I admit I had to check the definition of "bulwark" just to be sure I had it straight. From *dictionary.com*:

> a wall of earth or other material built for defense; a rampart; any protection against external danger, injury, or annoyance; any person or thing giving strong support or encouragement in time of need, danger, or doubt

Okay, so I get that God is a bulwark, and builds bulwarks in our lives, and generally brings on the bulwark just when we need it most. But, what do the mouths of babes and infants have to do with God founding a bulwark in order to silence God's enemies?

Unless it's such a fundamentally obvious thing that God will protect us that even babes and infants know it down deep in their souls — which is why, perhaps, they're never afraid to cry when they need a little help?

Hebrews 1:1-4, 2:5-12

For the writer of Hebrews, Jesus is simply "above all."
There are no powers of heaven, nor is there anything on earth that even comes close to being what Jesus is and doing what Jesus does.

Fine.
Punto.
結束.
 Diwedd.
The End.
-30-

Mark 10:2-16

Men, women, divorce, adultery. It's all a little mind-boggling trying to get at what Jesus really wants to say here. I know the literalist arguments built from this text that have bound many a miserable marriage partner in difficult and untoward situations. I am also fully in favor of marriage partners doing everything they can to hang in there when times are tough.

But I have seen with my own eyes — and counseled from my very own pastoral couch — couples that simply needed to let it go, dissolve a marriage, and move on. It happens.

The best news is that the grace of God is present and available in even the most difficult situations. And I think it is no accident that we have another "child story" to salve the wounds of the marital dissolution discourse here.

Even a hellish union can produce the marvelously grace-filled gift of a child. With God, nothing is impossible.

Sermon

"When God is Hard to Find"

As it is, we do not yet see everything in subjection to them, but we do see Jesus . . .

Almost every Saturday afternoon, I listen to the opera on the Public Radio station. Don't be so surprised. I like opera. Not as much as I like Lynard Skynard or ZZ Top, but I like opera.

Well, okay, I don't.

Not really, but I like the idea of liking opera. Deep down inside, I feel like I ought to like opera, that a well-educated person should like opera, and so . . . on Saturday afternoon's I listen to opera.

This is kind of like the theory my wife used in trying to feed our two sons liver and broccoli. She thought if she put it in front of them often enough eventually they would walk in the house one day and say, "Gee Mom, what's for supper? I could sure go for some liver and broccoli right about now."

Anyway, I listen to opera in the vague hope that someday, somehow, I'll start to like it and then I can count myself as a genuinely educated and cultured person. Every once in a great while I find myself kind of liking a piece, nodding my head and humming along and I think, "Gee, I'm starting to like this opera stuff after all."

But then I realized that the opera pieces I like are the ones they used as soundtracks for the Bugs Bunny and Elmer Fudd cartoons I watched as a child — and I'm back to square one. It's not music appreciation; it's just nostalgia for my childhood. I'm still listening, and I'm still hoping, but I'm 58. I don't think this plan is working.

"As it is, we do not see everything in subjection to them, but we do see Jesus . . ."

Many people in our world today are seeking Spiritual Enlightenment. In recent public opinion polls, more people are willing to claim being "spiritual," than are willing to say that they are "religious." Some people go looking for "spirituality," the way I have gone looking for "culture and sophistication," and with about the same level of success.

People explore the latest prayer techniques and different churches and praise bands and labyrinth walks and Alpha Bible Studies and the Wild Women of the Bible Weekends and Seeking Your Inner Child Men's Drum Circle Sweat Lodge and I don't know what all.

And whatever it is they think they're looking for, if it isn't where they are, well, it must it over the hill or around the corner or in the next place they look or the next.

"As it is, we do not yet see everything in subjection to them, but we do see Jesus . . ."

The author of the book of Hebrews is, in this text, dealing with the fact that while the biblical witness is that God is in charge of the world; when we look around us, it is difficult to see the evidence that God (or God's angels, "them") is actually in charge of much of anything.

As one of my unbelieving college professors put it, "If God is really in charge, he, she or it is doing a lousy job." War, drugs, disease, natural disaster, economic collapse, starvation: need I go on? Does this look like "everything in subjection. . ." to God?

And let's be honest with one another. The church, the place those of us gathered here have traditionally looked for hope and meaning is in a confused place right now.

In almost all denominational families it is a time of change and uncertainty and discomfort. Arguments about sexuality and theology and worship and decline fill all our churches. It is a time when people are searching for what a prayer in the Lutheran Funeral Service calls a "sure and certain hope." The little word "yet," is vital to understanding not only this text, but also the promise of the Gospel to us at times like these. "As it is, we do not yet see . . ." As much as we yearn for and look for and yes, do battle for, certainty and security, the Bible constantly reminds us of what Luther referred to as the "hiddenness of God." It is sometimes referred to as the "already-but-not-yet" Kingdom of God.

As we look around the world for God, God is often difficult to see, difficult to pin down. And sometimes, just when we think we have the holy in our hands, it slips away as we realize we were mistaken; as I was when I thought I liked opera but it turned out to be cartoons I liked.

The author of Hebrews reminds us that we are to look to Jesus to see what God is doing in the world. We are to look particularly at the fact that Jesus gave up his place at the right hand of God to become human like us. "Who for a little while became lower than the angels," the text says. And that as a result of this coming into humanity with us, Jesus suffered and died and "tasted death for everyone."

"....we do not yet see everything in subjection to them, but we do see Jesus. . . ." is the promise that in Jesus all we hope for and all we need is present.

In the community of faith we see Jesus in the midst of a world where God is often hard to find.

We hear Christ's voice in the readings and hymns and songs and liturgies and sermons. We see our Lord's face in the faces around us; we feel the divine touch in the touch of another's hand at the passing of the peace. Most of all we see and feel and receive Christ in the meal, in the bread and wine, the body and blood of Jesus. "We do not yet see everything in subjection to them, but we do see Jesus . . ."

And we are called to go out into the world and help it to see and hear and feel Jesus too. There is a post-communion prayer from the United Methodist service of Holy Communion that goes something like this, "Just as this bread and cup have been Christ for us; send us out to be Christ for the world."

Amen and amen.

Proper 23 – Season after Pentecost Sunday Closest to October 12

The scripture commentaries are based on the readings for **Canadian Thanksgiving Day**. The sermon is based on the gospel text for Proper 23. We try to cover all the bases here at the Lab!

Joel 2:21-27

English is such a bothersome language sometimes.
The English word "fear" is prominent in the Bible; for most of us, its connotations pack pretty powerful negative images. From it we get words like "afraid" and "frightening" and "fearful."

Thus, when we read the ancient wisdom of Proverbs 9:10 — "The fear of the Lord is the beginning of wisdom…" — we can get the idea that God is simply an angry deity, waiting to strike down unrighteous sinners with lightning bolts of wrath (or natural disasters or any number of diseases du jour popular with for-profit prophets and disgruntled pulpiteers.)

Of course, in the original languages of scripture, there is often a great deal of nuance and shading of meaning for these terms; the writer of Proverbs means no such thing. Rather, fear is used in its foundational context of "reverence, respect, awe" — realizing that there is and ought to be a discrete distance to be kept because of the nature of the object or person to be "feared."

Joel gives a healthy corrective to the angry-god-in-the-sky mantra. The Creator God is one who cares for the creation — do NOT fear, this God says to the soil, the animals, the pastures, the growing things. God's people will be vindicated, the days of sin and sorrow will be repaid with a great bounty.

Most importantly, there will be a day when God's words ring true for all of God's people: "And my people shall never again be put to shame."

Psalm 126

Like many a poor joke about children in worship, I was actually one of those youngsters who thought the old gospel song based on this text was, "Bringing in the Sheeps." (Sheaves…get it?)

What is really impressive to me now, as I read the words of the beautiful psalm, is the "dream-like" state of those whose fortunes the Lord has restored. When times are tough and the days look dark, deliverance does, indeed, seem only to be a dream — one that may never become reality.

I've never seen the watercourses of the Negev — though I did find a pretty awesome picture of the region.

http://commons.wikimedia.org/wiki/File%3ASunset_in_the_Negev_Desert_near_Yeruham%2C_Israel.jpg

Thanks to Wikipedia. I have seen the lakes and ponds in my area of the country awfully low (even dry, in some cases) during a drought. It is a genuine relief — and an abundant blessing — when the rains come and begin to restore the water levels in such a situation.

This image gives some real power to the prayer of v.4 — "Restore our fortunes, O LORD, like the watercourses...."

1 Timothy 2:1-7

It is election season in America — and a bitter one, at that (aren't they all, these days?)

Citizens of countries around the world would do well to remember — and preachers would do well to remind them — of the prayer urged upon young Timothy by his older, wiser mentor, Paul.

I would venture to say that genuine prayer is never partisan — may it be passionate and persistent, however!

Matthew 6:25-33

There has simply never been a better explication of faith than this snippet of Jesus' "Sermon on the Mount."

Need to understand faith in the sustaining presence of the world's Creator? Look at the birds — gaze at the flowers in the field. They get along just fine — they get up and get dressed every single morning with complete confidence in God's supply.

Been a little worried lately, and you just can't seem to let it go? Try this: get a yardstick or tape measure, and see just how tall you are. Write it down.

Now, worry for the next 24 hours about getting taller, then measure yourself again. How did that work for you? (The alternate translation for v.27 has always been my favorite — which of you can add a single cubit to your height by worrying?)

I suppose I could even make do with a sort of "urban slang" translation of v.33, which has the advantage of being succinct: "God's got this!"

Sermon

"Eternal Life"

Some years ago I found myself at a revival meeting in a small rural church. One of the young women from my Lutheran youth group had been asked to sing a solo so I went to support her.

The preacher was a traveling evangelist and he put on quite an exhibition; shouting and hollering and stomping his feet and breaking into song and denouncing sins, some of which I had never heard of. It was quite a show; both his theatrics and the crowd's reactions. One little boy in particular caught my eye.

While his grandmother tried to pay attention, he kicked the pew in front of him, he laid down, he slid off the pew into the floor, he drew in the back of the hymnal with that stubby little pencil you can usually find in a pew rack, he loudly chewed gum and he sucked on a mint, he played with Grandma's car-keys, and he asked if it was time to go, oh, about every two minutes.

Finally, as the Preacher launched into a fire-breathing altar call, with the congregation standing, every head bowed, every eye closed, I saw the little boy stand on tip-toe in the pew and whisper loudly into Grandma's ear, "Are you sure this is the only way to get to heaven?"

This is a question that in one way or another, all of us get around to asking eventually.

The man in our Gospel lesson asked, "What must I do to inherit eternal life?" When Jesus tells the disciples that rich people are going to have a hard time getting in, they ask, "Well, who can be saved then?' "What must I do to be saved?" says one. "How can I get right with God?" says another.

There are secular, non-religious versions of the question: "What is the meaning of life?" "How can I be fulfilled?" "What does success look like for me?" To me, it's all a part of the same question.

In the Gospel, a man came up and knelt in front of Jesus. We have traditionally referred to him as the "Rich Young Ruler." This is a composite name from three gospel writers. Matthew calls him "young," Luke calls him a "ruler," and all three say he's "rich."

The man came asking a question to which he thought he already knew the answer. He's like the wicked witch in Snow White talking to the mirror. "Mirror, Mirror, on the wall, who's the fairest of them all." The rich Young ruler believes he is, and comes to Jesus for affirmation, not information.

He wants Jesus to give him a benediction, a good word. He wants the JESUS OF NAZERETH, PROPHET AND TEACHER, seal of approval on his life. And much to his surprise he doesn't get it, not in the way he had expected.
You see, he had rested his claim on the Kingdom of God on the twin pillars of righteousness and riches. Obey the Ten Commandments and enjoy worldly success. And worldly

success is an outward and visible sign of God's inward and visible blessing.

So the young man believed. And honestly, so did everyone else in that time and place. That very debate was part of what the book of Job was about. Do we love God because we're blessed with material things; or are we blessed with material things because we love God?

If we're not blessed, does that mean we're bad? And if we're clearly good, and we have nothing, does that mean God's not fair? The people in Jesus' world, including his disciples, believed that morality and material blessing went hand in hand. If you were good, God would bless you with riches and comforts in this world.

So, when Jesus said to the young man, "You lack one thing, go and sell all and give it to the poor. . ." it wasn't just the giving up of his money and stuff that bumfuzzled him; the rich young ruler's whole world view, his entire way of looking at how the world works, has been turned upside down and inside out.

Remember the little boy at the revival meeting? After church I was standing in the parking lot chatting when Grandma came marching him out the door; hat squarely on her head, suitcase-size pocketbook on her arm, holding him by the neck with one hand and swatting at this behind with the other. He danced ahead of her with that pelvis-forward, swat-avoiding, Michael Jackson moon walk we've all seen. He yelled back at her, "What you hitting me for? I ain't done nothing."

The rich young ruler hasn't done anything either, and that's just the point. Though he has lived a fastidiously moral life, ("All these I have kept from my youth"), he had never learned that there is more to the moral life, to life in the Kingdom of God, than being good and safe and not wrong. He had never learned to go the extra mile, to take a risk, to boldly go where he has never gone before.

Jesus looked upon him with love and spoke to him out of that love when he said to him, "You lack one thing." Because Jesus then tells him to get rid of his wealth and give it to the poor, we can become confused about what Jesus sees as missing in his life.

The man doesn't lack generosity, he doesn't lack compassion for others, he doesn't lack doesn't lack morality; he doesn't lack an awareness of call of God on the Jews to hospitality to the stranger. This man lacks faith. He lacks a willingness to trust God both now and into the future. He lacks a confident and joyous reliance upon the love and generosity of God.

He is relying upon his goodness and his goods to get him through this life and into the next, and Jesus says, "Friend, that's just not good enough. "Why is it hard for a rich person to get into heaven, harder than for a camel to get through the eye of a needle? Because when you're rich, it's really hard to realize how much you need God and other people.

Being rich is not evil; it is just exceptionally dangerous to your spiritual health. The question for us today is this: what are we depending on in our relationship with God? Are we depending on our rightness, our ability to discern and know the right answer to spiritual and religious questions? Are we depending on our righteousness, on our goodness, on our obedience to the Ten Commandments? What is it that keeps us trusting ourselves and not fully trusting God?

What is the one thing that we lack, the one thing that keeps us from totally and completely committing ourselves to

God's will and God's way? What keeps us from doing wild and wonderful right things in the name of the Living Christ?

The Good News is that Jesus has come to transform the impossible into the possible. Jesus has come to release us from our bondage of serving ourselves and our things. Jesus has come to take us by the scruff of the neck and to drag us kicking and screaming through the eye of that needle, into the center of God's love.

Amen and amen.

Proper 24 – Season after Pentecost Sunday Closest to October 19

Job 38:1-7, (34-41)

Be careful what you pray for.

Job spends the better part of 37 chapters (assisted by his "friends," no doubt) bellyaching before God and demanding to speak face-to-face with the Almighty. Then, his request is granted.

Kind of puts a feller in his place, if you know what I mean. The questions that God asks Job are a masterful exposition of God's nature, character, abilities — of God's "God-ness," if you will.

Like any good courtroom exposition, by the time God has finished deposing the witness (Job, in this case) there is very little doubt left in the minds of the jury. God really is God, so I think I'll just hush now and go on back to the business of being mortal.

To quote Bill Cosby in another biblical context (his awesome monologue between God and Noah): "You and me, Lord — right?"

Psalm 104:1-9, 24, 35c

This psalm text forms the basis of one of my favorite hymns, "O, Worship the King." I prefer to sing it with voices and organ, but Chris Tomlin has brought it to a new generation in his contemporary version (you can check it here:

> https://www.youtube.com/watch?v=E280L4wNs0s)

The psalm is a powerful complement to the Job reading — the opening sentences are a masterpiece of understatement: "Bless the Lord, O my soul. O Lord my God, you are very great."

Isaiah 53:4-12

The Song of the Servant depicts the other side of greatness — one who is willing to suffer the greatest sorrow imaginable in order to "make many righteous." (v.11)

Christians most often read this passage with Jesus in mind. It is indeed fitting to do so. The passage serves as a guide and as inspiration for all who would suffer righteously, as well. God's presence with us allows us to see light and find satisfaction beyond the injustice and pain of suffering. May we live as our Savior has lived, with no deceit in our mouths.

Psalm 91:9-16

Lynn Anderson made a hit song out of it: "I beg your pardon, I never promised you a rose garden." (Of course, you can hear her at this link:

https://www.youtube.com/watch?v=2-eclUz-RYI)

One might be tempted to think that God's promise of refuge would mean that all our troubles will go away. Not so fast, my friend!

God is awfully good to have around when trouble comes, no doubt; but notice that the text says, "I will be with them in trouble…." The troubles do still come, but God is right there in the midst of the trouble with us.

God is a dwelling place (a shelter, a safe space) when the *skubala* is hitting the fan, so to speak!

Hebrews 5:1-10

No one should ever presume to take the honor of service to God on for themselves; the Hebrew priests didn't do it, and neither did Jesus, the Great High Priest.

God calls, we answer. That call may involve all sorts of trouble, pain, and suffering — but the glory is God's.

Mark 10:35-45

Now, in Mark's version of this tale, James and John come asking for themselves about the best seats in the house when Jesus comes into his glory. (Matthew says it was their momma what came and asked this for them — see Matthew 20:20-21)

Either way, the main question Jesus has for the boys is, "Do you think you really can follow me? Do you think you can handle the truth?"

Following Christ in his glory is something we all would like to get in on — entering into his suffering is another matter entirely.

Sermon

"Bad for Business"

Father Ed was pastor of a small Catholic Church at the beach. One Good Friday morning, he removed the purple Lenten banners from the three wooden crosses in the churchyard and carefully draped the crosses with long black shrouds.

Early that same afternoon, the priest received a phone call from the local Chamber of Commerce. A tense and angry voice said, "Look Preacher, we've been getting some complaints about those black crosses out in your churchyard. Now inside the church, who cares? But out front, where everybody can see them, they're offensive. The retired people here don't like them–they're depressing! And the tourists don't like them either. People come down here to get happy and have a good time, not to get depressed. It will be bad for business!"

The cross was, and still is, offensive, depressing and bad for business.

All three of our scripture lessons make reference to the offense of the cross, the suffering and death of Jesus offered as a sacrifice to Gad and a ransom for our souls.

In Isaiah 53, we read of the person whom the scholars called "The Suffering Servant" Though it is doubtful that the prophet Isaiah clearly foresaw a person like Jesus fulfilling this role far into the future, it is clear that Jewish religious thinking had made a connection between one or a few suffering and dying to spare and free the many. And it is no surprise that the early Christians, all Jews and all familiar with the Prophetic writings, immediately recognized in Isaiah's description of the Suffering One the life and death of Jesus.

Immediately before our Gospel reading, Mark shows Jesus clearly explaining to the disciples what is going to happen to him. Listen: "The son of man will be handed over to the chief priests and the scribes, and they will condemn him to death; then they will hand him over to the Gentiles; they will mock him, and spit upon him, and flog him, and kill him; and after three days he will rise again." And almost as soon as these words were out of his mouth, James and John ask him, "Can we be the #1 and #2 power people in a Jesus administration?" Obviously, they didn't get what he was talking about.

So Jesus tries again. The talk about cup and baptism refer to the cup of God's wrath and the baptism of death. Jesus refers to the cup again in the Garden of Gethsemane when he prays that the cup might pass over him. They still don't get it, so Jesus just shakes his head and says, "You will suffer and die, but honors are up to God, not me."

Hebrews 5:7-9 point again to the cross: "In the days of his flesh, Jesus offered up prayers and supplications, with loud cries and tears, to the one who was able to save him from death, and he was heard because of his reverent submission. Although he was a Son, he learned obedience through what he suffered; and having been made perfect, he became the source of eternal salvation for all...."

Jesus was not suicidal, not a "willing martyr," happily going to his death with visions of grandeur in his mind. He was not deluded. He was very much aware of what this meant and he struggled over it, crying out, as the text says: "to the one who was able to save him from death and he was heard. . ."

This cuts to the very heart of the issue. Jesus knew that his path led to death. Jesus knew that God could save him from this fate. And Jesus was not ashamed to let his fears and feelings be known. What agony! "You could save me if you would! But you won't! Why won't you? Why won't you? My God, my God; why have you forsaken me?"

"He was heard . . ." the text says, and yet he died. And yet he died.

When I was about 12 or 13, I was in the Boy Scouts. My Daddy was one of the Dads who helped out. One night we were playing around in the parking lot and I fell while racing some other boys. I hit squarely on my forehead in the gravel, and a piece of gravel got lodged under the skin against my skull. You can still see the scar.

Our Scoutmaster was also the local doctor and his clinic was across the road, so he and Daddy took me in there to tend to my wound. I was scared and hurting as I shivered on the cold examining table. He was a good doctor, but he had a lousy bedside manner, more appropriate for crusty farmers than little boys.

He washed his hands and then made some instruments ready, all the while chatting with Daddy. Suddenly he turned toward me with a needle the size of a baseball bat, or so it seemed to me. I never did like needles. I looked at Daddy and started crying and yelling "DADDY, DADDY, DADDY don't let him hurt me. Please, Daddy, please!"!

The doctor threw a huge leg over me to hold me down and put his left arm across my chest and swabbed my wound with alcohol, then approached me with that needle. I continued to cry and beg Daddy to make him stop. And just as the needle entered my forehead, I saw my daddy's hands, clutching my jacket. The knuckles had turned white. I looked up at his face and saw a tear in the corner of his eye; the only time I ever saw him cry. "DADDY, DADDY, DADDY!" I was heard, Oh yes, I was heard. And I was denied."

"Although he was a Son, he learned obedience through what he suffered, and having been made perfect, he became the source of eternal salvation . . ." That is the great mystery of our faith: that where we are; in the midst of sin and suffering, decay and death; Christ has been, fully completely, totally.

Whatever is the worst that you have been through; no matter how scared, lonely, lost and forsaken you have been; Jesus has been there! Have you ever felt abandoned by God? Jesus has been there! Have you ever wondered how you were going to make it one more day? Jesus has been there!

And the promise of the Gospel is that where Jesus is now, we are going. The Gospel is that God brought Jesus through to the other side of the Cross. The Gospel is God can and will carry you through as well.

God calls us to follow Him. It is not an easy way, it is not a painless path, it is not smooth sailing. Jesus' way is the Way of the Cross. But the joyous paradox and mystery of the Gospel is – the way of the cross leads home.

For all of us, from the greatest to the least, from the oldest to the youngest, from the power brokers to the powerless, from the first to the last; all roads lead to, and through and beyond the Cross to Christ.

"Who was wounded for our transgressions, crushed for our iniquities, upon him was the punishment which made us whole, and by his bruises we are healed."

Amen and amen.

Proper 25 – Season after Pentecost Sunday Closest to October 26
Job 42:1-6, 10-17

What is the best we can hope for out of life? Job's epitaph is, "And Job died, old and full of days."

Beyond numerical substance, the context indicates that Job's days (*yom*, in Hebrew) were full — full of joy, full of sorrow, full of exhilaration, full of frustration.

We often describe someone who is undergoing a particularly trying time — and somehow managing to find grace and peace in the midst of it — as having "the patience of Job." Certainly, that patience was hard-earned in Job's instance.

There is something to be said for simply never giving up; I am reminded of Viktor Frankl, the Holocaust survivor and prominent psychotherapist who became a proponent of Kierkegaard's "will to meaning."

Beyond the simple will to live, there is the ultimate human urge for life to have meaning. (A nice, ultra-brief review of Frankl's classic text, *Man's Search for Meaning*, may be found at http://books.google.com/books?id=F-Q_xGjWBi8C)

Psalm 34:1-8, (19-22)

Why should I bless the Lord at all times?

Psalm 34 acknowledges that "many are the afflictions of the righteous." There's no sense in pretending that life is all A-OK, peachy keen, *no problemo*, etc., just because one has placed one's trust in God. Life is difficult, as M. Scott Peck (among others) has reminded us.

The kicker comes with the other half of the psalm's message: "...the LORD delivers them from them all." Most especially, v.4 gives the operative phrase, "I sought the LORD, and he answered me, and delivered me from all my fears."

Franklin Delano Roosevelt is over-quoted, but he defined the paucity of fear's power over us when addressing a distraught nation in 1933: "So, first of all, let me assert my firm belief that the only thing we have to fear is fear itself — nameless, unreasoning, unjustified terror which paralyzes needed efforts to convert retreat into advance."

In the presence of the LORD, our fears may be named, our reason restored, our terror replaced with calm assurance. THAT is why I bless the Lord at all times!

Jeremiah 31:7-9

The path of return to the Lord — to the safety and sanity of God's refuge — is quite often through weeping and consolations. But God is the God who, like a father, walks alongside his children and leads them so that they will not stumble.

Psalm 126

Weeping to laughter, tears to joy. God sure does good work!

Hebrews 7:23-28

I remember the conversation with an older (in those days, as a young "preacher boy," older was probably anyone over 40 from my perspective) church member who wryly commented, "I appreciate all you're doing, but remember: preachers come and go. Some of us have to stay here all our lives."

The writer of Hebrews reminds us that God has always had to have a steady supply of priests and preachers in order to minister among God's people — for one very simple reason: preachers come and go. Or, at least, they eventually die.

But, Jesus is not like any mere human priest. He is the Great High Priest, and he will never die again. His priesthood, his ministry, is forever. It has been given to him by God, and he is now and ever will be doing what priests do — interceding on our behalf.

Mark 10:46-52

Blind Bart. What a great character!
- Several points come to mind when I read this story:

- Don't let other people discourage you or shout you down when you know what it is that you need
- Never give up — keep praying — in fact, don't be afraid to shout at the Lord!
- When Jesus invites you to come, jump at the chance
- When Jesus asks you what you need, tell him (no need for hem-hawing, eh?)
- Faith is awfully strong

Sermon

"A New Language"

See, I am going to bring them from the land of the north, and gather them from the farthest parts of the earth, among them the blind and the lame, those with child and those in labor, together, a great company, they shall return here.   Jeremiah 31:8

A young priest was assigned to the staff of a large cathedral. He soon noticed a woman who came in every day before mass and knelt before the statue of the Blessed Virgin and prayed for an hour.

He commented on the woman's obvious holiness to an elderly priest who had served the cathedral for decades. The old priest smiled and said. "Things are not always what they seem. Years ago, that woman was the model for the statue of the Virgin. She's not worshiping God. She's worshiping who she used to be." (Apocryphal: told by various sources about a variety of famous clergymen.)

Worshiping who we used to be; it's a bad habit that all of us with a few years on us can fall into. The older we get the smarter, hipper and more successful many of us apparently once were.

Churches and denominations often fall into this habit as well. I have served two churches in North Carolina with histories dating back into the 1700's and they both had walls filled with portraits of former pastors (referred to by the less reverent as "the rogues gallery") and a history room stocked with artifacts (dare I say relics?) from an earlier time.

And there is nothing particularly harmful in any of that. It's good to know about and honor those who came before us. It's also good to learn from their mistakes, if we can. George Santayana said, "Those who cannot remember the past are condemned to repeat it."

Things get messy when we adore the past more than remember it. Oct. 31 is not only Halloween, it is also Reformation Day and this is a time when many Lutherans are sometimes guilty of "worshiping who we used to be" rather than worshiping God.

A recent poll showed that for the first time in a long time less than half of the people in America identify as Protestants. The days when the grand old churches of the Reformation dominated the religious landscape are far gone.

Too many Lutherans and Methodists and Presbyterians and Episcopalians and Congregationalists are left looking back at a rich heritage while scratching their heads and wondering what in the world happened. We must avoid the temptation of worshiping (and trying to recreate) who we used to be and get on with the business of worshiping God and sharing God's story now, in this place and in this time.

Writing in America magazine and quoted in the *Huffington Post*, Jesuit priest James Martin shared an interesting sidebar to the recent vice-presidential debate.

". . . listeners may have been flummoxed by the Vice President's offhand reference to de fide doctrines of the church, which simply refers to the most basic Catholic beliefs, which cannot be denied by any Catholic in good standing. (Think, for example, of what is contained in the Creed.) Ironically, this was such an abstruse theological reference that the official transcription CNN simply wrote 'inaudible.' " (*Huffington Post*, Oct. 12, 2012)

"Inaudible." Basically it means "un-hearable," "incapable of being heard." It could be a metaphor for the voice of the church in the modern world. No matter what we say, the world no longer hears us.

It's like my favorite line from the Chris Tucker/Jackie Chan movie Rush Hour: "Do you understand the words that are coming out of my mouth?" Faced with a world that stares at us uncomprehendingly, we try saying the same old thing louder and more slowly.

It's not going to help. They don't know our language. And they are not running out to get a religious Rosetta Stone course in order to learn it. It is on us, the church, to learn the new languages the world is speaking so that we can talk with the world about the gospel of God's love.

The text from Jeremiah gives us a vision of those whom God desires to bring together in one holy community. "From the farthest parts of the earth," "the blind and lame," "those with child and those in labor," "a great company."

Jesus' healing of the blind man in the gospel lesson is a sign that this holy community is here in the world now.

God has chosen us to be the ones who call the world to participate in the community of love that is being created.

We are the tellers of the tale, the proclaimers of the promise, the speakers of the spiel; the witnesses to the world.

What story are we telling? Are we talking about who we used to be, inviting the world to join us in restoring our imagined former glory?

Or are we telling God's "old, old" story in a new, interesting and exciting way, inviting the world to join us in the healing, loving, sacrificing and joyful work of God in today's world?

Amen and amen.

Proper 26 – Season after Pentecost Sunday Closest to November 2

Today, the Lab does some "double duty." There are many congregations that will observe All Saints Day on the first Sunday in November, while others will follow the lectionary for the 23rd Sunday after Pentecost. It may not be the best decision on our part, but below you will find commentary for the latter, and a sermon for the former.

Ruth 1:1-18

What's a woman to do?

The upshot for Naomi, widowed and childless in a foreign land, is that she's in a mess of trouble! There is no visible means of support for her, or for her daughters-in-law (Orpah and Ruth,) given the cultural and financial constraints of the time.

So, Naomi follows the only viable course for herself — she makes plans to return to her home. She releases her d-i-l's from any sense of responsibility they might feel for her and basically has to say to them, "You're on your own, kids!"

There's a bit of a protest from the younger women, after which Orpah says, "You're right, mom; guess I'll be seeing you," and promptly hits the trail. But Ruth — well, her response is another matter.

I like the little phrase that is tucked into the story in v.14: "…but Ruth clung to her." Ruth is holding on for dear life; she is tenacious, persistent, unyielding. Maybe she has nowhere else to go, but one gets the sense that there is more to her insistence than that.

There is something to be said for the "Ruth Response" to life's challenges and deepest difficulties. Sometimes, you just gotta' hang on and see what God is about to do!

Psalm 146

An excellent psalm for worship anytime, of course. For those of us in America, these words are an appropriate reminder on this weekend before our national election day.

"Do not put your trust in princes, in mortals, in whom there is no help.

When their breath departs, they return to the earth; on that very day their plans perish."

As God's faithful people, we should and must pray for our leaders; however, never doubt for a moment that our trust is not ultimately in any human wisdom or strength.

"Happy are those...whose hope is in the LORD their God."

Deuteronomy 6:1-9

This beautiful, powerful section of Jewish Torah introduces the "Shema Yisrael" — Hear, O Israel — the communal prayer that forms the centerpiece of Hebrew morning and evening prayer.

Jesus uses these verses to answer the question, "What is the most important commandment?" (cf. Mark 12:28ff, below) It's loving God with all your heart (and stuff!)

All followers of the Creator God and of Jesus the Christ do well to remember and practice the Shema's admonition: "Keep these words...in your heart; recite them to your children and talk about them when you are at home and when you are away, when you lie down and when you rise."

Psalm 119:1-8

Psalm 119 follows closely on the heels of the Shema (see above) and lays out the significant benefits of keeping God's decrees and walking in the way of God's laws.

It is important to note that both the Shema and the Psalm call for "whole-hearted" devotion to God's way. Nothing "half-hearted" about it — just part of your attention will not do!

Hebrews 9:11-14

The writer of Hebrews has spent much time building up the great high priestly role of Jesus; in so many ways, he is uniquely qualified to do what he does, which is to make atonement for the sins of the world. V.12 makes the poignant summation toward which this preacher has been building: Christ's sacrifice is "once for all."

There is no need for his ministry ever to be repeated — the salvation (redemption) that Christ accomplishes is eternal. That's a long, long time, my friends.

Mark 12:28-34

There was a popular contemporary Christian song (although we didn't call it that, yet, in those days) back in the 1970's — it's title was, "Hand Grenades and Horseshoes."

Coming out of the evangelical Jesus Movement, it was about making your decision for Christ before things got out of hand and it was too late. The "hook" line was this: "Close only counts in hand grenades and horseshoes — even though you are not far, you still lose."

Certainly, there is a tinge of something missing in this dialogue between Jesus and the scribe who brought the BIG question ("Which commandment is first of all?")

Jesus says, after the scribe's wise explication of the scripture and its theological significance: "You are not far from the kingdom of God."

Not far. Close — but no cigar.

Maybe I'm still a bit of that evangelical teenager deep down inside, but I think it bears asking: When it's all said and done, do I want to find myself "close" to the kingdom, or more like "in-the-door-safe-and-sound?"

Sermon (All Saints Day)

I go to a lot of family reunions as a pastor, especially those that happen at the church after worship. People graciously invite me to stay for lunch and I seldom decline.

I remember one reunion when a woman had gotten all excited about doing the family history. So after dinner, she began to give everyone a report.

She started with the first settlement in North Carolina in the 1700's and worked her way back up the Great Wagon Road through the Shenandoah Valley of Virginia to the Pennsylvania Dutch area back over to Germany, to the time of Luther and beyond.

It was kind of interesting for a while, but it then dragged on and on for an hour and people started getting bored. As usual, I was sitting with the teen-agers and as she drew to a close, she asked, "Did I leave anyone else?" The kid next to me muttered, "Yeah, Adam and Eve."

Today is All Saints Sunday. It is a day when we remember those who have gone before us in the faith. It is a day to trace our Christian family history, yes, all the way back to Adam and Eve.

It is a day when we thankfully remember those of our church members and friends and relatives who have died in the last year, who have gone on to join the saints in heaven.
It is also a day when we are called to examine our own saintliness, a time to remember our call to follow in the footsteps of our ancestors.

As Christians, our family tree is not limited to nor defined by our biological connectedness. We are all grafted into the family tree of God through the sacrament of baptism; we have all been adopted as children of God and sisters and brothers of Christ through the working of the Holy Spirit in our lives.

When I look back at "the saints," the ones I have known personally and the ones I have only heard or read about, I don't feel very saintly myself. I feel like the little boy Lois Wilson wrote about meeting at her door on Halloween.

He was about four and he was wearing a Superman outfit. He reached out his hand as he said trick or treat. Ms. Wilson couldn't resist teasing him a bit, "Where's your bag?," she said. He replied, "My Mom's carrying it. It's too heavy for me." Ms. Wilson smiled and said, "But you're Superman!"

He looked down at the S on his chest and looked back at Ms. Wilson and whispered, "Not really, these are just Pajamas." Though the Scriptures tell us that because we're Christians, we're also saints; most of us don't believe it. We look down at the S on our chest and then plead with God, "Not really, I'm only human."

Which is the great mystery of All Saints Day. We are indeed only human, but we are also "The saints who gather" at Such-and-Such church, as Paul put it in many of his letters. We are, as Martin Luther said, saint and sinner at the same time. While we do not go around in Christian Pajamas, with a big haloed S on our chest, we do have an invisible cross on our foreheads, put there at our baptism with the words; "Delmer Lowell Chilton, child of God, you have been sealed by the Holy Spirit and marked with the Cross of Christ forever."

Each of us has that mark on our lives; a mark which calls us forward into saintliness. We are called to continually try to live into our name as Children of God, as baptized saints.

And, we never quite make it. We're always aware of falling short, of not measuring up. We are also always aware that the other people in our family seldom measure up either. Unfortunately, we are sometimes more aware of the failures of others that we are of our own.

Someone sent me a little poem a few years ago. It's one of those things that got tucked away in a file. I ran across it the other day;

> "Oh, to live above, with Saints we love,
> Oh, that will be Glory.
> Oh, to live below, with Saints we know,
> Well, that's a different story!"

The struggle of the Christian life is to remember that we are Saints in spite of our failures, and to remember that the other people in our Church Family are Saints as well, in spite of their imperfections.

One of the things I love about Family Reunions and Church Homecomings is that they are the most grace-filled moments we share. It is a time when we look beyond the surface to see the mark of the family, the mark of Christ on everyone.

Regulars and irregulars, the faithful and the wandering, the staunch believers and "barely hanging on to their faith by the skin of their teeth," doubters, those close at hand and those who came from far off; all together in one place, celebrating and enjoying their relatedness to each other and to God.

Our calling on this All Saints Sunday is to remember our saintedness, our blessedness, our holiness; which is a gift from God, a gift we were given for the benefit of the world.

It is also a day to remember the saintliness, the blessedness, the holiness of others. To remember that they too are the beloved Children of God and that we are to treat them that way.

Amen and amen.

Proper 27 – Season after Pentecost Sunday Closest to November 9
Ruth 3:1-5; 4:13-17

I loved the old Rocky and Bullwinkle Show. They had such catchy episode titles that always included an optional subtext featured prominently — to wit, the title of Episode 1 — "Rocky and His Friends: Knock on Wood, OR Bullwinkle Takes the Rap!"

(for more Rocky/BW nostalgia, check out the titles here: www.imdb.com/find?q=Rocky+and+Bullwinkle&s=ep)

I wonder how we might title this episode from the ongoing saga of Ruth and Naomi? I admit that it has always made me a bit uncomfortable for the seemingly questionable (according to our modern sensibilities) situation it puts young Ruth into.

"Fix up real nice, darlin', and go on down to the threshing floor after Boaz has had plenty to eat and drink. Lay right there next to him, and then do whatever he tells you to do!"

Of course, it works out all right — Boaz is, after all, the kindly kinsman-redeemer (and soon-to-be great grandpappy of King David, the messianic forerunner.)

So, here goes — "Widowed Women: Where There's a Will There's a Way, OR Kindly Kinsman Plants a Kiss, Saves the Day (and the Kingdom, Too!)"

Psalm 127

According to Psalm 127, the Eldridge* Family must have been the happiest bunch in Martin, Tennessee, my hometown. (Which, incidentally, was named as one of "Nine Happy Towns in the USA" in 1970 by Esquire Magazine. See, you just can't get this stuff anywhere else!)

There were 9 of them, seven children with the two parents. They all had bright red hair and rode in one of those way-cool 1970's station wagons with the wood panels on the side. I'm certain that the psalmist's rejoicing over the Lord's addition of happy little arrows to the quiver of the blessed had something to do with familial success and security. We tend to rejoice to this day over the addition of little ones in a family, do we not?

   * Not their real surname, though the family did exist — I promise!

1 Kings 17:8-16

As Dr. Chilton points out in the sermon below, this is the first of two "widow-stories" in our lessons for today (I suppose it would be three, if you count Ruth/Naomi in the first story, above.)

Both are stories about little becoming much when given in faith. Just how far and for how long does the blessing of God go in lives that are surrendered to God's care?

Psalm 146

See previous commentary for this psalm on September 9, 2012 and November 4, 2012.

Hebrews 9:24-28

Hebrews has been remarkably important on the doctrinal development of the church in so many ways. Today there are two important points to notice:

- The continuing emphasis on Christ's sacrifice as a "once for all" event
- The sure and certain return of Christ to once-and-for-all effect God's salvation (redemption, not the removal of sin)

Mark 12:38-44

Widows vs. Scribes — Choose a Side!

Sermon

"Widow's Work"

Today, we have read Bible lessons about two widows, both of whom were poor, and both of whom were generous with what they had. The story of the widow's mite in the gospel was a little tough on ministers and other official church folk.

"Beware of scribes, who like to walk around in long robes . . .," Well, I wear them during service, but I don't walk around in them, much. " . . . and to be greeted with respect in the marketplaces," Okay, I do like it when people in grocery stores and restaurants call me Father or Reverend or Padre and treat me a little extra nice. " . . . and to have the best seats in the synagogue," Well, I don't know if it's the best, but it is bigger and it is different. " . . .and places of honor at banquets." What can I say, I obviously like to eat!

"They devour widow's houses and for the sake of appearance say long prayers." Okay, I'm clean on these two; I've never tricked a widow out of her house, and I'm famous for short prayers, not long ones; so perhaps I've escaped the "greater condemnation" by a narrow margin.

Whenever we hear a Bible story, one of the most important things we can ask ourselves is, "With whom do I identify, who in this story feels like me?" Of course, none of us would like to think we're like the scribes, making a big, loud public display of our religion; in particular, none of us wants to look like a hypocrite. And we all want to believe that we're like the widow, doing all we can with what little we have.

Most of us, most of the time, hear the widow's mite story and think it means something like this: "See, it's not how much you give that matters, it's the spirit with which you give it that counts. A little bit is just as important as a lot." That is true, as far as it goes.

But most of us miss an important point here; Jesus did not say that the widow gave all she could afford; Jesus said she gave all she had.

"Truly I tell you, this poor widow has put in more than all those who are contributing to the treasury. For all of them have contributed out of their abundance, but she out of her poverty has put in everything she had, all she had to live on."

Truth be told, most of us, myself included, most of the time, give out of our abundance.

We give what we think we can afford to give without seriously affecting our standard of living. What Jesus points to in the widow is another thing entirely; her total commitment of everything she has, all her resources, "all she had to live on," to the Kingdom of God. At root, this story is not so much about giving and generosity as it is about trust in God.

That is why the Hebrew story of Elijah and the Widow of Zarephath is paired with the story of the widow's mite in the appointed readings for today. These two stories are not only about widows, they are about putting your complete trust in God as well.

The Widow of Zarephath also gave all she had. She shared with the Prophet of the Lord the last of her food in a time of famine. Yet, when she did, she discovered she had enough, enough at least to keep going, day by day; the jar of meal and the jug of oil having in them each day enough for that day's needs.

This is the way God operates. This is the way God provides for God's people. Remember the manna from Heaven, the bread upon the ground provided to the Israelites as they went from Egypt to the Promised Land? If they took more than they needed for the day, the extra would rot before the next morning. It was a lesson in trusting God to provide each day's needs.

What Jesus noticed and commented upon with the widow is not the size of her gift, but the fact that she gave her all, trusting that God would provide for the next day. This is the Biblical Principle of God's economy; this is the way God always works. God's promise is not: If you return to me a tithe, I will make you rich. God's promise is: If you commit to me your all, I will provide for your needs.

The Bible stories about the widow's and their generosity are not so much about finances as they are about the relationship of trust we are called upon to have with God. And, we must admit, this is hard for us, we like to hedge our bets, hold a little something back, play it safe.

A number of years ago I heard a story about a college student who went into a camera store to have a picture enlarged. It was a framed 8×10 of the young man and his girlfriend. When the clerk took the picture out of the frame, he read the writing on the back:

"My dearest Tommy, I love you with all my heart. I love you more and more each day. I will love you forever and ever. I am yours for all eternity. With all my love, Diane. PS – If we ever break up, I want this picture back!"

Today God call us to quit hedging our bets, to stop holding back. God calls us toward making a complete and total commitment of ourselves to Christ and the Kingdom of God. We are called upon to make all that we are and all that we have available to the work of spreading the Good News of Jesus Christ into all the World.

And the Gospel for us today is that we can make that leap, that commitment, with full confidence in God's promise to provide our every need, now and forever more.

Amen and amen.

Proper 28 – Season after Pentecost Sunday Closest to November 16

1 Samuel 1:4-20

Some of the most effective praying that is done may be with "wordless prayers," such as that of Hannah. Nothing audible, no profundity of phrasing. Just straight up "pouring out my soul before the Lord." (v.15)

1 Samuel 2:1-10

Hannah's response to God's goodness in answering her prayer (see above) functions as the psalm text for those using these readings. She certainly does as well as anything David or any other psalmist ever wrote!

One of my favorite questions to ask when the scripture is laid out before me – during those moments when I am simply seeking to let the text speak – is, "What do I learn about God from this text?"

- There is no Holy One like the LORD
- God is a God of knowledge
- God weighs God's every action
- God holds the power of both death and life
- God is in the midst of both poverty and wealth
- God may be found at the ash heaps of life, as well as in the seats of power
- God guards the feet of those who are faithful; God's adversaries will be shattered (ouch!)

Daniel 12:1-3

An apocalyptic portion from Daniel; in chapter 11, he has told us that the vision speaks of "the time of the end." We have one of the Bible's four mentions of Michael, the archangel of God (there is a second in Daniel, as well as others in Jude and Revelation.) Michael is one of seven angels of this rank according to some Jewish and Orthodox Christian sources (a pretty decent article from Wikipedia here: http://en.wikipedia.org/wiki/Archangel)

Whatever one's views of end times and angelology might be, we certainly have a text of hope and comfort in the midst of great anguish here. Daniel's vision has a formative influence on the eschatology of the early church, which knew its share of suffering, persecution, and anguish.

Psalm 16

Another passage with the theme of God's protection. Notice that faith in God affects the whole person — physically, mentally/emotionally, and spiritually: "Therefore my heart is glad, and my soul rejoices; my body also rests secure." (v. 9)

Hebrews 10:11-14, (15-18), 19-25

The preacher of Hebrews places his assurance and hope squarely on the success of Jesus' atoning sacrifice. Jesus has opened a "new and living way" for us to approach God — and we may now do so boldly and with great confidence.

With our eternal destiny secured, the preacher would have us turn to love and good deeds — "provoking" one another in these endeavors. What a different take on our usual impression of the word "provoke!"

Instead of provoking one another with political jabs, insults, taunts, and mocking — can you imagine what public discourse would be like if we substituted encouragement to love and good deeds, instead?

> "Yeah, well your mother was so nice, she used to bake cookies for the whole neighborhood!"

> "Aw, that's nothing — yo' momma was so generous, she used to give us all a quarter for picking up the sticks on Old Man Johnson's yard!"

> "Yeah, well if you don't stop it, I'm gonna have to go over and help your little brother with his homework."

> "You better watch out; if you do that — I'll be forced to fix your sister's bike!

Mark 13:1-8

The prognosticators of doom and gloom are quick to arise whenever there is a major tragedy. In recent memory, there have been all sorts of predictions and pronouncements of the judgment of God attached to everything from the World

Trade Center attacks of September 11, 2001 — to Hurricane Katrina in 2006 — and the recent Superstorm Sandy that affected millions on the East Coast of the U.S.

Worldwide, wars and famine and struggles for justice drag on day after day, year after year. Many people are prone to ask the question, "Is this the end of the world?"

Well, I admit that one does have to wonder — just as the disciples in Jesus time wondered. We are there when Peter, James, John, and Andrew (notice the addition of Andy to the usual inner circle of the Big Three) pop the question to Jesus : "When will this be, and what will be the sign?"

I do like Jesus' response, though it isn't designed to answer the question directly: "Beware that no one leads you astray. Many will come in my name and will say, 'blah, blah, blah, blah....'"

Provides a nice filter for the talking heads and non-stop purveyors of agony that fill the airwaves. They don't know any more than you or I; whatever is going on around us, it's all like birth pangs. Expectant parents all have to learn the same lesson: the baby will come when the baby is ready to come.

So it is with the final chapter of the coming kingdom of God....

Sermon

"The Wild Whirlwind of Life"

Morgan Wooten was a basketball coach. He coached at DeMatha High School in the DC area. His teams won 1274 games while losing only 192 times. He was considered by everyone who knew him to be one of the great ones. Well, everyone except his grandson.

Wooten is one of only three high school coaches in the Basketball Hall of Fame. At his induction, he told a story about his grandson's first day of school. The teacher asked Nick, "What's your favorite sport?" "Baseball," he said.
The teacher knew who Nick's grandfather was. She was surprised, "Not basketball?" Nick said, "Nope. I don't know anybody who knows anything about basketball."

The teacher was even more surprised, "But Nick, a lot of people think your Grandfather Wooten knows a lot about basketball. Nick snorted and laughed, "Oh no! He doesn't know anything about basketball. I go to all his games and he never gets to play."

Sometimes we see God the way Nick saw his grandfather. Because we see the game of life going on and have a hard time seeing the hand of God anywhere in it, we think, "God knows nothing about it," or, "God cares nothing about it," or, "God can't do anything about it," because, after all, we never see God get in the game.

The Scripture readings today talk about the art of having faith in a world gone mad, of seeing God's hand in the wild whirlwind of life around us. Each is an example of apocalyptic literature. Though many use these types of writings to try to make predictions about the future and to frighten people in the present; that is not what these Bible readings are about. They are intended to bring us reassurance of God's love when we go through hard times and God seems to be very far away.

Daniel was written at a time when the Hebrew people and the Jewish faith were in a tough spot. They were in exile, they were oppressed, they were persecuted. Daniel was written to give hope to a people who had lost all hope; to give faith to those who were losing touch with God.

Chapter thirteen of Mark's Gospel was written about thirty years after the death of Jesus, to the early Christians, a community of faith that was also in a tough spot, they were a people who were fearful and hesitant about the future. These words were written to give them hope and faith in the God of the future.

Hebrews was written to the Jewish Christian Community in Rome. They were struggling with the Romans on the one hand and their Jewish brothers and sisters on the other. They needed a word of hope in a time of distress.

Each of these communities was like Morgan Wooten's grandson. They saw the activity in front of them, but they couldn't see the hand of the one running the show; and so they were afraid, they were anxious, they were losing hope.

Have you ever seen the Carl Reiner and Mel Brook skit called the 2000 year old man? Reiner plays a TV reporter and Brooks plays, well, a 2000 year old man.

> Newsman: "Well did you worship God in your village?"
> Old Man: "No, at first we worshipped this guy in our village named Phil."
> Newsman: "You worshipped a guy named Phil? Why?"
> Old Man: "Well, he was bigger than us, and faster than us, and he was mean, and he could hurt you; break your arm or leg right in two; so we worshipped Phil."
> Newsman: "I see. Did you have any prayers in this religion?"
> Old Man: "Yeah. Want to hear one? – PLEASE PHIL NO! PLEASE PHIL NO!"

Newsman: "Okay. When did you stop worshipping Phil?"
Old Man: "Well One day we were having a religious festival. Phil was chasing us and we were praying. (PLEASE PHIL NO! PLEASE PHIL NO!) And suddenly a thunderstorm came up and a bolt of lightning struck and killed Phil. We all gathered around and stared at Phil awhile and then we realized:
THERE'S SOMETHING BIGGER THAN PHIL.

That is the ultimate message of apocalyptic literature; there's something bigger than Phil, there's something bigger than the bad stuff that happens in our lives. And that something bigger is God. That something bigger is faith in God's tomorrow overcoming our yesterdays and todays. That something bigger is the faith that God is indeed very much in the game. God is involved in all our pain and sorrow, our suffering and disappointment. God is bigger, much bigger than all those things that frighten and haunt us.

Almost every church sings the Hymn, *Now Thank We All Our God*, around Thanksgiving. As you sing it this year, reflect upon this: Pastor Martin Rinkhart wrote that hymn in the early 1600s, in the midst of the Thirty Years War. Six to eight thousand people in his village and territory died in an epidemic including the other two clergymen in town. For weeks at a time he buried as many as fifty people a day, including his own wife and children.

Either Rinkhart was heartless and a bit crazy, or he was in touch with a deep, deep spiritual truth about a God whose promises are ever sure and whose love never fails. If Reinhardt was right, if our Bible readings are telling us the truth that in the midst of this world's trouble and sorrow, pain and disappointment; we can hold fast to the assurance of God's concern and involvement in our lives; what are we to do, how are we called to live our lives?

There's a fascinating line in our Hebrews lesson, verse 24: "And let us consider how to provoke one another to love and good deeds," Usually the word provoke is used in a negative sense; as in "Honest Officer, I didn't aim to hit him, but he, he provoked me!" but here it is used positively, as encouragement, as stirring up, as prodding and pushing and being active in love.

We are called into a world full of scared, lonely, hurting people, and we are called to provoke one another into acts of love and works of mercy, into commitments to compassion, into doing the right thing for all the right reasons. We are called to be the hand of God in the world, touching all with the gentle and healing caress of divine love.

Amen and amen.

Proper 29 – The Reign of Christ Sunday Closest to November 23

2 Samuel 23:1-7

David speaks the words to which we all, as preachers, aspire every time we stand and deliver: "The spirit of the Lord speaks through me, his word is upon my tongue." N'est-ce pas?

This word outlines the character of the righteous ruler: one who rules justly, in the fear of God. This ruler brings light and life to the land.

In true Hebrew literary form, there follows a contrasting vision of the godless: thorns that prick and tear, worth nothing but to be piled together and burned.
Let us pray for righteous rulers!

Psalm 132:1-12, (13-18)

The psalmist remembers David's passion for the worship of God, for a place to serve as God's dwelling place. Rooted in that same passion and commitment, the psalm prays for God's blessing on the "sons of David" that will follow as God's righteous rulers over God's people in Zion.

Daniel 7:9-10, 13-14

Daniel's apocalyptic vision is of God, the Ancient One, on the exalted throne of heaven. God is joined by "one like a human being" who is given the authority to rule over all peoples, nations, and languages on earth.

This imagery is picked up by John, in the opening chapters of Revelation, and reworked brilliantly into the theme of God's great power and authority over even sin and death — made known to all of creation in the Lamb of God (and a slaughtered lamb, at that.)

The power and might of the Ancient One, the King of heaven, the ruler of an eternal dominion — in the end will lay claim to the throne through nothing other than sacrifice and love.

Psalm 93

It is the LORD who is robed with majesty, who has acted in strength to establish the world.

While the image of floodwaters roaring through our neighborhoods is not a particularly comfortable one (just ask those affected by the recent Superstorm Sandy, the Christmas tsunami of 2004, or the still-memorable Hurricane Katrina in 2006) — there is no denying the power and awe of the metaphor.

Revelation 1:4b-8

Jesus rules the kings of the earth, by virtue of his rule over death itself (a power that conquers even the most venerable kings — cf. King Tut, King Nebuchadnezzar, King Henry VIII, and so on.)

One of the connections with the Daniel passage (see above) appears here as Jesus Christ is envisioned "coming with clouds."

Not insignificant is the appointment of Christ's followers as "kings and priests" in his name. What import does this have for the church's ministry on this Sunday of Christ, the King?

John 18:33-37

Pilate senses that something is up with this Jesus fellow. He seems to be more than the local rulers have cracked him up to be. Pilate's questions are probing, intense.

"Are you the King of the Jews? What have you done? Tell me, are you a king?"

Those are questions that we are still answering to this day, I think. What does it mean for me to offer my allegiance to a king whose kingdom, by his own admission, is "not of this world?"

Sermon

"Citizens of Two Worlds"

In his book *The Canadians*, Andrew Malcolm writes about Cecille Bechard. She is "a Canadian who visits the United States several dozen times a day; when she goes to the refrigerator or to the backdoor or to make tea for instance. To read and sleep, she stays in Canada. And she eats there too, as she at the north end of her kitchen table. Mrs. Bechard's home is in Quebec and Maine at the same time." This is because her house was already there in 1842 when diplomat's sat down in London to create the official boundary line.

Hmm; a citizen of one country who spends most of her time in another country, all the while staying in the same place, somehow that feels familiar. We, as Christians, are also citizens on two worlds, of two kingdoms.

Most of our life is lived in the urgent now of eating and sleeping and working and playing. Most of our thinking is governed by the culture in which we live; indeed most of our opinions about most things are shaped by being citizens of and participants in the secular world around us.

But, to be a person of faith is to perceive another reality besides the one that is easily and readily apparent. To be a person of faith is to live in two worlds at the same time. It is to perceive the reality everyone else sees but also to see a reality that can only be seen with the eyes of faith.

In our Gospel lesson these two worlds collide. At the trial of Jesus we find Pilate, a thoroughly secular pragmatist; deciding what to do with hard, cold, real politik calculation. And we find Jesus, no less aware of the stark reality of his situation and the cross that stands before him, but also aware of another reality, another "kingdom" to which he belongs.

Pilate is both amused and annoyed by the whole thing. He can't figure out why this man is standing before him, accused of being, of all things, "the king of the Jews." This guy? This backwoods Bible thumper? After staring at him and his accusers awhile, Pilate asks, "Okay, what have you done?"

This doesn't really help, because he can't understand Jesus' answers either. Oh, he understands the words; he just can't decipher the meaning. "So, you are a king. Or not. What are you talking about?"

The problem is that Pilate, and the social and political leaders of Judea, and most of the people who had been following Jesus around and listening to him preach, were aware of only one world and Jesus was living in two.

"My kingdom is not of this world," he says, and in that moment he is like Mrs. Bechard, looking across her kitchen table to the "other country" where her refrigerator sits.

We are called to live each day in two worlds, two realities, two kingdoms. We cannot and should not permanently retreat from the real world which surrounds us with its pain and suffering, hunger and disease, wars and violence of all description. We are called of God to follow Christ and put ourselves into the midst of the worlds need.

We are called of God to struggle with the world we see all around us, to be active participants in making this world a better place for everyone. We are called to plunge into the secular now, to dive into the messiness that is the world; we are called to get into it up to our necks.

But we are also called to look beyond the obvious to the really real; to look past the daily to see the eternal; to look within the moment to see the mystery; to stare into the face of the truly human to perceive there the image of the truly divine.

For we live in two worlds at the same time and the trick is to not become so enamored of the one that we lose sight of the other.

With Christ the King as our guide, we are called to see the hand of God moving in our midst, holding us up with the divine love, pointing and gently nudging us in the right direction when we lose our way, holding us back from danger and harm, filling the ordinary with mystery and the mysterious with meaning, that we; like Daniel and the Psalmist and Saint John the Divine and Jesus himself; we will be able always to hold on to faith in the "already but not yet" divine world of which Christ is the one and only King.

Amen and amen.

ABOUT THE AUTHORS

John Fairless and Delmer Chilton have been writing, speaking, and just plain fooling around as "Two Bubbas and a Bible" for the past fifteen years or so, having met as two dads on a field trip with their seventh-grade sons. Friendship, colleagueship, and partnership have ensued.

They write a weekly weblog, **The Lectionary Lab**, available at www.lectionarylab.com; they also produce a weekly podcast, **Lectionary Lab Live**, which is available as a link on the Lectionary Lab website.

This volume is their third book together, with more to come ("Good Lord willing and the Creek don't rise!") Look for not only the third and final volume in the *Lectionary Lab Commentary* series (Year C) – but also the forthcoming book of the Bubbas' favorite stories, *The Gospel According to Aunt Mildred*.